Bible Brain Busters

Bible BRAIN Busters

Tyndale House Publishers, Inc.
WHEATON, ILLINOIS

Visit Tyndale's exciting Web site at www.tyndale.com

Edited by:
Christopher D. Hudson
J. Michael Kendrick

Contributors:
Greg Asimakoupoulos
Betsy Rossen Elliot
Lauran Bell Harrison
Shawn Harrison
Amber Rae
Carol Smith
Randy Southern
Neil Wilson
Len Woods

Library of Congress Cataloging-in-Publication Data
Bible brain busters.
   p. cm.
  ISBN 0-8423-0182-8 (pbk.)
  1. Bible—Miscellanea. 2. Bible games and puzzles. I. Tyndale House Publishers.
BS612.B5 1998
220—dc21   97-41075

Printed in the United States of America

05 04 03 02 01 00 99 98
9 8 7 6 5 4 3 2 1

TABLE OF CONTENTS

INTRODUCTION

Most Bible-trivia collections have a straightforward approach: They ask you a question, and you provide the answer. It's a great way to learn new facts and to share that knowledge with other people. But after a while, the same old thing gets boring. You need new challenges. You yearn for something more compelling, more tantalizing.

For those of you in the same old trivia rut, *Bible Brain Busters* springs to the rescue! We've packed this volume with more than a dozen intriguing approaches to Bible knowledge. You'll find scrambled numbers, tangled timelines, baffling crimes, rhyming tombstones, holiday quizzes, puzzling definitions, and mystery guests. Your job is to solve the conundrums we have placed before you.

You'll notice that all the puzzles are arranged according to difficulty. So if you feel intimidated, begin slowly. Start with the easy questions; then move to the intermediate and advanced levels. The expert-level questions will challenge even the most intrepid Bible scholar. If you master these incredibly challenging puzzles, congratulations!

But don't keep the fun to yourself! *Bible Brain Busters* can be a great way to kick off a small group, a youth gathering, or a family event. Let these amazing facts from God add life to your next get-together!

Name That Book
(PART 1)

In which book of the Bible will you find . . .
(Extra credit if you can name the chapter and verse, too!)

EASY

1. Songs written by the sons of Korah
2. The woman named "Babylon the Great, Mother of All Prostitutes and Obscenities in the World"
3. The wise men who followed the star to Bethlehem
4. Eli, who mistakes Hannah's fervent prayer for drunkenness
5. The water that was turned to wine
6. The walls of Jericho that collapsed
7. Queen Vashti, who was banished
8. The valley of dry bones that became alive again
9. Four things that make the earth tremble
10. Four things that are small but wise
11. Gabriel telling Mary she will give birth to a son
12. Enoch taken by God
13. "The sword of the Spirit, which is the word of God"
14. Miriam struck with leprosy for criticizing Moses
15. The stones used to kill Stephen
16. The stone and sling that killed Goliath
17. The still, small voice of God
18. The statue of a man with a head of gold, chest and arms

of silver, belly and thighs of bronze, legs of iron, and feet of iron and clay

19. God speaking to Job from the whirlwind
20. A song to be accompanied by an eight-stringed instrument
21. King Solomon declaring that obtaining wisdom is like chasing the wind
22. Joseph's silver cup
23. Paul's shipwreck on the island of Malta
24. The shepherds who visited Jesus at his birth
25. Samson's shaved head
26. Quail sent to the complaining Israelites
27. The scarlet rope that guaranteed Rahab's safety
28. The scales that fell from Saul's eyes when his sight was returned to him
29. The robe that set Joseph apart from his brothers
30. A river that cleansed Naaman's leprosy
31. Zechariah regaining his power of speech at his son's birth
32. The poisonous snake that failed to harm an apostle
33. Paul pleading for kindness on behalf of Onesimus
34. Ten plagues against Egypt
35. The people of Nineveh who turned from their evil ways—in stark contrast to the disobedience of Israel at the time
36. The tree of life
37. The number of the beast—666
38. The mysterious hand that spelled out Belshazzar's coming demise
39. The mark required on the right hand or on the forehead by the two-horned beast
40. The lots used to choose Matthias

INTERMEDIATE

1. Moses' death
2. Jacob blessing Pharaoh
3. Israel's request for a king
4. The prophecy that a virgin would conceive a child and call him Immanuel
5. The beauty of a gentle and quiet spirit, which is precious to God
6. Epaphroditus sent home again after his illness

7. Herod ordering killed all the boys in Bethlehem under two years old
8. The decree that allowed the Jews to defend themselves against anyone who attacked them
9. Twelve-year-old Jesus, who amazed the religious teachers in the temple
10. The leafy plant and worm that God used to teach a prophet a lesson about mercy
11. The loud gong and clanging cymbals that represent speaking without love
12. Samuel anointing David as king
13. Stephen's face bright as an angel's
14. The Samaritan woman at the well who spreads the news about Jesus
15. The tower of Babel
16. A Jew who becomes the prime minister of King Artaxerxes of Persia
17. John seeing the bride, the wife of the Lamb
18. The fleece used by Gideon to test God's promise
19. The sickle used by the Son of Man to harvest the earth
20. The strips of cloth used to wrap the newborn baby Jesus
21. The worms that consumed Herod's body
22. Boaz marrying Naomi's daughter-in-law
23. Jesus commissioning the disciple John to care for his mother
24. Jesus washing the disciples' feet
25. A coat that divided a family
26. A pharaoh who dreams about grain and corn
27. Ananias and Sapphira dying for their deception
28. The medium at Endor
29. The mountain of fire that was thrown into the sea, turning one-third of the sea into blood
30. The leaves used for medicine to heal the nations
31. The vine and gardener that illustrate Jesus and the Father
32. The believers first given the title "Christians"
33. Six things God hates
34. The eye-covered wheels in the prophet's vision
35. A ram stuck in a bush
36. A baby floating in the reeds
37. Priscilla and Aquila instructing Apollos

38. The stone that Jacob used as a pillow
39. Thomas believing in Jesus' resurrection
40. The prophecy about John the Baptist that said he would
    not touch liquor, would be filled with the Holy Spirit before
    his birth, would persuade many to turn to the Lord, and
    would have the spirit and power of Elijah

ADVANCED

1. The young women of Jerusalem who talk with Solomon's
   bride
2. Jesus writing in the dust with his finger and driving away
   the accusers of an adulterous woman
3. The woman who declares herself to be the rose of Sharon,
   the lily of the valley
4. The parable about the woman whose persistence earned
   her justice from an exasperated judge
5. The window that a king shot arrows through
6. The whip Jesus used to chase the merchants and money
   changers from the temple
7. The warning from Paul's nephew
8. The walls Sanballat, Tobiah, and Geshem opposed
   rebuilding
9. The wall of hostility between Jews and Gentiles broken down
10. The vineyard that Ahab wanted
11. The two stone tablets God wrote on
12. Jesus' trial before Herod
13. Paul torn between wanting to live and wanting to go and be
    with Christ
14. The tiny rudder to which the tongue is compared
15. The ten bridesmaids whose story illustrated the kingdom
    of heaven
16. Paul telling his child in the faith to drink a little wine for the
    sake of his stomach
17. The sting that results in death
18. Red stew that gained a birthright
19. The small bit to which the tongue is compared
20. The seven bowls holding the seven plagues of God's wrath
21. The seal on Jesus' tomb with guards to protect the grave

22. The scrolls on which Baruch recorded the words of the prophet
23. Barnabas sailing to Cyprus with John Mark
24. A sacrifice that carried its own wood
25. The robe for which the soldiers threw dice
26. Lazarus rising from the dead
27. The rebuilt walls of Jerusalem
28. The raven that brought Elijah food
29. A queen from Sheba brings gifts to Solomon
30. Eliashib provides Tobiah with a temple storeroom
31. The prophet appointed as a watchman for Israel
32. A prophet helps Solomon become king
33. Simeon prophesying that Jesus will reveal the deepest thoughts of many
34. The prophecy of Enoch
35. Jesus promising paradise to the criminal hanging beside him
36. Anna praising God for Jesus
37. The potter and clay that God used as an illustration of his authority to destroy Judah
38. Jesus' post-resurrection appearance to Peter when Peter was alone
39. Paul pleading with Euodia and Syntyche to settle their disagreement
40. The plans David made to help Solomon build the temple

EXPERT

1. The Nicolaitans
2. Miriam's tambourine
3. Antipas martyred
4. The hundred bulls, two hundred rams, and four hundred lambs sacrificed at the dedication of the rebuilt temple after the Exile
5. The man on a red horse among the myrtle trees in the prophet's vision
6. Goatskin used as a disguise
7. The church that acted as Paul's letter of recommendation
8. A divine judgment against Solomon
9. The cutting, swarming, and stripping locusts that invaded the land of Israel

10. Paul turning Hymenaeus and Alexander over to Satan so they would learn not to blaspheme God
11. A smoking firepot and a flaming torch
12. Jonathan and his armor bearer defeating the Philistines
13. A bandage used as a disguise
14. The prophet who ate a scroll covered with funeral songs, words of sorrow, and pronouncements of doom
15. Adonijah plotting to become king in place of David
16. The star named Bitterness
17. The Field of Blood receiving its name
18. A palace that burned with the king still inside
19. Abishag warming King David
20. Nadab and Abihu's death because they disobeyed God
21. Ehud's dagger disappearing beneath King Eglon's fat
22. Agabus predicts a famine that would affect the entire Roman world
23. Paul greeting Epenetus—the first person to become a Christian in the province of Asia
24. The Recabites commended for their faithfulness
25. The baskets of good and bad figs in the prophet's vision regarding the exiles and the people left in Jerusalem
26. Paul as a guest in Gaius's home
27. The false prophet Hananiah, who broke the yoke worn by the true prophet of God
28. The basket that held the woman named Wickedness
29. Members of Chloe's household informing Paul of arguments in the church
30. The plumb line in the prophet's vision
31. The tabernacle that is set up for the first time
32. The food that is for the stomach, and the stomach that is for food
33. The inheritance that is beyond the reach of change and decay
34. The people of Israel compared to the people of Sodom and Gomorrah
35. Timothy's release from jail
36. The bones of Joseph that are buried at Shechem
37. A lion who killed but did not eat a prophet
38. The sword that killed James (John's brother)
39. The bears that mauled forty-two youths
40. Tertius writing a letter for Paul

Name That Book (Part 1, Answers)

EASY

1. Psalms (42 and others)
2. Revelation (17:5)
3. Matthew (2:9)
4. 1 Samuel (1:12-14)
5. John (2:9)
6. Joshua (6:20)
7. Esther (1:19)
8. Ezekiel (37:1-8)
9. Proverbs (30:21-23)
10. Proverbs (30:24-28)
11. Luke (1:31)
12. Genesis (5:22-24)
13. Ephesians (6:17)
14. Numbers (12:1-15)
15. Acts (7:58-60)
16. 1 Samuel (17:49)
17. 1 Kings (19:12)
18. Daniel (2:31-33)
19. Job (38:1)
20. Psalms (12 and others)
21. Ecclesiastes (1:17)
22. Genesis (44:2)
23. Acts (28:1)
24. Luke (2:20)
25. Judges (16:19)
26. Numbers (11:31)
27. Joshua (2:17-18)
28. Acts (9:18)
29. Genesis (37:3)
30. 2 Kings (5:14)
31. Luke (1:63-64)
32. Acts (28:3)
33. Philemon (1:10)
34. Exodus (7–11)
35. Jonah (3:5)
36. Genesis (3:22) and Revelation (2:7; 22:2)
37. Revelation (13:18)
38. Daniel (5:5)
39. Revelation (13:16)
40. Acts (1:26)

INTERMEDIATE

1. Deuteronomy (34:5)
2. Genesis (47:1-12)
3. 1 Samuel (8:4-5)
4. Isaiah (7:14)
5. 1 Peter (3:4)
6. Philippians (2:25-27)
7. Matthew (2:16)
8. Esther (8:11)
9. Luke (2:46-47)
10. Jonah (4)
11. 1 Corinthians (13:1)
12. 1 Samuel (16:13)
13. Acts (6:15)
14. John (4:39)
15. Genesis (11:1-9)
16. Esther (10:3)
17. Revelation (21:9)
18. Judges (6:36-40)
19. Revelation (14:14-16)
20. Luke (2:7)
21. Acts (12:23)
22. Ruth (4:13)
23. John (19:26-27)
24. John (13:5)
25. Genesis (37:3)
26. Genesis (41:17-21)
27. Acts (5:1-11)
28. 1 Samuel (28)

29. Revelation (8:8)
30. Revelation (22:2)
31. John (15:1-4)
32. Acts (11:26)
33. Proverbs (6:16-17)
34. Ezekiel (1:18)
35. Genesis (22:13)
36. Exodus (2:3)
37. Acts (18:26)
38. Genesis (28:10-11)
39. John (20:27-28)
40. Luke (1:15-17)

ADVANCED

1. Song of Songs
2. John (8:6-9)
3. Song of Songs (2:1)
4. Luke (18:3-5)
5. 2 Kings (13:17)
6. John (2:15)
7. Acts (23:20-21)
8. Nehemiah (2:18-19)
9. Ephesians (2:14)
10. 1 Kings (21)
11. Exodus (24:12)
12. Luke (23:9)
13. Philippians (1:23)
14. James (3:4)
15. Matthew (25:1-13)
16. 1 Timothy (5:23)
17. 1 Corinthians (15:56)
18. Genesis (25:30)
19. James (3:3)
20. Revelation (15:6-8)
21. Matthew (27:65-66)
22. Jeremiah (36)
23. Acts (15:39)
24. Genesis (22:6)
25. John (19:23-24)
26. John (11:44)
27. Nehemiah (6:15)
28. 1 Kings (17:4-6)
29. 1 Kings (10) and 2 Chronicles (9)
30. Nehemiah (13:4-5)
31. Ezekiel (3:17)
32. 1 Kings (1:11-40)
33. Luke (2:35)
34. Jude (1:14-15)
35. Luke (23:43)

36. Luke (2:38)
37. Jeremiah (18:4)
38. Luke (24:34)
39. Philippians (4:2)
40. 1 Chronicles (22)

EXPERT

1. Revelation (2:6)
2. Exodus (15:20)
3. Revelation (2:13)
4. Ezra (6:17)
5. Zechariah (1:8)
6. Genesis (27:16)
7. 2 Corinthians (3:2)
8. 1 Kings (11:9-13)
9. Joel (1:4)
10. 1 Timothy (1:20)
11. Genesis (15:17)
12. 1 Samuel (14:13)
13. 1 Kings (20:35-43)
14. Ezekiel (2:9–3:3)
15. 1 Kings (1:5)
16. Revelation (8:11)
17. Matthew (27:5-8)
18. 1 Kings (16:18)
19. 1 Kings (1:1-4)
20. Leviticus (10:1-2)
21. Judges (3:22)
22. Acts (11:28)
23. Romans (16:5)
24. Jeremiah (35:12-19)
25. Jeremiah (24)
26. Romans (16:23)
27. Jeremiah (28:10)
28. Zechariah (5:7-8)
29. 1 Corinthians (1:11)
30. Joel (7:7-9)
31. Exodus (40)
32. 1 Corinthians (6:13)
33. 1 Peter (1:4)
34. Isaiah (1:10)
35. Hebrews (13:23)
36. Joshua (24:32)
37. 1 Kings (13:23-25)
38. Acts (12:2)
39. 2 Kings (2:24)
40. Romans (16:22)

Tombstones

The poems below could have been engraved on the headstones of famous Bible people. After reading each one, try to guess who is being described.

1. To me, Christians were worse than debtors;
   I would chain them up in iron fetters.
   But God changed my name,
   Forgave my blame,
   Had me travel and write letters.

2. You know me as the girl
   God chose to bear his only Son.
   I was scared but bravely dared
   To let his kingdom come.

3. My sheep knew me as shepherd.
   The king enjoyed my strumming.
   But when I was anointed by Sam,
   Saul's behavior became unbecoming.

4. When my boss died I took over.
   We crossed over a dry riverbed,
   And the walls of the city we conquered collapsed
   Just the way that the Lord had said.

5. I learned the hard way
   It doesn't pay
   When God says, "Go!"
   To run away.
   Your boat may toss.
   The wind may blow.
   And a giant fish
   May swallow you whole.

6. I used to pray three times a day,
   Windows open, facing the east.
   How would I know I'd end up thrown
   Into the den of a beast?

7. I lived in a garden.
   My wife made me glad.
   I never had a mother.
   And I never had a dad.

8. The hair on my head grew long as can be.
   And strong were my muscles, 'twas easy to see.
   But I had quite a temper and liked pagan maids,
   Which cost me my eyes and wondrous braids.

9. It really was a tiring chore
   To build a floating zoo.
   But I was the Lord's "yes man" for sure,
   And I did what he said to do.

10. When I was a baby, I lived in a boat
    That my mother had made from reeds.
    Rescued by royalty, I lived a fine life
    Till God called me to do his deeds.

11. I had a captive audience
    With the one who filled the stands.
    But when I gave in to the crowd
    I simply washed my hands.

12. When I left Haran,
    I walked through barren
    Land till God said stop.
    He alone knew

When the trip would be through
And if I'd ever be called someone's pop.

13. The prophecies within my book
    Announce the Lord's anointed.
    Although I don't come out and say it
    It's clear to whom they pointed.

14. With boils and heartache and trouble
    I sat in some sackcloth and said,
    "Why is it that God keeps me living?
    I would surely be better off dead!"

15. The king had a way to fire us up
    For the task we were called to perform.
    All three of us prayed
    He would let up someday
    On his edict to make all conform.

16. His mother told him, "Stay away, Son,
    From Philistine girls, though they look like fun!"
    Like me, a pagan woman from Sorek Valley,
    To whom Samson was just another tally.
    Don't blame me that he lies in his grave;
    All I did was give him a shave.

17. I stood head and shoulders above all the rest;
    My words were always profane,
    Till a shepherd boy took a stone from a brook,
    Spun it round, let it go—what an aim!

18. Balak, king of Moab, was pretty scared.
    The Israelites stood on his plain.
    So I was hired to curse them
    And send them back east again.
    On my way to visit the king
    My donkey's words left their mark.
    And so I became a blessing to all
    Who called Abraham patriarch.

19. The servant knew when I watered the camels
    I would be given to Isaac to wed.

And after our marriage I blessed him with twins—
One a schemer, the other nicknamed "Red."

20. My husband lost a rib one day
In a most unusual way.
He fell asleep, and when he woke,
He fell in love. And that's no joke!

21. After a long day of working with wood
I had a dream where an angel said I should
Go ahead and marry a woman named the same
Even though a baby was growing in her frame.

22. I was simply known as Simon
Before the Rabbi came.
But when Jesus changed my aim in life,
He also changed my name.

23. My brother was a big shot,
But from public talks he would run.
So I became his toastmaster.
And my family? Just call us Priest and Sons.

24. The mother of Messiah
Is a relative of mine.
And when she came and stayed with me,
We had a "magnificent" time.

25. I've been in the pits and in prison.
I've been next in line to the throne.
But an old faded coat from my father
Is the most treasured item I own.

26. My father placed me upon the altar;
It was not what he wanted to do.
He raised the knife, was about to strike
When an angel came to my rescue.

27. Never has a man seen such visions!
A valley of bones, amazing creatures, a turning
wheel.
But the most beautiful sight I saw
Was the temple and the waters that heal.

28. You could say that I'm well versed—
    After all, I have *four* books to my name.
    But if you just called me the one Jesus loved
    That would be worth more than all the fame.

29. When I ran from a queen
    I used all my steam
    And felt like I wanted to die.
    But an angel said, "Sleep,"
    And then let me eat
    And God spoke to me with a sigh.

30. The Pharisees and all the scribes
    Came out to see me preach.
    But when I started splashin' folks
    They'd mock the things I teach.

INTERMEDIATE

1. When I was just a baby
   My daddy, David, wore the crown.
   And when it became my turn
   Adonijah tried to bring me down.

2. I wasn't able to please the Lord
   With my bloodless sacrifice.
   Since my brother did as he was told,
   I didn't treat him nice.

3. I kept the books for Jesus' men
   Even though I wasn't "born again."
   That I liked the Teacher there's no doubt.
   But I set him up to see what he was about.

4. Ever since my wife looked back
   I haven't had the guts
   To salt my eggs or popcorn
   Or eat dry roasted nuts.

5. My younger brother was a cheat;
   He stole my recipe for meat.
   He even faked my hairy arms
   While I was hunting on Dad's farm.

6. I had my doubts about such talk
   Of empty graves and ghosts.
   But when I saw those ugly scars
   I worshiped more than most.

7. I had a case of leprosy.
   It gobbled up my skin.
   But when the prophet said "Go wash,"
   I stripped and took a swim.

8. I was carried away by the Spirit
   To a chariot down Gaza way.
   And he told me to tarry with a black dignitary
   And I baptized him that very day.

9. The king granted my request
   So I rode my horse back home.
   The Holy City was such a pity.
   No walls! All rubble. I moaned!

10. I told the king a sorry tale
    About a little lamb.
    It made him mad and then quite sad
    When I said, "You're the man!"

11. Herod was carried away, I guess
    My dancing he approved.
    So I made an outrageous request
    And the Baptist's head was removed.

12. Jesus was my brother.
    He also is my Lord.
    I learned from him the truth I wrote
    That rich folk shouldn't hoard.

13. I was called Elijah's disciple.
    When he took off, I put on his coat.
    And God showed me more wondrous sights
    Like an ax head that actually floats.

14. Who would have guessed that one of my boys
    Would one day rule Israel as king?
    Especially the one who reclines in the sun
    And teaches his sheep how to sing.

15. There was a bullfrog named for me
    But that's not what I am.
    God chose me in my mother's womb
    In keeping with his plan.

16. I couldn't have a baby
    No matter how I tried.
    But soon after the Lord heard me praying
    I had a baby growing inside.

17. It fell to me to choose a king
    When Saul fell into sin.
    It grieved my heart to see him replaced.
    I really cared for him.

18. I have no proof of being born,
    But I really was alive.
    The king of Salem I was called
    By him who brought a tithe.

19. They buried me right near the town
    Where Jesus Christ was born.
    I was my husband's favorite;
    My sister was forlorn.

20. I chased my father from Jerusalem,
    And I caused him many tears.
    I might have lived to be an old man
    If I'd owned a pair of shears.

21. I ran and got my brother
    And told him near the dock,
    I had found the Messiah.
    And Jesus called him "Rock."

22. I shouldn't have an epitaph—
    After all, I didn't die.
    After three hundred years of godly life
    I walked into the sky.

23. My father pulled the bait and switch
    To keep my cousin workin'.
    My sister was who Jacob loved
    But he married me for certain.

24. My lady Sapphira's my partner in crime.
    We thought we'd make some dough on the side.
    But Peter got wise and told us
    We'd drop dead because we had lied!

25. A murderous thug and a criminal
    Is what I was known to be.
    Although Jesus deserved a pardon
    I'm the one Pilate set free.

26. I was a cousin of King Saul,
    General of his armed detail.
    But when David took control
    I deserted the wimpy Ish-baal.

27. I loved Hadassah as a daughter
    And raised her as my own.
    And in return she honored me
    When Xerxes gave her the throne.

28. My name may ring a bell with you.
    I hunted Jehovah's prophets.
    Because I worshiped Baal with no shame,
    I gave old Elijah real fits!

29. There was no way the Jews would live
    If it all had been left to me.
    But my wicked plans were exposed,
    And I was hanged by order of Xerxes.

30. Our mama was determined
    That her boys would get their due.
    If Jesus was God's number one
    She thought we should be number two.

ADVANCED

1. They called my boy a Baptist,
   But not because of me.
   Our family had been Levites
   Since Moses set us free.

2. My name is in the Bible,
   And so is my worst sin.

When Barnabas and Paul went on
I quit, went home, gave in.

3. A "lady of the night" I'm called.
   I've known a lot of men.
   But God forgave my sordid past
   When I took two strangers in.

4. I'd been sick, and Jesus knew it.
   Instead of coming he delayed.
   And by the time he finally showed
   I'd been dead for several days.

5. When I was called Levi and raked in the bucks
   Jesus challenged me to share.
   He came for dinner at my place,
   Then I followed him everywhere.

6. I loved to slap folks on the back
   And say, "Great job! You're neat!"
   My friends gave me a nickname
   To go with my missionary feet.

7. When Paul and I were jailbirds
   You should have heard us sing.
   The earth was quakin', our cells were shakin',
   So the jailer claimed Jesus as King.

8. Sticks and stones can break your bones—
   I know, they took my life.
   But when I looked in the sky, I had courage to die
   As I left all Jerusalem's strife.

9. It was the Passover feast
   And I was high priest
   The night their King Jesus was "crowned."
   My Pharisee friends
   Cursed him time and again
   While he made not even one sound.

10. I marveled at the wonders
    Done in Jesus' name.
    In fact, I offered money
    If I could do the same.

11. My prophetic pen expressed God's wrath
    For those who steal him blind
    And for those who break their wedding vows.
    My book's not hard to find.

12. My great-grandson was Israel's king.
    I was not a Jew, but a careful gleaner.
    When back to Bethlehem I went
    I wed my kinsman-redeemer.

13. Why not take a census? It makes sense to me
    To find out who's living 'round here.
    So what's all the fuss? Don't you trust
    A man the Romans hail as Caesar?

14. Paul preached until the night was long;
    I felt myself begin to nod and yawn.
    And because I was sitting up high on a sill
    You could say it was a view to a kill.

15. My precious young daughter was dying,
    And so I stalked Jesus to see
    If this miracle-working young Rabbi
    Could help a synagogue ruler like me.

16. I deal a lot in purple cloth.
    I worship at the river.
    It's there I met a man who said
    In Christ we live forever.

17. The townsfolk of Tekoa
    Thought it kind of odd
    That one who is a farmer
    Would claim to speak for God.

18. My husband was rightly called a fool.
    God judged him and he died.
    But my offer of food so improved the king's mood,
    He asked me if I'd be his bride.

19. I never got an M.B.A.,
    But my son-in-law thinks otherwise
    Ever since I showed him the Midianite way
    To govern any size.

20. When the exiled Hebrews began to return
    To rebuild Jerusalem's walls,
    We taunted and mocked them, but we couldn't stop them.
    The best we could do is stall.

21. Our jobs were "in-tents," you could say.
    We labored with needle and thread
    And that zealous convert from Tarsus
    Learned our trade so he could eat bread.

22. Long before Jesus was born
    I lived in the town of his birth.
    My field of dreams
    Grew only barley it seems
    Until a young widow brought mirth.

23. A youngun' was I when they crowned me.
    I learned as I went how to reign.
    But when the Law of God was found,
    My eyes blinked tears like rain.

24. You probably know me as one of the spies
    Who entered the land just to see
    If all we'd been told
    Was as good as fine gold—
    Sure 'twas for Joshua and me!

25. Once when my troops were in battle
    God told me to do as he said.
    And though our enemies held sword and spear,
    My musicians led our army instead.

26. Deborah and I looked to the sky
    As we sang our duet to heaven.
    And after we ceased the land was at peace
    For forty years. What a blessing!

27. Who said we women are not skilled to lead
    Our mighty men in battle?
    I killed Sisera! Is that so amazing?
    A woman does more than just prattle.

28. Abraham's bride had a personal servant
    Who bore him a surrogate son.

I am that person in question,
And for me Ishmael's number one.

29. I saw my father naked
    When he was sleeping off his wine.
    And when he found what I had done
    He cursed me like a swine.

30. David's best friend was my father.
    As a baby I fell to the ground.
    And though as a cripple I've suffered,
    The king really wanted me around.

EXPERT

1. Quilts and clothes and comforters.
   Those who know my way
   Know my heart's a servant's kind.
   "Sew what?" I humbly say.

2. A runaway slave is who I am,
   Guilty and filled with regret.
   But the man in jail who sends all the mail
   Had my master cancel my debt.

3. My two daughters needed a husband,
   And I needed help with my flocks.
   Because I was shrewd and deceitful
   My nephew had to work 'round the clock.

4. I ran from my man and my children
   And tried to leave them for good.
   But my husband's love, as if from above,
   Pursued me like God would.

5. Always something's doing!
   There's never time to rest.
   And yet my sister always
   Finds the time to do what's best.

6. It was at my house a woman broke
   Her alabaster vase
   And expressed her love for Jesus
   While tears fell from her face.

7. After I sat on the branch I wondered
   Who is this amazing gent
   Who talked me into giving
   A refund of 400 percent!

8. I lived in a town named for Caesar.
   I was one of his trusted execs.
   But one day I had a strange vision
   And wondered, "For Pete's sake, what's next?"

9. I waited inside the temple
   For years and years and years.
   My husband died when I was young
   But God comforted my fears.
   He let me know that I would live
   To see "his promised" born.
   And I will never forget the day
   I held him. What a blessed morn!

10. I was a sorcerer of sorts.
    That's how I got my Greek name.
    But my powers shriveled at their source.
    A guy named Paul was to blame.

11. My father was the first king.
    After him, my husband reigned.
    But when David danced in his underpants,
    I looked at him with shame.

12. The year they buried my body
    Isaiah saw the Lord.
    He wept at the news (like all of the Jews)
    Because I was dearly adored.

13. My brother the prince abused me.
    He tricked me, that horrid rat!
    But his sin would be shortly avenged—
    My brother Absalom saw to that.

14. The doctor wrote it out for me;
    You could say it was a prescription.
    Two books that taught me about God's Son,
    The very best in nonfiction!

15. My baby's name was Timothy;
    My mother's name was Lois.
    We are a home that trusted God
    Even when times were the lowest.

16. My brother's name was Hophni.
    Perhaps you know our dad.
    Eli was the fattest priest
    Israel ever had.

17. Up in my watchtower
    Patiently I waited.
    I just knew that by faith
    We would be vindicated.

18. They call me a minor prophet
    But my message isn't trite.
    Old men and young men will see
    Amazing things. What a sight!

19. A royal musician I've been called;
    My name's in the Psalter a lot.
    But though I am famous, know that my aim is
    To never act like a big shot.

20. The governor of Syria,
    That's what I was back when
    A couple trekked to Bethlehem
    To find a crowded inn.

21. When Joshua's men fled from Ai
    I knew I was in trouble.
    For stealing treasure that wasn't mine
    I'm buried beneath the rubble.

22. My employer was a prophet,
    And I profited much from him.
    My ears perked up when he would speak;
    I'd jot down his words with my pen.

23. That so-and-so down at the church
    Gives my soul a blister.
    Paul wrote that we should get along
    But Syntyche's not my sister.

24. When I carried money to our brother in jail
    His spirits were high as the sky.
    He wasted no time to scrawl out his thanks
    To my church back in ol' Philippi.

25. God gave me what I asked for;
    He delivered me from pain.
    So in his list the Chronicler couldn't resist
    Accentuating more than my name.

26. When Samuel saw me in Jesse's home,
    He thought that I would be anointed.
    Although I'm handsome, muscular, and tall,
    Alas! that didn't get me appointed.

27. Joshua prophesied I would be cursed by the Lord.
    I rebuilt Jericho and regret every board.
    When I laid the foundation my first son perished.
    When I finished, I lost the other I cherished.

28. I loved to be first, and I took on all comers.
    I'd gossip, lie, and blackmail.
    I'm not one for sharing with those who come carrying
    John's message. I'd put them in jail!

29. The roll of the dice determined the man.
    It chose Matthias, not me, that day.
    But even though I didn't win,
    I'd say God got his way.

30. I told David about the slaughter in Nob;
    I chose him over Absalom.
    Those facts kept me alive when
    I backed another, not King Solomon.

Tombstones (Answers)

EASY

1. Paul
2. Mary
3. David
4. Joshua
5. Jonah
6. Daniel
7. Adam
8. Samson
9. Noah
10. Moses
11. Pontius Pilate
12. Abraham
13. Isaiah
14. Job
15. Shadrach, Meshach, and Abed-nego
16. Delilah
17. Goliath
18. Balaam
19. Rebekah
20. Eve
21. Joseph
22. Peter
23. Aaron
24. Elizabeth
25. Joseph
26. Isaac
27. Ezekiel
28. John
29. Elijah
30. John the Baptist

INTERMEDIATE

1. Solomon
2. Cain
3. Judas
4. Lot
5. Esau
6. Thomas
7. Naaman
8. Philip
9. Nehemiah
10. Nathan
11. Salome
12. James
13. Elisha
14. Jesse
15. Jeremiah
16. Hannah
17. Samuel
18. Melchizedek
19. Rachel
20. Absalom
21. Andrew
22. Enoch
23. Leah
24. Ananias
25. Barabbas
26. Abner
27. Mordecai
28. Jezebel
29. Haman
30. James and John

ADVANCED

1. Zechariah
2. John Mark
3. Rahab
4. Lazarus
5. Matthew
6. Barnabas

7. Silas
8. Stephen
9. Caiaphas
10. Simon the sorcerer
11. Malachi
12. Ruth
13. Augustus
14. Eutychus
15. Jairus
16. Lydia
17. Amos
18. Abigail
19. Jethro
20. Sanballat and Tobiah
21. Aquila and Priscilla
22. Boaz
23. Josiah
24. Caleb
25. Jehoshaphat
26. Barak
27. Jael
28. Hagar
29. Ham
30. Mephibosheth

EXPERT

1. Dorcas
2. Onesimus
3. Laban

4. Gomer
5. Martha
6. Simon the Pharisee
7. Zacchaeus
8. Cornelius
9. Anna
10. Elymas
11. Michal
12. Uzziah
13. Tamar
14. Theophilus
15. Eunice
16. Phinehas
17. Habakkuk
18. Joel
19. Asaph
20. Quirinius
21. Achan
22. Baruch
23. Euodia
24. Epaphroditus
25. Jabez
26. Eliab
27. Hiel of Bethel
28. Diotrephes
29. Barsabbas
30. Abiathar

Famous Phrases

Name the book of the Bible from which these famous expressions, titles, or phrases are derived.

EASY

1. A Good Samaritan
2. A Judas
3. *Adam's Rib,* 1949 movie
4. An eye for an eye, a tooth for a tooth
5. A Goliath
6. Pride goes before a fall.
7. Born again
8. Prodigal Son
9. Coat of many colors
10. The salt of the earth
11. Sodom and Gomorrah
12. The pearly gates
13. "Let there be light!"
14. "This do in remembrance of me."
15. "The greatest of these is love."
16. "Thy rod and thy staff comfort me."
17. "Death, where is thy sting?"
18. "You shall not make any graven images."
19. "Am I my brother's keeper?"
20. Jacob's ladder

21. Wonderful Counselor, the Mighty God, the Everlasting Father, Prince of Peace
22. "Man shall not live by bread alone."
23. Doubting Thomas
24. Golden calf
25. "The walls came a-tumblin' down."

INTERMEDIATE

1. Vanity, vanity, all is vanity.
2. "A house divided against itself cannot stand."
3. "The truth shall set you free."
4. The handwriting is on the wall.
5. A thorn in the flesh
6. There's nothing new under the sun.
7. Money is the root of all evil.
8. The apple of his eye
9. Spare the rod, spoil the child.
10. Forbidden fruit
11. A Jezebel
12. "Don't hide your light under a bushel."
13. Four horsemen of the Apocalypse
14. Have someone's head on a platter
15. "Thou art the man."
16. Wrestling with the angels
17. "The Gift of the Magi," short story by O. Henry
18. Man after my own heart
19. Physician, heal yourself.
20. "A prophet is not without honor, except in his own country."
21. Eat, drink, and be merry.
22. A cross to bear
23. A land flowing with milk and honey
24. Fight the good fight.
25. "It is more blessed to give than to receive."

ADVANCED

1. Keep to the straight and narrow
2. *Absalom, Absalom!* novel by William Faulkner
3. "The Lord gives, and the Lord takes away; blessed be the name of the Lord"

4. What therefore God hath joined together, let not man put asunder.
5. Feet of clay
6. A wolf in sheep's clothing
7. A still small voice
8. Cast your bread upon the waters.
9. Entertaining angels unaware
10. How the mighty have fallen!
11. A stranger in a strange land
12. Go the way of all the earth.
13. The queen of Sheba
14. *To a God Unknown,* book by John Steinbeck
15. Out of the mouths of babes
16. Laughter is the best medicine.
17. Give up the ghost.
18. By their fruits you shall know them.
19. Let us eat and drink, for tomorrow we die.
20. Sign of the times
21. Many are called, but few are chosen.
22. The spirit is willing, but the flesh is weak.
23. To suffer fools gladly
24. Wars and rumors of wars
25. Don't let the sun go down on your anger.

EXPERT

1. To fall from grace
2. Filthy lucre
3. A labor of love
4. [God is] no respecter of persons.
5. The four corners of the world
6. *Leviathan,* political treatise by Thomas Hobbes
7. At their wits' end
8. Absent in body, but present in spirit
9. Through a glass darkly
10. Land of the living
11. "The laborer is worthy of his hire."
12. The cattle upon a thousand hills
13. Set thine house in order
14. *East of Eden,* novel by John Steinbeck

15. Balm in Gilead
16. *Chariots of Fire*, 1981 movie
17. *Lilies of the Field*, 1963 movie
18. Can a leopard change his spots?
19. *The Sun Also Rises*, novel by Ernest Hemingway
20. *The Power and the Glory*, novel by Graham Greene
21. *The Weight of Glory*, book by C. S. Lewis
22. *The Little Foxes*, play by Lillian Hellman
23. *The Skin of Our Teeth*, play by Thornton Wilder
24. *Inherit the Wind*, play by R. E. Lee about the Scopes trial of 1925
25. *How Should We Then Live?* book by Francis Schaeffer

Famous Phrases (Answers)

EASY

1. Luke
2. Matthew, Mark, Luke, John, or Acts
3. Genesis
4. Exodus, Leviticus, Deuteronomy, or Matthew
5. 1 Samuel
6. Proverbs
7. John
8. Luke
9. Genesis
10. Matthew
11. Genesis
12. Revelation
13. Genesis
14. Matthew
15. 1 Corinthians
16. Psalms
17. 1 Corinthians
18. Exodus or Deuteronomy
19. Genesis
20. Genesis
21. Isaiah
22. Deuteronomy, Matthew
23. John
24. Exodus
25. Joshua

INTERMEDIATE

1. Ecclesiastes
2. Mark or Luke
3. John
4. Daniel
5. 2 Corinthians
6. Ecclesiastes
7. 1 Timothy; the phrase actually reads: "The love of money is the root of all evil" (KJV).
8. Deuteronomy, Psalms, Proverbs, or Zechariah
9. Proverbs; the phrase actually reads: "He that spareth the rod hateth his son" (KJV).
10. Genesis
11. 1 Kings
12. Luke
13. Revelation
14. Matthew
15. 2 Samuel
16. Genesis
17. Matthew
18. 1 Samuel
19. Matthew
20. Matthew, Luke, or John
21. Ecclesiastes, Luke
22. John
23. Exodus, Leviticus, Numbers, Deuteronomy, Joshua, Jeremiah, or Ezekiel
24. 1 Timothy
25. Acts

ADVANCED

1. Matthew, Luke
2. 2 Samuel
3. Job
4. Matthew
5. Daniel
6. Matthew
7. 1 Kings
8. Ecclesiastes

9. Hebrews
10. 2 Samuel
11. Exodus
12. Joshua
13. 1 Kings
14. Acts
15. Psalms
16. Proverbs
17. Genesis, Job, Jeremiah, Lamentations, Matthew, Mark, Luke, John, or Acts
18. Matthew
19. Isaiah or 1 Corinthians
20. Matthew
21. Matthew
22. Matthew or Mark
23. 2 Corinthians
24. Matthew or Mark
25. Ephesians

EXPERT

1. Galatians
2. 1 Timothy
3. 1 Thessalonians

4. Acts
5. Isaiah or Revelation
6. Job
7. Psalms
8. 1 Corinthians
9. 1 Corinthians
10. Job, Psalms, Isaiah, Jeremiah, or Ezekiel
11. Luke
12. Psalms
13. 2 Kings or Isaiah
14. Genesis
15. Jeremiah
16. 2 Kings
17. Matthew
18. Jeremiah
19. Ecclesiastes
20. 1 Chronicles or Matthew
21. 2 Corinthians
22. Song of Songs
23. Job
24. Proverbs
25. Ezekiel

They Said What?

(PART 1)

*Guess the identity of the speaker from the statements
or questions below.*

EASY

1. "Fix your thoughts on what is true and honorable and right. Think about things that are pure and lovely and admirable. Think about things that are excellent and worthy of praise."

2. "Anyone who is willing to hear should listen to the Spirit and understand what the Spirit is saying to the churches."

3. "As surely as the Lord, the God of Israel, lives—the God whom I worship and serve—there will be no dew or rain during the next few years unless I give the word!"

4. "At last! She is part of my own flesh and bone! She will be called 'woman,' because she was taken out of a man."

5. "Brothers, I am a Pharisee, as were all my ancestors! And I am on trial because my hope is in the resurrection of the dead!"

6. "I will give half my wealth to the poor, Lord, and if I have overcharged people on their taxes, I will give them back four times as much!"

7. "But why did you need to search? You should have known that I would be in my Father's house."

8. "Come to me, all of you who are weary and carry heavy burdens, and I will give you rest."

9. "Cut the living child in two and give half to each of these women."

10. "Do not be afraid, Abram, for I will protect you, and your reward will be great."

11. "Am I my brother's keeper?"

12. "Do you need a whole army to settle this? Choose someone to fight for you, and I will represent the Philistines. We will settle this dispute in single combat!"

13. "Don't be troubled. You trust God, now trust in me."

14. "Even if everyone else deserts you, I never will."

15. "Everything is meaningless, utterly meaningless!"

16. "Follow me now! Let those who are spiritually dead care for their own dead."

17. "For God so loved the world that he gave his only Son, so that everyone who believes in him will not perish but have eternal life."

18. "Go and marry a prostitute."

19. "I won't believe it unless I see the nail wounds in his hands, put my fingers into them, and place my hand into the wound in his side."

20. "Go through the camp and tell the people to get their provisions ready. In three days you will cross the Jordan River and take possession of the land the Lord your God has given you."

21. "Go to Bethlehem and search carefully for the child. And when you find him, come back and tell me so that I can go and worship him, too!"

22. "Greetings, favored woman! The Lord is with you!"

23. "Here I am living in this beautiful cedar palace, but the Ark of the Lord's covenant is out in a tent!"

24. "How could I become a father at the age of one hundred?"

25. "How much will you pay me to betray Jesus to you?"

26. "I accept all blame in this matter, my lord. Please listen to what I have to say. I know Nabal is a wicked and ill-tempered man; please don't pay any attention to him. He is a fool."

27. "I came naked from my mother's womb, and I will be stripped of everything when I die. The Lord gave me

everything I had, and the Lord has taken it away. Praise the name of the Lord!"

28. "Come, be my disciples, and I will show you how to fish for people!"

29. "I have sinned, for I have betrayed an innocent man."

30. "I will go in to see the king. If I must die, I am willing to die."

INTERMEDIATE

1. "Am I a dog, that you come at me with a stick?"

2. "If anyone adds anything to what is written here, God will add to that person the plagues described in this book. And if anyone removes any of the words of this prophetic book, God will remove that person's share in the tree of life and in the holy city that are described in this book."

3. "Why all this weeping? You are breaking my heart! For I am ready not only to be jailed at Jerusalem but also to die for the sake of the Lord Jesus."

4. "Ah, my lord! It was a borrowed ax!"

5. "I have heard all this before. What miserable comforters you are!"

6. "Dear friends, do not believe everyone who claims to speak by the Spirit. You must test them to see if the spirit they have comes from God. For there are many false prophets in the world."

7. "For a child is born to us, a son is given to us. And the government will rest on his shoulders. These will be his royal titles: Wonderful Counselor, Mighty God, Everlasting Father, Prince of Peace."

8. "What have I done to you that deserves your beating me these three times?"

9. "From the one who eats came something to eat; out of the strong came something sweet."

10. "Give me children, or I'll die!"

11. "How can a poor man from a humble family afford the bride price for the daughter of a king?"

12. "I baptize with water; but someone is coming soon who is greater than I am—so much greater that I am not even worthy to be his slave. He will baptize you with the Holy Spirit and with fire."

13. "You are blessed by God above all other women, and your child is blessed."

14. "I have fought a good fight, I have finished the race, and I have remained faithful."

15. "If you have two coats, give one to the poor. If you have food, share it with those who are hungry."

16. "Let a curse fall on anyone who eats before evening—before I have full revenge on my enemies."

17. "My destruction is sealed, for I am a sinful man and a member of a sinful race. Yet I have seen the King, the Lord Almighty!"

18. "O Lord, I'm just not a good speaker. I never have been, and I'm not now, even after you have spoken to me. I'm clumsy with words."

19. "How foolish! You have disobeyed the command of the Lord your God. Had you obeyed, the Lord would have established your kingdom over Israel forever. But now your dynasty must end, for the Lord has sought out a man after his own heart."

20. "O my father, bless me, too!"

21. "Please, my lord, let me stay here as a slave instead of the boy, and let the boy return with his brothers. For how can I return to my father if the boy is not with me? I cannot bear to see what this would do to him."

22. "So let it be clearly known by everyone in Israel that God has made this Jesus whom you crucified to be both Lord and Messiah!"

23. "The Lord has kept me from having any children. Go and sleep with my servant. Perhaps I can have children through her."

24. "The voice is Jacob's, but the hands are Esau's."

25. "This is a true saying, and everyone should believe it: Christ Jesus came into the world to save sinners—and I was the worst of them all."

26. "We have the wood and the fire, but where is the lamb for the sacrifice?"

27. "I see very clearly that God doesn't show partiality. In every nation he accepts those who fear him and do what is right."

28. "Whom would the king wish to honor more than me?"

29. "Skin for skin."

30. "You must not build a temple to honor my name, for you are a warrior and have shed much blood."

1. "If you are really serious about wanting to return to the Lord, get rid of your foreign gods and your images of Ashtoreth. Determine to obey only the Lord; then he will rescue you from the Philistines."

2. "A vast horde of people has arrived from Egypt. They cover the face of the earth and are threatening me. Please come and curse them for me because they are so numerous."

3. "Lord, if it's really you, tell me to come to you by walking on water."

4. "Brother Saul, the Lord Jesus, who appeared to you on the road, has sent me so that you may get your sight back and be filled with the Holy Spirit."

5. "If you follow this advice, and if God directs you to do so, then you will be able to endure the pressures, and all these people will go home in peace."

6. "Come and meet a man who told me everything I ever did! Can this be the Messiah?"

7. "Even though the fig trees have no blossoms, and there are no grapes on the vine; even though the olive crop fails, and the fields lie empty and barren; even though the flocks die in the fields, and the cattle barns are empty, yet I will rejoice in the Lord! I will be joyful in the God of my salvation."

8. "Have you forgotten about the time he risked his life to kill the Philistine giant and how the Lord brought a great victory to Israel as a result? You were certainly happy about it then. Why should you murder an innocent man like David?"

9. "My father has made trouble for us all! A command like that only hurts us. See how much better I feel now that I have eaten this little bit of honey."

10. "He must become greater and greater, and I must become less and less."

11. "I am a Hebrew, and I worship the Lord, the God of heaven, who made the sea and the land."

12. "If the Lord were going to kill us, he wouldn't have accepted our burnt offering and grain offering. He wouldn't have appeared to us and told us this wonderful thing and done these miracles."

13. "Lord, how often should I forgive someone who sins against me? Seven times?"

14. "We will die, for we have seen God!"

15. "Lord, show us the Father and we will be satisfied."

16. "May the Lord, the God of Israel, under whose wings you have come to take refuge, reward you fully."

17. "No, Father, this one over here is older. Put your right hand on his head."

18. "O Lord, please hear my prayer! Listen to the prayers of those of us who delight in honoring you. Please grant me success now as I go to ask the king for a great favor."

19. "Paul, you are insane. Too much study has made you crazy!"

20. "Peter is standing at the door!"

21. "Should I go out to fight the Philistines? Will you hand them over to me?"

22. "That's fine with us! There's nothing for us here—none of our father's wealth will come to us anyway."

23. "But will God really live on earth? Why, even the highest heavens cannot contain you. How much less this Temple I have built!"

24. "The day of judgment is coming, burning like a furnace. The arrogant and the wicked will be burned up like straw on that day. They will be consumed like a tree—roots and all."

25. "Why are you so sad? You aren't sick, are you? You look like a man with deep troubles."

26. "The man who finds a wife finds a treasure and receives favor from the Lord."

27. "What is this you have done to us? What have I done to you that deserves treatment like this, making me and my kingdom guilty of this great sin? This kind of thing should not be done!"

28. "God turned into good what you meant for evil."

29. "You may kill my two sons if I don't bring Benjamin back to you. I'll be responsible for him."

30. "Why aren't you eating? Why be so sad just because you have no children? You have me—isn't that better than having ten sons?"

EXPERT

1. "Go and get your wife again. Bring her back to you and love her, even though she loves adultery. For the Lord still loves Israel even though the people have turned to other gods, offering them choice gifts."

2. "A star will rise from Jacob; a scepter will emerge from Israel. It will crush the foreheads of Moab's people, cracking the skulls of the people of Sheth."

3. "I am here to tell you what will happen later in the time of wrath. What you have seen pertains to the very end of time."

4. "At last I know that I have gained your approval, for you have granted me this request!"

5. "But you, O Bethlehem Ephrathah, are only a small village in Judah. Yet a ruler of Israel will come from you, one whose origins are from the distant past."

6. "Dress yourselves in sackcloth, you priests! Wail, you who serve before the altar! Come, spend the night in sackcloth, you ministers of my God! There is no grain or wine to offer at the Temple of your God."

7. "Gentlemen, you know that our wealth comes from this business."

8. "Where is another God like you, who pardons the sins of the survivors among his people? You cannot stay angry with your people forever, because you delight in showing mercy."

9. "Greetings, Teacher!"

10. "He will bring us relief from the painful labor of farming this ground that the Lord has cursed."

11. "Well, I'll tell you what to do. Go back to bed and pretend you are sick. When your father comes to see you, ask him to let Tamar come and prepare some food for you. Tell him you'll feel better if she feeds you."

12. "How long, O Lord, must I call for help? But you do not listen! 'Violence!' I cry, but you do not come to save. Must

I forever see this sin and misery all around me? Wherever I look, I see destruction and violence. I am surrounded by people who love to argue and fight."

13. "I suggest that you mobilize the entire army of Israel, bringing them from as far away as Dan and Beersheba. That way you will have an army as numerous as the sand on the seashore. And I think that you should personally lead the troops."

14. "Listen to me, Asa! Listen, all you people of Judah and Benjamin! The Lord will stay with you as long as you stay with him! Whenever you seek him, you will find him. But if you abandon him, he will abandon you."

15. "Why are you now questioning God's way by burdening the Gentile believers with a yoke that neither we nor our ancestors were able to bear?"

16. "Look, I am sending you the prophet Elijah before the great and dreadful day of the Lord arrives."

17. "Must I die on foreign soil, far from the presence of the Lord? Why has the king of Israel come out to search for a single flea? Why does he hunt me down like a partridge on the mountains?"

18. "No, sir, please listen to me. I will give you the cave and the field. Here in the presence of my people, I give it to you. Go and bury your dead."

19. "Go where your followers can see your miracles! You can't become a public figure if you hide like this! If you can do such wonderful things, prove it to the world!"

20. "On that day a fountain will be opened for the dynasty of David and for the people of Jerusalem, a fountain to cleanse them from all their sins and defilement."

21. "Shimei should die, for he cursed the Lord's anointed king!"

22. As far as I'm concerned, you're as perfect as an angel of God. But my commanders are afraid to have you with them in the battle. Now get up early in the morning, and leave with your men as soon as it gets light."

23. "Son of man, prophesy against the shepherds, the leaders of Israel. Give them this message from the Sovereign Lord: Destruction is certain for you shepherds who feed

yourselves instead of your flocks. Shouldn't shepherds feed their sheep?"

24. "The scepter will not depart from Judah, nor the ruler's staff from his descendants, until the coming of the one to whom it belongs, the one whom all nations will obey."

25. "The glory has departed from Israel, for the Ark of God has been captured."

26. "Today I am eighty-five years old. I am as strong now as I was when Moses sent me on that journey, and I can still travel and fight as well as I could then. So I'm asking you to give me the hill country that the Lord promised me. . . . If the Lord is with me, I will drive them out of the land, just as the Lord said."

27. "Give me a further blessing. You have been kind enough to give me land in the Negev; please give me springs as well."

28. "What are you trusting in that makes you think you can survive my siege of Jerusalem?"

29. "My soul is crushed with grief to the point of death. Stay here and watch with me."

30. "Will you choose three years of famine throughout the land, three months of fleeing from your enemies, or three days of severe plague throughout your land?"

They Said What? (Part 1, Answers)

EASY

1. Paul (Philippians 4:8)
2. Jesus (Revelation 3:22)
3. Elijah (1 Kings 17:1)
4. Adam (Genesis 2:23)
5. Paul (Acts 23:6)
6. Zacchaeus (Luke 19:8)
7. Jesus (Luke 2:49)
8. Jesus (Matthew 11:28)
9. Solomon (1 Kings 3:25)
10. God (Genesis 15:1)
11. Cain (Genesis 4:9, KJV)
12. Goliath (1 Samuel 17:8)
13. Jesus (John 14:1)
14. Peter (Matthew 26:33)
15. Solomon (Ecclesiastes 1:2)
16. Jesus (Matthew 8:22)
17. Jesus (John 3:16)
18. God (Hosea 1:2)
19. Thomas (John 20:25)
20. Joshua (Joshua 1:11)
21. Herod (Matthew 2:8)
22. Gabriel (Luke 1:28)
23. David (1 Chronicles 17:1)
24. Abraham (Genesis 17:17)
25. Judas Iscariot (Matthew 26:15)
26. Abigail (1 Samuel 25:24-25)
27. Job (Job 1:21)
28. Jesus (Matthew 4:19)
29. Judas Iscariot (Matthew 27:4)
30. Esther (Esther 4:16)

INTERMEDIATE

1. Goliath (1 Samuel 17:43)
2. John (Revelation 22:18-19)
3. Paul (Acts 21:13)
4. Elisha's student (2 Kings 6:5)
5. Job (Job 16:2)
6. John (1 John 4:1)
7. Isaiah (Isaiah 9:6)
8. Balaam's donkey (Numbers 22:28)
9. Samson (Judges 14:14)
10. Rachel (Genesis 30:1)
11. David (1 Samuel 18:23)
12. John the Baptist (Luke 3:16)
13. Elizabeth (Luke 1:42)
14. Paul (2 Timothy 4:7)
15. John the Baptist (Luke 3:11)
16. Saul (1 Samuel 14:24)
17. Isaiah (Isaiah 6:5)
18. Moses (Exodus 4:10)
19. Samuel (1 Samuel 13:13-14)
20. Esau (Genesis 27:34)
21. Judah (Genesis 44:33-34)
22. Peter (Acts 2:36)
23. Sarai (Genesis 16:2)
24. Isaac (Genesis 27:22)
25. Paul (1 Timothy 1:15)
26. Isaac (Genesis 22:7)
27. Peter (Acts 10:34-35)
28. Haman (Esther 6:6)
29. Satan (Job 2:4)
30. The Lord (1 Chronicles 28:3)

ADVANCED

1. Samuel (1 Samuel 7:3)
2. King Balak of Moab (Numbers 22:5-6)
3. Peter (Matthew 14:28)
4. Ananias (Acts 9:17)
5. Jethro (Exodus 18:23)

6. The Samaritan woman (John 4:29)
7. Habakkuk (Habakkuk 3:17-18)
8. Jonathan (1 Samuel 19:5)
9. Jonathan (1 Samuel 14:29)
10. John the Baptist (John 3:30)
11. Jonah (Jonah 1:9)
12. Manoah's wife (Judges 13:23)
13. Peter (Matthew 18:21)
14. Manoah (Judges 13:22)
15. Philip (John 14:8)
16. Boaz (Ruth 2:12)
17. Joseph (Genesis 48:18)
18. Nehemiah (Nehemiah 1:11)
19. Festus (Acts 26:24)
20. Rhoda (Acts 12:14)
21. David (1 Chronicles 14:10)
22. Rachel and Leah (Genesis 31:14)
23. Solomon (1 Kings 8:27)
24. The Lord Almighty (Malachi 4:1)
25. Artaxerxes (Nehemiah 2:2)
26. Solomon (Proverbs 18:22)
27. King Abimelech (Genesis 20:9)
28. Joseph (Genesis 50:20)
29. Reuben (Genesis 42:37)
30. Elkanah (1 Samuel 1:8)

7. Demetrius the silversmith (Acts 19:25)
8. Micah (Micah 7:18)
9. Judas Iscariot (Matthew 26:49)
10. Lamech (Genesis 5:29)
11. Jonadab (2 Samuel 13:5)
12. Habakkuk (Habakkuk 1:2-3)
13. Hushai (2 Samuel 17:11-12)
14. Azariah (2 Chronicles 15:2)
15. Peter (Acts 15:10)
16. Malachi (Malachi 4:5)
17. David (1 Samuel 26:20)
18. Ephron the Hittite (Genesis 23:11)
19. Jesus' brothers (John 7:3-4)
20. Zechariah (Zechariah 13:1)
21. Abishai (2 Samuel 19:21)
22. Achish (1 Samuel 29:9-10)
23. The Lord (Ezekiel 34:2)
24. Jacob (Genesis 49:10)
25. Phinehas' wife (1 Samuel 4:22)
26. Caleb (Joshua 14:10-12)
27. Acsah (Judges 1:15)
28. Sennacherib (2 Chronicles 32:10)
29. Jesus (Matthew 26:38)
30. Gad (2 Samuel 24:13)

EXPERT

1. The Lord (Hosea 3:1)
2. Balaam (Numbers 24:17)
3. Gabriel (Daniel 8:19)
4. Joab (2 Samuel 14:22)
5. Micah (Micah 5:2)
6. Joel (Joel 1:13)

Whodunit?

You've been appointed to investigate the scene of a crime found in the Bible. Using the clues provided, solve the mystery and determine the culprit.

EASY

1. **Crime:** Fraud
   Location: Prime section of real estate
   Clues: Perpetrator lured victim with deceitful promises of a better life. Only crime in Bible committed by an animal. Victim also involved husband in cover-up scheme.
   Hint: Read the crime report in Genesis 3:1-7.

2. **Crime:** Breach of contract, illegal confinement
   Location: Egypt
   Victims: Residents of Goshen in Egypt
   Clues: Perpetrator was the most powerful man in the land. Had an annoying habit of rescinding promises made to Hebrews who wanted to worship. Perpetrator continued in his ways despite loss of livestock and natural disasters. Eventually suffered great loss in his own family.

3. **Crime:** Cruelty to animals
   Location: Timnah
   Victim: A young lion
   Clues: Perpetrator was known for prodigious strength and

tore the lion apart with his hands. Some claim he acted in self-defense. Young man would later become a judge of Israel. He was also a Nazirite.

4. **Charge:** Illegal worship
   Location: Babylon, then under the rule of the Medes
   Defendant: Able administrative officer of one of the most powerful kingdoms on earth. Reached his position despite the fact that he belonged to a conquered people.
   Clues: Others in the kingdom were jealous of administrator's power and position. They decided to frame him by making prayer to anyone (save the king) illegal. Conspirators knew that the defendant had a habit of praying three times each day. He continued his practice and was arrested in the act. He was sentenced to death.

5. **Crime:** Murder
   Location: Jerusalem
   Means: Hasty, farcical trial and quick execution
   Clues: The crime had countless witnesses, and its results are still being felt today. The form of death is one of the most agonizing and painful. Victim was put to death with two others charged with unrelated crimes.
   Hint: The crime is retold in all four Gospels—Matthew, Mark, Luke, and John.

6. **Crime:** Attempted rape
   Location: One of the notorious cities of the Plain
   Victims: Two mysterious visitors to city, who were visiting Lot, himself a newcomer to the area
   Clues: Fiends attempted to break into Lot's house, but were struck blind. Villains most certainly died the next day in tremendous firestorm.

7. **Crime:** False worship, fornication, drunkenness
   Location: Wilderness of Sinai
   Clues: Out of boredom and disobedience, people fashioned an idol out of their own jewelry and worshiped it. Ringleader was brother of the religious leader of the nation. Incident brought severe reprisals.

8. **Crime:** Cursing and blasphemy
   Location: Elah Valley, between Israel and the Philistine city-states
   Weapon: Boastful tongue
   Clues: Perpetrator was a feared warrior in the Philistine army. He challenged the armies of Israel to produce an appropriate match for him. Warrior stood between nine and ten feet tall. Despite his strength, he was stunned by a high-velocity rock and killed with his own sword.

9. **Crime:** Adultery
   Location: Jerusalem
   Circumstances: A military leader failed to lead his troops but remained at home, restless. His boredom left him open to temptation.
   Clues: Perpetrator was in a position to view the victim as she was taking an evening bath. Perpetrator had the power to order the victim to appear in his home. Victim became pregnant as a result of the perpetrator's actions.
   Hint: This event is recorded in 2 Samuel 11:1-5.

10. **Crime:** Murder, resisting arrest, and obstruction of justice
    Location: Goshen, Egypt
    Weapon: Unknown
    Clues: Fugitive is alleged to have murdered a member of the ruling class. Public awareness of the crime resulted in his loss of royal stature and his escape from Egypt. Fugitive suspected of having ties with Hebrew slaves.
    Hint: The fugitive's identity can be found in Exodus 2:11-17.

INTERMEDIATE

1. **Crime:** Attempted murder
   Location: Jerusalem
   Weapon: Spear
   Clues: Just before the incident, the intended victim was playing harp in the king's palace. The intended victim was an extremely popular young soldier who would eventually become king. The perpetrator had reason to feel jealous toward the young musician.
   Hint: This incident is described in 1 Samuel 18:1-13.

2. **Crime:** Manslaughter
   Location: The city of Rabbah
   Circumstances: An outstanding soldier was deliberately placed in harm's way so that he was killed.
   Clues: Soldier had recently been ordered home on leave to try to hide the fact that his wife had just been made pregnant by his commander in chief. Out of solidarity with his fellow soldiers, he refused to spend time with his wife, ruining the plan. Apparently, losing face with one of his brave soldiers seemed worse to the commander than having him killed. The soldier returned to the battleground unknowingly carrying his own death orders.
   Hint: This tragic episode is recorded in 2 Samuel 11:6-27.

3. **Crime:** Murder
   Location: Perpetrator's farm
   Weapon: Unknown
   Clues: Perpetrator reportedly both angry and jealous of victim. Perpetrator and victim were brothers.
   Hint: The details are recorded in Genesis 4:1-14.

4. **Crime:** Fraud
   Location: Land of Canaan
   Method: Roast venison and animal skins
   Clues: Victim was deceived by the perpetrator's clever disguise. Perpetrator's accomplice was his own mother. Still other clues: Item taken was a valuable birthright blessing. Victim was the father of the perpetrator.
   Hint: Read the crime report in Genesis 27:1-29.

5. **Crime:** Assault
   Location: Near the Jabbok River
   Clues: Perpetrator engaged a stronger opponent in a wrestling match. The match was a draw, but the perpetrator was left with a limp.
   Hint: The fight report is found in Genesis 32:22-30.

6. **Crime:** Illegal pro-life activity
   Location: Goshen, Egypt
   Clues: Fear of a population explosion among tribes of Israel led to aggressive infanticide laws. Partial-birth and even post-birth killing of Hebrew male children was legally

required. Medical staff took drastic measures to keep the children alive anyway. Parents hid newborns. Male children continued to survive and multiply.

Hint: This exciting episode is told in Exodus 1:15-22.

7. **Crime:** Thirty killings that could be called the "Wardrobe Murders"
   Location: Ashkelon, city-state of the Philistines
   Weapons: Unknown
   Clues: Victims were all known as stylish dressers whose bodies were found missing their clothing. Young men in Timnah were reportedly seen wearing the missing clothing. When questioned, the young men claimed the fine robes had been given to them as a present by the groom at a recent wedding they had attended.
   Hint: This episode in one judge's life is recorded in Judges 14:10-20.

8. **Crime:** Rape
   Location: Jerusalem
   Setting: The royal palace
   Clues: The victim tried to avoid the shame by agreeing beforehand that she would marry the perpetrator. Perpetrator despised and rejected the victim after the rape. Victim was the half sister of the perpetrator.
   Hint: This shameful crime is recorded in 2 Samuel 13:1-19.

9. **Crime:** Attempted genocide
   Location: Suza, capital of the Medo-Persian empire
   Means: Intended victims were targeted for reprisals because their faith made them unwilling to bow before a prideful government official.
   Clues: The official was willing to manipulate the king and his power to take vengeance on an entire ethnic group. The king gave the official permission to act without full knowledge of the plan. The queen became the key person to thwart the planned genocide. She was actually part of the targeted group herself.
   Hint: This story of political intrigue is recounted in Esther 3:1–4:14.

10. **Crime:** Treason
    Location: Jerusalem
    Means: A clever public relations campaign stole the loyalty of the king's subjects.
    Clues: Rebel was a charismatic man whose father had never disciplined him. One of his most notable features was his thick, long hair. He had also been involved in a sordid murder and was estranged from the king for some time.
    Hint: The details of this episode are recorded in 2 Samuel 15:1–16:23.

ADVANCED

1. **Crime:** Theft
   Location: Paddan-aram
   Weapon: None
   Clues: Victim's relatives disappeared suddenly. The household shrine was apparently looted. Jacob left his father-in-law's neighborhood unannounced and traveled back to Canaan.
   Hint: The thief is revealed in Genesis 31:17-21.

2. **Crime:** Rape
   Location: City of Shechem in Canaan
   Weapon: None reported
   Clues: Perpetrator offered to marry the victim. Father of the perpetrator approached father of the girl with an offer of marriage.
   Hint: Find the names of those involved in Genesis 34:1-6.

3. **Crime:** Attempted rape
   Location: Egypt
   Weapon: None
   Clues: Victim claimed she was attacked by her husband's administrator. Accused claimed he was sexually harassed by the wife. Accused fled the scene, leaving his coat behind. Until this incident, the accused had been trusted with the husband's entire estate.
   Hint: The rest of the story can be found in Genesis 39:1-19.

4. **Crime:** Unlawful offering
   Location: The Hebrew tabernacle of worship in the desert of Sinai
   Physical evidence: Nothing left of the bodies. Some badly scorched religious censers for carrying holy fire were found at the scene.
   Clues: Perpetrators were seen lighting their worship censers from a common fire. Perpetrators displayed no concern about their actions. God had given strict instructions about every detail of worship, including the keeping of holy fire to be used in lighting ceremonies. Perpetrators related to the high priest Aaron.
   Hint: The report of God's judgment is recorded in Leviticus 10:1-3.

5. **Crime:** Murder
   Location: The city gate at Hebron
   Weapon: Dagger
   Clues: Victim had killed the brother of the killer in combat earlier. The killer excused his deed by claiming that the victim had come to spy on the king.
   Hint: This act of vengeance is recorded in 2 Samuel 3:22-30.

6. **Crime:** Murder
   Location: The great stone in Gibeon
   Weapon: Dagger
   Clues: The victim had recently been designated commander in chief of the army of Israel after Absalom's revolt. The victim knew and trusted the killer. Both the victim and the killer were on special assignments for the king, but the killer had reason to want the victim dead. Killer had a reputation for bumping off rivals.
   Hint: This treacherous act is described in 2 Samuel 19:11-14; 20:1-13.

7. **Crime:** Attempted political coup
   Location: Jerusalem
   Circumstance: Like Absalom before him, a member of David's family tried unsuccessfully to take the throne before David could name an heir.

Clues: Perpetrator first tried to generate public support for his claim to the throne. He recruited some of David's inner circle (General Joab and Abiathar the priest). Nathan the prophet and Bathsheba were able to derail the coup by having David make his choice of heir public.

Hint: The identities of David's chosen heir and this pretender are recorded in 1 Kings 1:28-53.

8. **Crime:** Fraud

   Location: Outside Samaria

   Background: The victim had recently been healed of leprosy. The victim was a Syrian military leader.

   Clues: The healing had been accomplished without charge. Even gifts of appreciation had been refused. Perpetrator worked for the healer. Perpetrator decided to pursue the victim and convince him that "gifts" would, after all, be appropriate and accepted. His violation was made known, and his punishment resulted in him receiving the leprosy from which his victim had been healed.

   Hint: The details of this crime can be found in 2 Kings 5.

9. **Crime:** Murder

   Location: Jerusalem

   Details: A royal grandmother tried to kill all of her grandchildren when she learned that her son, the king, had been murdered. Only one of the grandchildren was rescued and later became the king.

   Clues: Although this grandmother was part of the royal household in Judah, she was born in the royal household of Israel. Her family was cursed by God for its unspeakable acts of evil. Her only surviving grandson, Joash, was rescued by his aunt Jehosheba, who was married to a priest named Jehoida. The murdering queen was later overthown and killed.

   Hint: This story of shame is recorded in 2 Kings 11:1-16.

10. **Crime:** Assault with a deadly weapon

    Location: Mount of Olives, outside Jerusalem

    Weapon: Sword

    Clues: Crime was committed at night, there were numerous witnesses, and both attacker and victim were

underlings to more senior people. Jesus rebuked the attacker even though he was on Jesus' side.
Hint: The account in John 18:1-11 cuts to the heart of the matter.

1. **Crime:** Multiple homicide
   Location: Shechem in Canaan
   Weapons: Swords
   Clues: The victims were all adult men. They were practically helpless because they had recently been circumcised. The murders turned out to be an act of vengeance by brothers of a girl who had been raped.
   Hint: This tragic event is retold in Genesis 34:7-29.

2. **Crime:** Assassination
   Location: Nineveh in Assyria
   Setting: Victim was assassinated in a pagan temple after returning from a military campaign.
   Clues: The accused were related to the victim. Victim had recently suffered a humiliating defeat at the hands of an obviously inferior opponent, King Hezekiah of Judah. The defeat was the result of humble prayer on the part of King Hezekiah and his spiritual advisor, the prophet Isaiah. Victim was killed by his own sons.
   Hint: This event is recorded in 2 Chronicles 32:20-22.

3. **Crime:** Incest
   Location: The mountains near Zoar
   Clues: Both daughters bore children fathered by their own father. The daughters' plan was deliberate and premeditated, as they got their father drunk before each act.
   Hint: This tragedy is recorded in Genesis 19:30-38.

4. **Crime:** Multiple homicide
   Location: Shechem
   Circumstance: Political struggle in royal family
   Clues: Gideon, the judge of Israel, died without naming an heir from among his seventy sons. Killers were hired using money that had been given in pagan worship by the people

of Shechem. All of Gideon's children were killed except
two: a son named Jotham and the perpetrator.
Hint: The grisly details of this crime are recorded in Judges
9:1-6.

5. **Crime:** Murder
   Location: Mahanaim
   Weapon: Probably swords
   Clues: Killers sneaked into the king's bedroom and
   murdered him while he slept. They cut off his head and
   took it to present to King David, whom they wanted to
   impress. The killers were themselves executed for having
   murdered a king.
   Hint: Discover the identity of the killers in 2 Samuel 4.

6. **Crime:** Treason
   Location: Jerusalem
   Circumstance: Rejected heir devised a simple and daring
   plan to steal the throne by marrying one of the dead king's
   former wives.
   Clues: The perpetrator was related to the former king. The
   perpetrator had already tried to take the throne once
   before. The king in power had warned the perpetrator that
   any further efforts to take the throne would lead to death.
   Hint: The tragic fate of this son of a king is recorded in
   1 Kings 2:13-25.

7. **Crime:** Theft
   Location: Jericho
   Items taken: A costly robe, some silver, and a valuable
   bar of gold
   Clues: The action occurred after God had given strict
   instructions that the only items to be kept from Jericho
   would be given to the Lord's treasury. God's displeasure
   with the theft was revealed when the people were soundly
   defeated in their next battle. The items were discovered
   hidden under the perpetrator's tent.
   Hint: You won't have to endure the painful process the
   Israelites went through to find the culprit. Read the report
   in Joshua 7.

8. **Crime:** Counterfeiting
   Location: Jerusalem
   Details: Perpetrator lost items of great value and had inferior replicas made to hide the loss.
   Clues: Items had dual use as elaborate decorations as well as parts of the honor guard's armor in the palace of a king. Originals were lost when an invader ransacked the temple and palace of Jerusalem. Fakes were made out of bronze to replace the gold originals.
   Hint: This fast switch is described in 1 Kings 14:25-28.

9. **Crime:** Assassination
   Location: Damascus
   Weapon: A wet blanket
   Clues: Victim was a king of Syria who had been ill. Killer was sent by the king to Elisha to find out whether he would recover. God revealed to Elisha that the king would recover but would soon die at the hands of another. Elisha knew and was grieved by the evil the killer/messenger would commit. Only the recovery part of the message was delivered to the king. The killer carried out his act the following day.
   Hint: This assassination is described in 2 Kings 8:7-15.

10. **Crime:** Murder
    Location: Land of Nod
    Weapon: Unknown
    Clues: Accused claimed he killed someone in self-defense who had wounded him. The first capital crime recorded after Cain's murder of Abel.
    Hint: The accused's confession is recorded in Genesis 4:23-25.

Whodunit? (Answers)

EASY

1. Satan's deception of Eve. Significance: Set up the human race for sin.
2. The pharaoh of Egypt. Significance: Pharaoh's willful disobedience of God's commands led him and his people into disaster.
3. Samson. Significance: Samson's great strength was a gift, but he did not always use it wisely.
4. Daniel. Significance: No one has a right to a higher allegiance from us than God.
5. The Sanhedrin and Pontius Pilate. Significance: Although Jesus' death was entirely unfair from a human point of view, he fulfilled God's purpose, took on our blame, and gave us eternal life through his death and resurrection.
6. The perverted inhabitants of Sodom, who lusted after Lot's visitors. Significance: This horrifying incident confirmed the necessity of the judgment that destroyed Sodom and Gomorrah.
7. The Israelite refugees from Egypt, who, led by Aaron, worshiped the gold calf. Significance: Aaron's foolish concession to the demands of the people led to widespread misery and death.
8. Goliath of Gath. Significance: God avenged the Philistine's curses through his servant David, an unlikely warrior.
9. David, with Bathsheba. Significance: This impulsive action opened David's family to a terrible series of sins.
10. Moses, who fled Egypt when his killing of the Egyptian guard was made public. Significance: Poor decisions often lead to actions of panic.

INTERMEDIATE

1. Saul, who attempted to pin David to the wall with his spear. Significance: Demonstrated the fact that Saul was rapidly losing control of himself and his kingdom.
2. David, who arranged for Uriah's death. Significance: David's original sin of adultery led to other sins, including murder.
3. Cain, who killed his brother, Abel. Significance: The crime of murder became a part of human history within one generation of Adam.
4. Jacob, who tricked his father, Isaac, into giving him the blessing meant for Esau. Significance: God's plan will work out in spite of humans' efforts to advance it improperly or alter it by their choices.
5. Jacob, who wrestled all night with God's messenger. Significance: Jacob was not too proud to cling to God desperately. His

unashamed desperation was rewarded with blessing.

6. The Hebrew midwives, Shiprah and Puah. Significance: God's laws supersede men's laws when they conflict.

7. Samson. Significance: One of the results of Samson's refusal to see his strength as a gift God meant to be carefully kept and used.

8. Amnon, son of David, who raped his half sister Tamar. Significance: Amnon's ugly deed would eventually result in his own death at the hand of Absalom.

9. The Jewish people were targeted for death by Haman, second highest official of Persia. Significance: God arranged people and events ahead of time to prevent the plan from being carried out.

10. Absalom, who tried to take the throne of Israel from his father, David. Significance: David's sin with Bathsheba (and his poor parenting skills) had resulted in family and national rebellion.

ADVANCED

1. Rachel, who stole the pagan idols from her father's house. Significance: The deception led to a tense standoff between Jacob and Laban, but the two were finally reconciled.

2. Shechem, son of Hamor, who raped Dinah, Jacob's daughter. Significance: One sin often paves the way for other tragedies.

3. Joseph, who was imprisoned after the accusation by Potiphar's wife, though he was innocent. Significance: Doing the right thing doesn't ensure that difficulties will not sometimes arise.

4. Nadab and Abihu, who were burned for dishonoring God's presence. Significance: Nothing profane or defiled should be brought into our worship of God.

5. Joab, who murdered Abner. Significance: Once again Joab's cold-hearted and calculating character caused him to murder another for the sake of his reputation.

6. Joab, who murdered his rival Amasa in cold blood. Significance: Yet another example of Joab's self-centered life.

7. Adonijah, who tried to take the throne before his half brother Solomon. Significance: In spite of human efforts to the contrary, God works out his will in human situations.

8. Gehazi, who embezzled gifts from Naaman. Significance: Gehazi was punished because his greed devalued the generosity of God.

9. Queen Athaliah, mother of King Ahaziah and daughter of Ahab and Jezebel. Significance: In spite of the atrocities that make up low points in human history, God maintains control.

10. Peter, who drew his sword and cut off the ear of Malchus, the high priest's servant (John 18:1-11; see also Matthew 26:47-55; Mark 14:43-48; Luke 22:47-53). Significance: Despite Jesus' attempts to prepare them for the inevitability of his death, the disciples tried to change the course of events. In desperation, Peter embraced a violent method to fight for the Prince of Peace.

EXPERT

1. Simeon and Levi, Jacob's sons, who murdered the men of Shechem. Significance: Revenge only begets more revenge. Jacob feared he would be hated by his neighbors.

2. The sons of Assyrian king Sennacherib. Significance: The king's arrogance before God was severely punished.

3. Lot's daughters. Significance: The children who came from this relationship were the ancestors of Israel's long-standing enemies, Moab and Ammon.

4. Abimelech, who conspired to have his seventy half brothers killed. Significance: Abimelech's sordid means of seizing the crown set in motion his own demise.

5. Rechab and Baanah, who assassinated Ishbosheth. Significance: David refused to take the throne by force, even though God had made it clear he would be the next king.

6. Adonijah, son of David, who tried a second time to take the throne of Israel from his half brother Solomon. Significance: King David left behind a family in disarray created by some of his own failures.

7. Achan. Significance: God does not overlook individual sin.

8. Rehoboam, who lost the gold shields of his father, Solomon, when he was defeated by King Shishak of Egypt. Significance: The episode represents how quickly the kingdom of Israel lost its glory and power.

9. Hazael, who murdered King Benhadad of Syria. Significance: God is never surprised by the events of history.

10. Lamech, who murdered an unnamed young man. Lamech's vengeful deed showed the rapid decline of human behavior after Eden.

Bible Dictionary

Select the definition or description that best matches these words.

EASY

1. **Abomination**
   a. The land where the Abomi tribe dwelled
   b. A word used to describe that which is morally offensive
   c. The divine act by which a person is cast into hell
   d. Head covering worn by women in New Testament churches

2. **Abraham's Bosom**
   a. The nickname for a mountain pass on the route from Ur to Jerusalem
   b. The affectionate name given to the tribe of Dan
   c. A figure of speech intended to indicate one's presence (with Abraham) in heaven
   d. An herb used to cure fevers

3. **Amen**
   a. A Greek word meaning "Let him preach!"
   b. The spoken command that formally ended temple worship
   c. A word intended to confirm the words, wishes, or predictions of another
   d. A word tacked onto prayers to signify that they are over

4. **Brimstone**
   a. A flammable resin from the gopher tree
   b. The kind of stone used to build Nehemiah's wall
   c. A weight used to measure the size of a fisherman's catch
   d. A rare mineral used to construct the walls of Solomon's temple

5. **Canon**
   a. The body of ancient writings that are recognized as divinely inspired
   b. Repetitive chant probably sung during temple ceremonies
   c. The currency of the Moabite peoples
   d. Forklike tool used on a threshing floor

6. **Cistern**
   a. A jeweled goblet
   b. A god worshiped in Ai, thought to control the weather
   c. A raised deck near the rear of some first-century fishing vessels
   d. A receptacle (usually underground) for holding water

7. **Dead Sea Scrolls**
   a. Maps of the Dead Sea region used by modern-day archaeologists
   b. Ancient manuscript copies of the Scriptures discovered by a Bedouin shepherd in 1947
   c. Detailed plans of Jericho used by Joshua as he planned his assault
   d. The original copies of the Bible that are kept in vaults near the Dead Sea because of the area's dry climate

8. **El**
   a. The name by which God is called in the Old Testament
   b. The fifth letter of the Hebrew alphabet
   c. The Jewish high priest during the time of Abraham
   d. A battle club used during the conquest of Canaan

9. **Ephod**
   a. A long stick used by shepherds to gather in wayward sheep

b. A sacred garment worn by the high priest

c. The original name of the city of Ephesus

d. A unit of measurement equal to about 1.6 gallons

10. **Flagon**

    a. A god worshiped by the Ammonites

    b. A city on the Appian Way known for its immorality

    c. A bottle or pitcher made of either earthenware or skin

    d. The servant of Onesimus, for whom Paul wrote his famous letter

11. **Gideon**

    a. The man who led a campaign to put Bibles in all the motel rooms in ancient Israel

    b. The manufacturer of prized trumpets

    c. The author of the Old Testament book that bears his name

    d. One of Israel's deliverers during the period of the judges

12. **Goads**

    a. Leather breastplates worn by Assyrian soldiers

    b. The most commonly used trade routes in Israel

    c. Instruments for guiding a team of oxen

    d. The name given to rural men during the time of King David

13. **Golgotha**

    a. The giant who fought with David

    b. Paul's sidekick on his trip to Rome

    c. The hill where Christ was crucified

    d. The Aramaic greeting Paul delivered to the Ephesian church

14. **Great Tribulation**

    a. Israel's eighty-year captivity in Babylon

    b. The period of lawlessness following the death of Joshua

    c. A future period of unparalleled worldwide suffering prophesied in Revelation

    d. Period of mourning for the thirty men killed by Samson during his wedding feast

15. **Habakkuk**

    a. A smoked meat enjoyed by the Israelites during a feast

    b. The saddle blanket used when traveling by camel

c. One of the minor prophets who ministered before the Exile

d. The rain goddess of the Syro-Phoenecian peoples

16. **Hades**
    a. The place where the dead are kept until the Day of judgment
    b. Roasted quail eaten during the wilderness wanderings
    c. The king who had Jeremiah thrown into the pit
    d. The Egyptian word for *scepter*

17. **Haggai**
    a. A common greeting in ancient Jerusalem
    b. A trouser-type garment worn by priests
    c. A prophet who urged the returning exiles to rebuild the temple
    d. The coastal city destroyed by David's army

18. **Hallelujah**
    a. Another name for the first forty-one Psalms
    b. A Hebrew phrase that means "Praise the Lord!"
    c. A cove in the Sea of Galilee known for its large fish
    d. Originally a baptism ritual in the river Jordan

19. **Haman**
    a. A rock badger
    b. A Persian official who tried to destroy the Jewish people
    c. A disgraced priest who died in battle against the Philistines
    d. The name for the cover of a well

20. **Heifer**
    a. A young cow
    b. A female sheep (ewe) that has not yet produced young
    c. Goats used in sacrifices
    d. The assistant to the high priest

21. **Heresy**
    a. A legal term referring to statements not actually heard but only reported
    b. One of the judges who presided over the trial of Paul
    c. Disrespect shown to a high priest
    d. A doctrinal deviation from revealed truth

22. Hittites
a. An ancient people, descended from Canaan, and settled in the Promised Land
b. The Praetorian Guard stationed in Judea during Jesus' time
c. A large, curved shield used by the Babylonians
d. What the ancients called leprosy

23. Hosanna
a. The name of Peter's mother-in-law
b. A common stew served in New Testament times
c. A cry of lament from exiles returning to the destroyed city of Jerusalem
d. A cry of pilgrims as they journeyed to Jerusalem that means "Save now!"

24. Immanuel
a. A common name for Baptist churches in North America
b. A name that means "God with us" and which is often ascribed to Christ
c. The guide who led Moses through the wilderness
d. Inland sea where Jesus walked on the water

25. Incarnation
a. Words spoken during a sacrifice
b. The act of taking on or assuming flesh
c. A flower related to the carnation and used in the temple because of its fragrant aroma
d. The theological term that means "God's justice must be satisfied"

26. Incense
a. The tax collected by officials such as Matthew and Zacchaeus
b. An aromatic compound that gives off a pleasant smell when burned
c. Sacrificial doves that Mary and Joseph presented at the temple
d. The gold inlay used to adorn the ark of the covenant

27. Iscariot
a. The surname of Judas

b. The last kingdom seized by Alexander the Great before his sudden death

c. A delicacy served at elegant banquets

d. A carriage usually pulled by two horses

28. **Jesse**

a. A wayward son of James the Elder, who became a most notorious criminal

b. The son of Obed and father of David

c. Warrior who struck down Jezebel

d. The daughter of King Jesimiel, who was known for her great beauty

29. **Jewry**

a. Term of disparagement used by Egyptian taskmasters

b. A term for the Jewish nation and/or kingdom of Judah (used in the KJV)

c. The third of the sons of Parosh

d. A term used to describe anyone who opposed the Jewish people

30. **Keturah**

a. The second wife of Abraham

b. The city to which Jonah tried to flee

c. A Hebrew word used to describe the state of being childless or infertile

d. Silversmith who started a riot in Ephesus

31. **Magi**

a. Deceptive people that tricked Joshua into signing a treaty

b. Small edible mushroom eaten by the poor

c. Ancient astrologers and/or mathematicians who were considered very wise

d. The name given for people from Magdala, the town of Mary Magdalene

32. **Matthias**

a. The prisoner released by Pilate

b. The disciple who was selected by lot to replace Judas among the twelve apostles

c. A popular name for the kind of fish that swallowed Jonah

d. Pharaoh who finally let the Israelites leave Egypt

33. **New Jerusalem**

   a. What Jerusalem was called by the residents after the Exile

   b. The northern part of the city where Solomon's temple resided

   c. The City of God that will come down from heaven as described in Revelation

   d. What Jeroboam called his capital city of Samaria after the kingdom split in two

34. **Omniscience**

   a. The slave who ran away from Philemon

   b. A theological term that describes God's complete and perfect knowledge

   c. The philosophy of Omnippocus, the Greek scholar who debated Paul on Mars Hill

   d. A word that describes God's inability to make a rock so large he cannot move it

35. **Orpah**

   a. A Moabite woman

   b. The sister-in-law of Ruth

   c. The name by which we would know a famous talk show host if not for a misspelling on her birth certificate

   d. All of the above

36. **Parable**

   a. A literary device used to illustrate unfamiliar truths by using common objects and relationships

   b. Another word for a myth or legend

   c. A nonrhyming poem

   d. Greek philosophical style that Paul relied on to refute heresy

37. **Patmos**

   a. A small rocky island in the Aegean Sea where the apostle John was banished

b. The name of Upper Egypt, the region around the mouth of the Nile

c. One of the Christians who brought Paul food when he was sick in Iconium

d. The name of a place rich in gold where Solomon sent workers to mine

38. **Perseverance**
   a. Woman encouraged by Paul during time of great hardship
   b. Continuing steadfastly in obedience and faithfulness to Christ
   c. A term that refers to the severe persecution to be unleashed in the Tribulation
   d. Fussiness about small details

39. **Pharaoh**
   a. Great palace near Luxor
   b. The title of the Egyptian kings
   c. Deity of Egyptian afterlife
   d. Mythical Egyptian bird that arose from its ashes

40. **Quicken**
   a. A word found in the KJV that means "to make alive"
   b. The system for managing the financial assets of the ancient temple
   c. To march (an army) double time
   d. The act by which news was delivered to each of the twelve tribes

41. **Redemption**
   a. A theological term that refers to God's act of freeing sinful people by paying a price for them
   b. The spiritual transaction in which we go to God and exchange our sins for his forgiveness
   c. A synonym for justification
   d. Another word for God's willingness to give Christians a second (and third) chance

42. **Repent**
   a. A term that literally means "Do what I am telling you!"
   b. To publicly declare one's innocence

c. A Greek word that literally means to change one's mind and is used to describe a person's desire to turn away from sin and to turn toward God and righteousness

d. A synonym for regret

43. **Ruddy**
   a. Wife of Haman who predicted her husband's death
   b. To be covered with rust
   c. A term used to describe a reddish complexion, like King David's
   d. The color of one of the horses mentioned in Revelation

44. **Sackcloth**
   a. Material that Rahab hung from her window to warn the Israelite spies
   b. A coarse fabric (often made of goat hair) worn during times of mourning
   c. The material used to make Joseph's coat of many colors
   d. The fabric used to make the veils in the temple

45. **Sanhedrin**
   a. A geometric name for any object shaped like the Great Pyramids of Egypt
   b. The gate through which the Babylonians entered Jerusalem
   c. The ruling party of the Samaritans
   d. The council of seventy prominent men that functioned almost as a supreme court in Israel

46. **Sapphira**
   a. The wife of Salome, King of Deuteros
   b. The Greek word from which we get our word *jewel*
   c. The wife of Ananias who was judged by God for a sinful act of hypocrisy
   d. A Philistine giantess who could lift six men at once over her head

47. **Vainglory**
   a. A Middle-eastern flower in the same family as the American morning glory
   b. The KJV translation of the Greek word *kenodoxia,* which means being prideful or haughty without reason

c. The name of the boat on which Jonah tried to flee to Tarshish

d. The preacher's familiar utterance in the book of Ecclesiastes

48. **Wave Offering**
    a. A halfhearted sacrifice that was criticized by the prophet Malachi
    b. A sacrifice in which offerings were moved back and forth in a horizontal fashion, usually to express thanks to God
    c. An annual worship ceremony held on boats in the Sea of Galilee
    d. The act of lifting one's hands in praise

49. **Worship**
    a. Literally, to bow or bend the knee
    b. A word taken from a Canaanite phrase meaning "to purge with fire"
    c. In the days of Joshua, a boat used to carry soldiers across the Dead Sea
    d. Originally, a flat stone used to make altars

50. **Zebedee**
    a. One of the five cities of the valley of Siddim
    b. The father of Peter and Andrew
    c. The father of James and John
    d. The father of Crispus and Charles

INTERMEDIATE

1. **Abaddon**
   a. A Canaanite game that Joshua refused to let the Israelites watch
   b. A word that means "destruction" in Greek and refers to a bottomless pit of torment (i.e., hades)
   c. One of the rivers of Damascus
   d. A mountain chain of which Mt. Moriah is a part

2. **Agabus**
   a. The ancient public roadway in Tarsus
   b. A New Testament prophet

c. An infectious skin disease that caused one to itch uncontrollably

d. A small coastal town on the east side of the Dead Sea

3. **Agape**

a. The Greek word that refers to pure, unconditional love (usually God's)

b. A simple meal celebrated in the early church as part of the Lord's Supper

c. A member of the Corinthian church who was disciplined for his immoral living

d. Both A and B

4. **Alamoth**

a. A giant winged insect found in the wilderness of Sin

b. Site of Saul's massacre of eighty-five priests

c. A Hebrew musical term

d. The servant who helped the blind Samson place his hands on the pillars of the Philistine temple

5. **Aleph**

a. The son of Olaph, leader of the Midianite army during the time of Judges

b. A Hebrew word that means "weary"

c. A city near Jericho

d. The first letter of the Hebrew alphabet

6. **Apocrypha**

a. The name of the Ethiopian eunuch evangelized by Philip

b. Lampstand that stood in the Holy of Holies

c. Golden statue on the Plain of Dura that Shadrach, Meshach, and Abednego refused to worship

d. The name given by church father Jerome to the books not considered among the canonical books of the Bible

7. **Belial**

a. Of or related to Bel, the god of Babylonia

b. A person who is untrustworthy

c. Another name for the city of Zoar

d. A euphemistic term for Satan, as the personification of all that is bad

8. **Book of Jashar**
   a. Book of Canaanite black arts burned by Joshua's men
   b. The Old Testament book that continues the story of Hezekiah
   c. A noncanonical collection of odes and stories
   d. The most popular book in ancient Israel that described life in Eden

9. **Castor and Pollux**
   a. Eli's wicked sons who were killed for their contempt of God's ways
   b. The sign on the ship in which Paul sailed from Malta
   c. The brothers who owned the upper room in which Christ met with his disciples
   d. A Jewish phrase that is the equivalent of our "Stay and eat!"

10. **Dodo**
    a. False prophet who declared that Hezekiah would live another fifty years
    b. A species of bird that became extinct shortly after the Flood
    c. The name of three different men in the Bible
    d. A place in the wilderness of Sinai

11. **Edification**
    a. The foundation of a giant edifice—for example, a temple
    b. The word used to describe the spiritual state of rebelliousness
    c. A word based on the Greek term meaning "to build up"
    d. A synonym for the theological concept of regeneration

12. **Elohim**
    a. The fifth month in the Jewish calendar year
    b. The birthplace of the prophet Jeremiah
    c. A Hebrew word meaning gods, both false and true ones
    d. One of the towns on the border of the tribe of Asher

13. **Epicureans**
    a. The people of the island of Epicurus, who assisted Paul on his second missionary journey

b. Followers of the philosopher Epicurus, who advocated the pursuit of pleasure

c. Jewish advocates of a legal system developed in Assyria

d. A notorious sect of Canaanites who practiced human sacrifice

14. **Frankincense**
    a. A fearsome giant from the city of Ashdod who tormented the tribe of Manasseh
    b. A common gift for newborn babies (as in the case of the infant Christ)
    c. A pale yellow, pungent resin burned for its pleasing aroma
    d. A salty substance used in sacrifices to prevent rotting and foul smells

15. **Gehazi**
    a. The king of Syria when David ruled Israel
    b. The name of the healed leper who returned to thank Jesus
    c. A village on the Sinai peninsula where Moses often took his flocks
    d. The servant of Elisha

16. **Gehenna**
    a. The daughter of Saul who ran away from home to marry a Gibeonite
    b. A glen south of Jerusalem where the Jews sacrificed their children to Molech
    c. A popular expression for the Pharisees used by Jesus and others
    d. The city where the witch of Endor lived

17. **Gershom**
    a. The levitical composer of all the music sung in the temple courts
    b. One of the twelve disciples
    c. The garden where Jesus prayed before his arrest
    d. The eldest son of Moses

18. **Gomer**
    a. A large basket for measuring flour

b. The faithless wife of the prophet Hosea

c. The lowest rank in the Chaldean military

d. A device used to sharpen iron in Bible times

19. **Hazor**

a. The cruel half brother of the queen of Sheba

b. A swordlike weapon with serrated edges

c. An important city in north Palestine

d. The name of the archangel of the Lord

20. **Heman**

a. The Israelite who molded the golden calf

b. First musician mentioned in the Bible

c. A very wise man who may have been the grandson of Judah

d. The only warrior who ever defeated Samson in a wrestling match

21. **High Places**

a. Mountains on which God revealed the law to Moses

b. Lush gardens situated near the top of the Mount of Olives

c. According to the Sadducees, the upper regions of heaven where the most glorious angels dwell

d. Elevated altars or sites of worship (usually devoted to false gods)

22. **Hyssop**

a. An Egyptian word for "king of the foreign lands"

b. A honeylike substance that the Israelites poured over their bread

c. A plant that figured prominently in Jewish sacrificial ceremonies

d. The name of Pontius Pilate's wife

23. **Ichabod**

a. The headless ghost that terrified Saul shortly before his death

b. The Hebrew word translated as "fat of the land"

c. A bottle used to hold perfume

d. The son of Phinehas; his name meant "Where is the glory?"

24. **Iconium**
   a. A precious metal used in making royal thrones, crowns, and scepters
   b. A pungent solution used by the Jews to wash down the altar area after sacrifices
   c. A city in Asia Minor visited by Paul
   d. A monument to a pagan god that Josiah burned during his reforms

25. **Intercession**
   a. The year of rest held every fifty years in Israel
   b. The act by which warring armies would declare a short, mutual truce
   c. A giant celebration held in conjunction with answers to national prayer
   d. The act of making petitions on behalf of another

26. **Kadesh**
   a. A kind of dance performed by worshipers at the temple
   b. A city near Mecca, founded by King Kabzeel
   c. One of the spies who came back with the negative report of the Promised Land
   d. A place where the Israelites encamped on their journey from Egypt to Palestine

27. **Kislev**
   a. A pastry prepared during the Passover
   b. A city near the Golan Heights
   c. An Aramaic word shouted to call sheep in from the high pastures
   d. The name of the third civil month (or ninth ecclesiastical month) in the Jewish calendar

28. **Laver**
   a. The basin in which the priests did their ceremonial washing
   b. The stone knife Abraham used to sacrifice a ram
   c. Tribe of Israel that disappeared after the Assyrian conquest
   d. A Christian who fell from a window during one of Paul's sermons

29. **Lo-Ammi**
   a. A gambling game played by Roman soldiers
   b. Curse placed on the rulers who opposed Nehemiah
   c. The name of Hosea's second son that means "not my people"
   d. The king of Ammon in the time of Joshua

30. **Malchus**
   a. Port city where Paul's shipwrecked companions washed ashore
   b. The type of rock used in building stone walls and fences
   c. The servant of the high priest, whose ear was cut off by Peter
   d. The son of Herod Antipas who tried to overthrow his father

31. **Mandrake**
   a. A river in present-day Lebanon
   b. A narcotic plant thought to be an aphrodisiac
   c. The process of installing princes in the royal court
   d. The official responsible for overseeing the construction of Solomon's palace

32. **Maranatha**
   a. Strict churches begun by Paul on his various missionary journeys
   b. The daughter of John Mark who was a beloved worker in the early church
   c. A term that is thought to mean "Come, Lord Jesus"
   d. A place four miles from Nazareth and mentioned in the Gospels

33. **Mount Tabor**
   a. The site where Jesus will one day return
   b. A limestone mound about six miles east of Nazareth
   c. The place where Noah's ark came to rest
   d. The place where Elisha was buried

34. **Nadab**
   a. A measure of pitch commonly used in the construction of city walls

b. The oldest son of Aaron who was killed by God for unholy behavior during his priestly service

c. The owner of a vineyard that was seized by Ahab and Jezebel

d. An ancestor of Jesus in his paternal line

35. **Negev**

a. A stringed instrument played by David

b. The dry, south country of Judah

c. A Hebrew word that means "to renege on a promise"

d. What Israelites would scream when they chopped off body parts that were causing them to sin

36. **Nimrod**

a. A name for someone with a penchant for acting impulsively and angrily

b. A very fertile tract of land near Bashan

c. The father of Cush

d. The son of Cush and founder of the kingdom of Babylon

37. **Publius**

a. The Latin word for *publican*

b. The governor of Malta, where Paul was shipwrecked

c. A pulpitlike structure upon which first-century missionaries often stood to preach

d. The man who carried the cross upon which Jesus was crucified

38. **Raca**

a. The daughter of Rachel

b. A city in the territory of Judah where hunting dogs were raised

c. An Aramaic verbal put-down (perhaps similar to *dummy* or *stupid*) meaning "empty-headed" or "worthless"

d. The Hebrew word that means "excellent"

39. **Reconciliation**

a. A theological term referring to the judicial act in which God declares us forgiven

b. A theological term referring to the sacrificial act in which Christ acted as our substitute, dying in our place

c. A theological term referring to the restoration of

friendship after a time of estrangement (i.e., an enemy is made a friend)

    d. A theological term referring to the divine act of making us ever like Christ

40. **Sabachthani**

    a. Messenger who warned David of King Saul's murderous plans

    b. An exotic perfume worn by wealthy women in Jerusalem

    c. A word that means "You have left me"

    d. A Semitic delicacy made from sardines, olive oil, and rolled grain

41. **Salamis**

    a. Judge who prostrated himself before the altar of Bethel

    b. The inhabitants of Salam (an island in the Dead Sea)

    c. An herb consumed in the belief that it would ward off illness

    d. A city on the isle of Cyprus

42. **Sanctification**

    a. The process in which the Holy Spirit consecrates (i.e., makes holy) believers in Christ

    b. Vow taken by Samson that forbade him from cutting his hair

    c. The process of setting up the tabernacle in the wilderness

    d. Another word for forgiveness

43. **Succoth**

    a. Squash eaten during Bible times

    b. The name of the village in which King David danced before the ark

    c. The father of Suah, wife of Gideon

    d. An ancient town in Palestine where Jacob built a house for himself after separating from Esau

44. **Tammuz**

    a. A hermit who prophesied the end of Assyria

    b. A resort near Mount Hermon where Philip had a fruitful ministry

    c. The wife of Er, the son of Judah

    d. An ancient Babylonian deity

45. **Tekel**
   a. Half a shekel
   b. Hebrew name for Day of Atonement
   c. Aramaic word meaning "weighed" that appeared on the wall during Belshazzar's feast
   d. One of the temple elders who sent away his Gentile wife

46. **Tenons**
   a. Dowel pins at the end of the planks of the tabernacle
   b. Clams served in a butter sauce
   c. Tribe in charge of setting up and taking down the tabernacle
   d. A Christian who reluctantly let Paul stay at his house

47. **Tishbite**
   a. A feared desert marauder
   b. A ceremonially unclean person who had to remain outside of the camp
   c. A resident of Tishbe, such as Elijah
   d. Small pieces of fish served in the miraculous mass-feedings of Christ

48. **Uz**
   a. The region north of the Philistine city-states
   b. A soldier who fought alongside his brother Buz in David's army
   c. The land in which Job lived
   d. A cohort of Korah during the great rebellion

49. **Zadok**
   a. Spring where Moses miraculously made bitter water drinkable
   b. The son of Nathan
   c. High priest in the time of King David
   d. A town in the low country of Judah

50. **Zedekiah**
   a. First judge of Israel who killed six hundred Moabites with an iron rod
   b. The son of Josiah and last king of Judah
   c. The writer of the Old Testament book that bears his name
   d. A prince of Midian who was defeated by Gideon

ADVANCED

1. **Akeldama**
   a. A notorious robber during the time of Christ
   b. A burial plot on the southern slope of the valley of Hinnom, the so-called field of blood
   c. An implement found near the altar and used in animal sacrifices
   d. The loophole by which the Pharisees avoided their obligations to their parents

2. **Anathema**
   a. The last word of the book of Revelation
   b. The writer of the Wisdom of Anathema, a book in the Apocrypha
   c. A Greek word that literally means "a thing laid by" and came to be used of cursed things or people
   d. A debating style enjoyed by Greek philosophers

3. **Antediluvian**
   a. Of or related to the Antediluvia region in southwestern Egypt
   b. A word used in reference to the time before the flood of Noah
   c. A dialect spoken in the high country of Edom
   d. A reference to Judah's so-called Golden Era before the invasion of King Diluv of Tyre

4. **Aramaic**
   a. Architectural style that flourished during the reign of Joachim, king of Aram
   b. Of or related to the country of Aramia, a fiercely independent kingdom one hundred miles west of Israel
   c. The language spoken by Jews during New Testament times
   d. A kind of pottery made by the peoples indigenous to the area around Mt. Ararat

5. **Bakbuk**
   a. The head of one of the Jewish families that returned from Babylon with Zerubbabel
   b. An honored Levite who had memorized the entire Torah

c. A deity in the Babylonian cosmos

d. A kind of mountain goat referred to in Job

6. **Ben-Hur**

    a. King of Judah known for his reckless chariot driving

    b. One of Solomon's twelve governors

    c. Jewish Christian who debated James over ceremonial rituals

    d. A Benjamite, son of Bela

7. **Besor**

    a. A city near Bethcar where many biblical manuscripts have been found

    b. A brook near Gaza where David and his men once camped

    c. The name of one of the survivors who fell from the Tower of Shechem

    d. Rebel swallowed up by the earth for opposing Moses

8. **Bilhah**

    a. Rachel's handmaid, given to her by Laban

    b. The mother of Dan and Naphtali

    c. The woman who had an affair with her stepson Reuben

    d. All of the above

9. **Cab**

    a. One of the seven churches John addresses in the book of Revelation

    b. A shortened version or nickname of Caleb

    c. A Hebrew measure equal to about two quarts

    d. A small Canaanite city conquered by Joshua

10. **Canticles**

    a. Brass containers used to keep manna

    b. Small crustaceans that attach themselves to fishing boats in the Sea of Galilee

    c. Another name for the Song of Songs

    d. Seven-pronged candelabras often seen at Jewish feasts

11. **Censer**

    a. Royal official who oversaw the King James Bible translation and deleted explicit phrases from the final version

b. The flint knife with which the high priest would kill the scapegoat during the Feast of Tabernacles

c. A vessel used in the burning of incense on the altar

d. The guard stationed next to the cross

12. **Cozbi**

a. A physician who approached Jesus about his sick daughter

b. A kind of sandal worn by Roman slaves

c. The name of the son of Zur, a Midianite prince

d. The daughter of Zur, a Midianite prince

13. **Daric**

a. A Persian unit of measurement (in weighing things)

b. Rebellious son who tried to overthrow King Solomon

c. A city near Sodom

d. A Hebrew word meaning "scroll"

14. **Decalogue**

a. A Jewish craft in which colorful pictures are cut, pasted, and shellacked

b. Ten cities located in the proximity of the Sea of Galilee

c. A fountain and pool located near the Acropolis

d. The name given the Ten Commandments by the Greek fathers

15. **Ebenezer**

a. Abraham's brother who refused to leave Terah

b. A stone set up by Samuel to commemorate the defeat of the Philistines

c. Mountainous region settled by Lot after he left Sodom

d. A city between Mizpah and Shen

16. **Elim**

a. To be thin from hunger

b. The eldest son of Eliphaz

c. A desert oasis where the Israelites camped during their desert journey

d. The name of a lost text written by Moses that described his years in Pharaoh's court

17. **Eschatology**
    a. The study of the marine life in the Middle Eastern bodies of water
    b. The science that has sprung up around the search for Noah's ark and other artifacts
    c. The study of the "lost years" of Christ (between ages twelve and thirty)
    d. The study of last things, especially the return of Christ

18. **Fair Havens**
    a. A phrase, found in Milton's *Paradise Regained,* thought to refer to heaven
    b. A harbor in the isle of Crete
    c. The Italian city that was the home of Priscilla and Aquila
    d. A mysterious inscription that has been found near the caves of Qumran

19. **Fleshhooks (KJV)**
    a. The spear tips used in battle by the brutal Babylonian army
    b. A device used by shepherds to hold sheep still so they could be sheared
    c. Metal bits used by pagan priests to pierce their lips, ears, nose, etc.
    d. Large forks used to handle animals being sacrificed

20. **Imputation**
    a. A theological term that means "to charge to another's account"
    b. The process by which missionaries gather the necessary funds to go overseas
    c. Another word for salvation
    d. A legal term that means "guilty as charged"

21. **Iota**
    a. The smallest letter of the Greek alphabet
    b. The name of the servant girl who accused Peter of being a follower of Christ
    c. A Hebrew word meaning "diminutive"
    d. A small village in Edom where the prophet Jonah lived

22. **Jabbok**
    a. The son of Lamech and Adah
    b. A river east of the Jordan where Jacob wrestled with God
    c. The father of Shallum
    d. A game played by Jewish youth similar to the modern game of dominoes

23. **Jambres**
    a. Shallow stream that David crossed while fleeing from Saul
    b. A musical instrument (like an oboe) played by the temple musicians
    c. The name of a magician who opposed Moses
    d. A colleague of Paul listed in Romans 16

24. **Japheth**
    a. One of the sons of Noah
    b. One of Pharaoh's priest-magicians
    c. A town of Judah close to Hebron
    d. A kind of fishing hook

25. **Jemimah**
    a. The first of three daughters of Job born to him after he regained his prosperity
    b. Town in Samaria whose name meant "well fed"
    c. The aunt of King David who lived with him and cleaned his palace
    d. The Jewish wife of Jekamiah, son of Shallum

26. **Joanna**
    a. The wife of John the Baptist
    b. An exotic dancer in the court of Nero who converted to Christianity
    c. The wife of Chuza, the steward of Herod Agrippa, who became a devoted follower of Christ
    d. The great female judge of Israel

27. **Junia**
    a. The Greek name for the month of June
    b. A pita-like bread used in eating the Passover meal

c. A Christian at Rome greeted by Paul in the letter to the Romans

d. Roman goddess of rain and fertility

28. **Kenosis**

    a. A dreamlike state in which one is able to receive divine visions

    b. Violent shaking caused by long periods of fasting

    c. A Greek word used to describe the self-denial of Christ in becoming incarnate

    d. A psychiatric condition in which one displays symptoms similar to demonic possession

29. **Lamed**

    a. Ishmaelite trader who purchased Joseph and took him to Egypt

    b. The Hebrew word for *physician*

    c. The twelfth letter of the Hebrew alphabet

    d. The name of a kind of lizard common in Israel

30. **Lois**

    a. Prophetess who blessed the infant Jesus in the temple

    b. The grandmother of Timothy

    c. The mother of Timothy

    d. The wife of Timothy

31. **Lydda**

    a. A mountainous province in the southwest of Asia Minor

    b. A town about eleven miles southeast of Joppa

    c. A seller of purple fabrics in the city of Thyatira

    d. The word used in the KJV for Lud

32. **Maher-Shalal-Hash-Baz**

    a. The symbolic Hebrew name of Isaiah's son

    b. A Jewish expression of contempt for Samaritans

    c. Arrogant king whose army was destroyed by the angel of death

    d. One of the stopping places for the children of Israel during their wilderness wandering

33. **Maskil**

    a. An obscure word that appears in the titles of many psalms

b. One of the guards whom Paul won to Christ during his Roman imprisonment

c. A kind of gourd used for food and for storage during times of famine

d. One of a shepherd's most important tools, used to shear tangled, matted wool away from a sheep's legs

34. **Nicanor**
    a. Flat bread eaten with olive oil
    b. Nicodemus' name before he met Christ and received the name by which we now know him
    c. A deacon of the church of Jerusalem
    d. Governor who ordered Paul to be sent to Rome for trial

35. **Nisan**
    a. Craftsman who manufactured chariots in ancient Egypt
    b. The name of the servant who accompanied Joshua during his conquest of Italy
    c. The first month in the Hebrew calendar
    d. A priest who served under Aaron

36. **Og**
    a. The Amorite king of Bashan
    b. Land where Job lived
    c. The third named of the sons of Simeon
    d. A frequent misspelling of the word *of* in the Gutenberg Bible

37. **Philologus**
    a. The official seal of the king found on many ancient documents
    b. The founder of a popular school of thought like Stoicus and Epictetus
    c. A Christian at Rome who was a friend of Paul's
    d. A city near Pamphylia

38. **Pishon**
    a. A diminutive Jewish man
    b. The Amorite king of Jarmuth
    c. The second named of the sons of Jethro
    d. One of the four rivers said to flow from Eden

39. Quartus
a. A Palestinian unit of liquid measurement
b. A Corinthian Christian known by Paul
c. An ancient kind of canteen worn by foot soldiers
d. A unit of four Roman soldiers

40. Regeneration
a. The spiritual act in which the Holy Spirit gives us new life and a new nature
b. Another word for being "born again"
c. A term sometimes used to describe a person's conversion
d. All the above

41. Reuel
a. Hebrew name meaning "despised by God"
b. The son of Phalec, an ancestor of our Lord
c. The name given to Jethro, the father-in-law of Moses
d. An outpost along the trade route through Asia Minor

42. Sanballat
a. Also called the Horonite, the man who opposed Nehemiah and his effort to rebuild the walls of Jerusalem
b. A device used to weigh out purchases
c. A kind of fishing vessel used in very shallow streams and creeks
d. One of the soldiers who witnessed the trial of Christ

43. Shallum
a. Bitter herb served during Passover
b. City burned by Dinah's brothers in retaliation for her rape
c. The sixteenth king of Israel
d. High priest killed at King Saul's behest by Doeg the Edomite

44. Shamgar
a. Son of David who conspired to take the throne from Solomon
b. A terrorist who led a revolt against Roman rule just before Judas Maccabaeus came on the scene

c. A Gaddite leader who advocated an end to idolatry during the settling of the land

d. The third judge of Israel

45. **Talmai**

a. One of the giants of Anak who lived in Hebron

b. The head of a family of doorkeepers at the temple

c. A spice used in cooking stews and soups

d. A city founded by Abram on his pilgrimage to Canaan

46. **Ur of the Chaldees**

a. A famous hunter who roamed the Chaldean countryside

b. Abraham's native city in southern Babylonia

c. The leader of the Chaldean resistance movement during Nebuchadnezzar's reign

d. Babylonian holy book that told the story of creation

47. **Uzzah**

a. Ornamental stone worn on the breastplate of the high priest

b. The man who tried to keep the ark of God from falling off an oxcart and died as a result

c. A war cry of the Israelite army that meant "Win for God!"

d. The son of Bukki, and brother of Walli and Beevah

48. **Vav**

a. Canaanite king who escaped from Ai and lived in hiding the rest of his life

b. The technical name for the kind of handle typically found on Jewish water wells

c. The sixth letter in the Hebrew alphabet

d. The brutal king of the Phoenicians who forced his people to build a tremendous papyrus statue

49. **Xerxes**

a. A scribe who copied biblical manuscripts

b. The ruler of the Persian Empire around 475 B.C., also known as Ahasuerus

c. Ephesian official who debated Paul in the marketplace

d. The ruler of the Babylonians during the life of Daniel

50. **Zilpah**

a. The Hebrew word for *zero*

b. The wilderness region south of Palestine

c. The mother of Lamech

d. The female servant of Leah who became the mother of Gad and Asher

1. **Adramyttium**
   a. A traveling companion and colleague of Paul
   b. The name given to sudden storms that often appeared on the Sea of Galilee
   c. A seaport of Mysia in Asia Minor
   d. The ruling council of the Babylonian government during the Exile

2. **Agora**
   a. The marketplace in a Greek city
   b. The first city visited by Paul on his missionary journey to Ireland
   c. A Greek city near Athens
   d. A highly valued breed of sheep in ancient Israel

3. **Agur**
   a. A tool used by the ancient Israelites to dig wells
   b. The author of the sayings found in Proverbs 30
   c. Mountain on which Moses died
   d. Host of the wedding in Cana where Jesus turned water to wine

4. **Amorites**
   a. The giant hailstones that fell from heaven during the ten plagues of Egypt
   b. A Canaanite tribe whose land was given to Israel
   c. The set of rituals performed during pagan marriage ceremonies
   d. The inhabitants of the Persian city of Amor

5. **Areopagus**
   a. The hill of Ares, the Greek god of war, northwest of the Acropolis in Athens
   b. The Thessalonian scribe who circulated Paul's books and letters

    c. An Arabian king, the father-in-law of Herod Antipas

    d. A blunt tool used to smash olives in the production of olive oil

6. **Baal-Berith**

    a. Another name for Satan; it means "Lord of the Flies"

    b. An herb that was used to treat snakebites during the wilderness wanderings

    c. A city near Jabneel known for its ungodliness

    d. A false god worshiped in Shechem

7. **Bashan**

    a. A Hebrew word that means "throw down" or "pummel"

    b. The priest who married beautiful Barzillai, daughter of Joab

    c. A fertile region of Israel famed for its fine cattle near the present-day Golan Heights

    d. Assyrian god of war

8. **Beulah**

    a. A figurative expression used in prophetic literature to describe restored Palestine

    b. Isaac's wife after Rebekah's death

    c. A prophetess Paul met on his third missionary journey

    d. A variation in the spelling of Bethuel, a southern city of Judah

9. **Biztha**

    a. Official who gave Absalom foolish wisdom that led to the collapse of his rebellion

    b. Jehu's captain and fellow officer

    c. A servant in charge of the harem of Xerxes/Ahasuerus

    d. A prosperous port city on the west side of Mount Bethlehem

10. **Blastus**

    a. Elder to whom the third epistle of John is addressed

    b. The mental state that afflicted Nebuchadnezzar, causing him to behave like a cow

    c. The steward of King Herod Agrippa

    d. A kind of igneous rock used in constructing Solomon's temple

11. **Corban**
    a. The term used to designate something as a sacred gift
    b. A kind of turban, worn most commonly in colder weather
    c. A colleague of St. Paul who, according to tradition, became the bishop of Alexandria
    d. A spice used to anoint the body of Jesus

12. **Dagon**
    a. Israelite stoned during wilderness wanderings for blasphemy
    b. The third of the ten sons of Haman
    c. The fourth letter of the Hebrew alphabet
    d. A fish god worshiped by the Mesopotamians

13. **Didymus**
    a. Woman in the courtyard who accused Peter of being Jesus' disciple
    b. Elevated plateau where Jesus delivered his Sermon on the Mount
    c. A town in the low country of Judah
    d. A surname of "Doubting" Thomas that means "twin"

14. **Eglon**
    a. Unit for measuring liquid volume
    b. One of David's wives during his reign in Hebron
    c. A fortified town of northern Palestine
    d. A Moabite king during the time of the judges

15. **Eldad**
    a. An outpost of ancient Baghdad
    b. One of the seventy elders appointed to assist Moses
    c. A prized strain of wheat known for its smooth texture and hearty taste
    d. A charismatic leader who lived in the period between the Testaments and claimed to be the Messiah

16. **Ephah**
    a. An Israelite of the tribe of Judah who tried to assassinate Hezekiah
    b. A common Egyptian expression of disgust
    c. The town at the foot of Mount Enosh
    d. A measure for grain

17. **Evil-Merodach**
    a. The name of a Babylonian king mentioned twice in the Old Testament
    b. The label given to Merodach of Capernaum so as to distinguish him from Merodach of Nain
    c. A nautical term describing sudden easterly winds that would inhibit travel
    d. Nomadic people who existed in what is now Saudi Arabia

18. **Gallio**
    a. A first-century wine maker
    b. The proconsul of Achaia
    c. Roman philosopher who speculated on the cause of gravity
    d. One of Paul's many traveling companions

19. **Hoshea**
    a. Exclamation shouted as Jesus made his triumphal entry into Jerusalem
    b. The prophet who married Gomer
    c. The last king of Israel
    d. The last book of the Old Testament

20. **Impeccability**
    a. The hardness of something (e.g., a pomegranate)
    b. The state of standing guilty before God
    c. The theological idea that seeks to show why Christ could not have sinned
    d. The theological idea that all people will eventually be saved

21. **Jabez**
    a. Woman who killed Abimelech with a millstone
    b. A city near Jabesh-Gilead
    c. A descendant of Judah who prayed for God to bless him
    d. Owner of the ephod taken by the tribe of Dan

22. **Jashobeam**
    a. Giant timbers used to construct the temple—imported from the forests of Jash
    b. High priest who succeeded Aaron

c. One of King David's warriors/servants

d. An intoxicating beverage consumed in pagan debauches

23. Jebus

a. The leader of the tribe of Jebusites

b. Prophet killed by a lion for disobeying God

c. The name of Jerusalem while it was under Jebusite control

d. The god of war worshiped by the Hittites

24. Joash

a. The son of Jehu and the twelfth king of Israel

b. The eighth king of Judah, son of Ahaziah

c. Hebrew name meaning "shifting sand"

d. A "poor man's stew" in Old Testament times made with leeks and lentils

25. Joppa

a. A very old city on the Mediterranean coast

b. A faithful servant of Elijah the prophet

c. A flowering plant that grows only in the high mountain pastures of Mount Hermon

d. The Egyptian name for *basket* (as in the one Moses floated in)

26. Jubal

a. The son of Lamech who invented the harp and/or organ

b. A kind of wild dog or wolf mentioned in the book of Ecclesiastes

c. A person who is joyful and jubilant

d. A time of rest celebrated every fifty years among the tribes of Israel

27. Justification

a. Giving the reason for one's sin

b. The divine act whereby a holy God declares a sinner to be righteous because of the work of Christ

c. The divine act of explaining the reason for meting out certain punishment

d. A synonym for the filling of the Holy Spirit

28. **Kenites**
    a. Marauders who defeated Joshua after his conquest of Jericho
    b. People who gave refuge to David after Absalom forced him to flee Jerusalem
    c. A group of metalsmiths who traveled throughout the Dead Sea region
    d. Residents of Kenah, a city of refuge located in the tribe of Dan

29. **Lachish**
    a. Tribute given by vassal state to a conquering king
    b. The son of Bethuel and brother of Rebekah
    c. A royal Canaanite city thirty miles southwest of Jerusalem
    d. The Hebrew word for *cheese*

30. **Leviathan**
    a. A name used to describe a large creature (either literal or symbolic)
    b. The name of the sword bearer of King David
    c. The youngest son of Levi
    d. An obscure musical term that appears commonly in Psalms

31. **Maccabees**
    a. Wandering Levites who sang for food and shelter
    b. The powerful Hasmonaean family, distinguished in Jewish history in the two centuries before Christ
    c. Division of temple priests to which Zechariah, father of John the Baptist, belonged
    d. The Gaddite warriors who sided with King David in his attempt to consolidate power

32. **Madmannah**
    a. Dissolute son of the prophet Samuel who was forced to abandon his priestly duties
    b. A town north of Jerusalem
    c. A town in the extreme south of Judah
    d. Persian official who helped Mordecai in his struggle with Haman

33. **Merab**
    a. Midwife who refused to kill the newborn Hebrew children
    b. A small rodent common in Palestine
    c. A chief priest who was a contemporary of Nehemiah
    d. The eldest daughter of Saul

34. **Muppim**
    a. The last day of the Feast of Tabernacles
    b. A potent beverage shared during feasts and celebrations
    c. A son of Merari
    d. A Benjamite and one of the descendants of Rachel

35. **Nehushtan**
    a. The daughter of Elnathan of Jerusalem
    b. The name given by King Hezekiah to the bronze serpent, then an object of idolatry
    c. The questioner who prompted Jesus to tell the story of the Good Samaritan
    d. Joseph's wife, given to him by Pharaoh

36. **Obil**
    a. Valley where Elijah put to death the prophets of Baal
    b. The son of Boaz and Ruth
    c. Rich perfume poured on Jesus' feet at Simon's banquet
    d. An Ishmaelite who kept camels during the reign of King David

37. **Phylactery**
    a. A song of mourning, such as the one sung by David for King Saul and Jonathan
    b. A strip of parchment on which Scriptures are written and fastened to the forehead or arm
    c. A physician's assistant, as John Mark was to Luke
    d. City near Thessalonica where Timothy ministered for a short time

38. **Queen of Heaven**
    a. The title given to Jezebel upon her marriage to Ahab
    b. In Syrian lore, the rival to Mother Earth
    c. A symbolic name for Israel

    d. A false goddess (such as Astarte) who was thought to
       bring about fertility

39. **Recab**
    a. A Hebrew verb that means "to heal"
    b. One of the men who killed Ish-bosheth, the son of Saul,
       in an attempt to win the favor of David
    c. Mother of Samson
    d. One of the Midianite kings whose death is recorded in
       Numbers 31

40. **Rehum**
    a. City where a war broke out between Benjamin and the
       rest of Israel
    b. Mysterious expression found five times in the book of
       Lamentations
    c. A city founded by Asshur
    d. A common name at the time of the Exile and the Return

41. **Samekh**
    a. The king of Edom just before the Israelites conquered
       the land
    b. The fifteenth letter in the Hebrew alphabet
    c. The name of the rainy season in Israel
    d. Temple scribe

42. **Satraps**
    a. Kneeling gestures made before a king
    b. High-ranking government officials in Persia
    c. The Hebrew name for the cities of refuge
    d. Special saddles used to ride camels long-distance

43. **Secundus**
    a. Gentile Christian who encouraged others to adopt
       Jewish dietary practices
    b. An opponent of Peter on one of his early preaching
       missions
    c. A Thessalonian Christian who traveled with Paul
    d. Governor who had James executed

44. **Taberah**
    a. Ornamental veil that hung in the tabernacle
    b. The father of Pekah, king of Israel in 735 B.C.

c. A place in the wilderness of Paran where God consumed the grumbling children of Israel

d. A royal city of the Canaanites conquered by Joshua

45. Tahpanhes

a. Taskmaster killed by Moses for his mistreatment of the Hebrew slaves

b. A site that figures prominently in the future battle of Armageddon

c. An important Egyptian city in the time of Jeremiah and Ezekiel

d. The chief of David's captains who was distinguished because of his left-handedness

46. Tattenai

a. A game played by Israelite children in which the object was to cast lots and gradually proceed to the Promised Land

b. The Hebrew word for "place mat"

c. A race of giants who lived in Canaan

d. The Persian governor of Samaria when Zerubbabel began rebuilding Jerusalem

47. Uel

a. Only surviving son of Samson who avenged his father's death

b. One of the sons of Bani mentioned among the returning exiles

c. Site where tower of Babel was likely built

d. The father of Melchizedek

48. Vulgate

a. One of the many entrances to the city of Jerusalem

b. Early church manuscript that describes the worship of first-century Christians

c. A Latin version of the Bible, usually attributed to Jerome

d. Roman soldier who guarded Paul during his house arrest in Rome

49. Zalmunna

a. One of the Midianite kings killed by Gideon

b. A wafer served with wine at weddings

c. A station of Israel in the wilderness

d. A disciple who deserted Paul during his Roman imprisonment

50. Zenas

a. A Christian lawyer in Crete

b. Follower of John the Baptist converted by Aquila and Priscilla

c. A town in Judah known as a leper colony

d. One of David's valiant men

Bible Dictionary (Answers)

1. b *(Mark 13:14)*
2. c *(Luke 16:22-23)*
3. c
4. a *(Genesis 19:24; Revelation 9:17)*
5. a
6. d *(Proverbs 5:15; Jeremiah 2:13)*
7. b
8. a *(Genesis 33:20)*
9. b *(Exodus 28; 39)*
10. c *(Isaiah 22:24, KJV)*
11. d *(Judges 6–8)*
12. c *(Ecclesiastes 12:11; Acts 26:14)*
13. c *(John 19:17)*
14. c *(Daniel 9:24-27; Revelation 11:2-3)*
15. c *(Habakkuk 1:1)*
16. a *(Luke 16:23; Revelation 1:18)*
17. c *(Haggai 1:1; Ezra 5:1; 6:14)*
18. b *(Revelation 19:1-6)*
19. b *(Esther 3:1-6)*
20. a *(Numbers 19:2)*
21. d *(2 Peter 2:1)*
22. a *(Genesis 10:15; Exodus 3:8)*
23. d *(Matthew 21:9, 15)*
24. b *(Matthew 1:23)*
25. b *(John 1:1-14)*
26. b *(Jeremiah 44:21)*
27. a *(Matthew 10:4)*
28. b *(Ruth 4:17, 22; 1 Samuel 17:12)*
29. b *(Daniel 5:13; Luke 23:5)*
30. a *(Genesis 25:1, 4)*
31. c *(Matthew 2:1-7, 16)*
32. b *(Acts 1:15-26)*
33. c *(Revelation 21)*
34. b
35. d *(Ruth)*
36. a
37. a *(Revelation 1:9)*
38. b *(2 Thessalonians 2:4; Hebrews 12:1)*
39. b *(Exodus 12:29)*
40. a *(Romans 8:11; 1 Corinthians 15:36)*
41. a *(Galatians 3:13; 1 Corinthians 15:56)*
42. c *(Matthew 3:8; Acts 5:31; Romans 2:4)*
43. c *(1 Samuel 16:12; 17:42)*
44. b *(Genesis 37:34; Psalm 35:13; Isaiah 50:3)*
45. d *(Mark 14:53-55)*
46. c *(Acts 5:1-10)*
47. b *(Philippians 2:3)*
48. b *(Exodus 29:24; Leviticus 7:30)*
49. a
50. c *(Matthew 4:21)*

1. b *(Revelation 9:11)*
2. b *(Acts 11:28-30; 21:10-12)*
3. d
4. c *(Psalm 46)*
5. d
6. d
7. d *(2 Corinthians 6:15)*
8. c *(Joshua 10:13; 2 Samuel 1:17-18)*
9. b *(Acts 28:11)*

10. c *(Judges 10:1; 2 Samuel 23:24; 1 Chronicles 11:26)*
11. c *(1 Corinthians 14:3-5; Ephesians 4:11-12)*
12. c
13. b *(Acts 17:18)*
14. c
15. d *(2 Kings 4)*
16. b *(Called Valley of Hinnom in 2 Kings 23:10; Jeremiah 7:31)*
17. d *(Exodus 2:22; 18:3)*
18. b *(Hosea 1)*
19. c *(Joshua 11:10)*
20. c *(1 Kings 4:31; 1 Chronicles 2:6)*
21. d *(Leviticus 26:30; Numbers 33:52; Deuteronomy 33:29)*
22. c *(Exodus 12:22; Numbers 19:6; Psalm 51:7)*
23. d *(1 Samuel 4:19-22)*
24. c *(Acts 13:51; 14:1, 19, 21; 16:2)*
25. d *(1 John 2:1; Romans 8:27; Hebrews 4:14-16)*
26. d *(Numbers 20)*
27. d *(Nehemiah 1:1; Zechariah 7:1)*
28. a *(Exodus 30:18)*
29. c *(Hosea 1:9)*
30. c *(John 18:10-15)*
31. b *(Genesis 30:14)*
32. c *(1 Corinthians 16:22)*
33. b *(Joshua 19:22; Judges 4:6-15)*
34. b *(Exodus 6:23; Numbers 3:2)*
35. b *(Genesis 20:14)*
36. d *(Genesis 10:8-10)*
37. b *(Acts 28:1-8)*
38. c *(Matthew 5:22)*
39. c *(2 Corinthians 5:18-19)*
40. c *(Matthew 27:46)*
41. d *(Acts 13:4-5)*
42. a *(Psalm 51:7-10)*
43. d *(Genesis 33:17)*
44. d *(Ezekiel 8:14)*
45. c *(Daniel 5:25-27)*
46. a *(Exodus 26:17; 36:22-24)*
47. c *(1 Kings 17:1)*
48. c *(Job 1:1)*
49. c *(1 Chronicles 24:3)*
50. b *(2 Kings 24:18-20)*

ADVANCED

1. b *(Acts 1:19)*
2. c *(Galatians 1:8-9)*
3. b
4. c
5. a *(Ezra 2:51; Nehemiah 7:53)*
6. b *(1 Kings 4:8)*
7. b *(1 Samuel 30:9)*
8. d *(Genesis 29:29; 30:3-8; 35:22; 46:25)*
9. c *(2 Kings 6:25)*
10. c
11. c *(Exodus 30:7-8; Leviticus 16:12-13)*
12. d *(Numbers 25:15-18)*
13. a *(1 Chronicles 29:7; Ezra 8:27)*
14. d
15. b *(1 Samuel 7:12)*
16. c *(Exodus 15:27)*
17. d
18. b *(Acts 27:7-8)*
19. d *(Exodus 27:3)*
20. a *(Romans 5:12-21; 2 Corinthians 5:21)*
21. a *(Matthew 5:18)*
22. b *(Genesis 32:22-32)*
23. c *(2 Timothy 3:8)*
24. a *(Genesis 5:32; 6:10; 7:13)*
25. a *(Job 42:14)*
26. c *(Luke 8:3; 24:10)*
27. c *(Romans 16:7)*
28. c *(see Philippians 2:7)*
29. c
30. b *(2 Timothy 1:5)*
31. b *(Acts 9:32-38)*
32. a *(Isaiah 8:1-3)*
33. a *(Psalms 32; 42)*
34. c *(Acts 6:1-5)*
35. c *(Nehemiah 2:1; Esther 3:7)*
36. a *(Numbers 21:33)*
37. c *(Romans 16:15)*
38. d *(Genesis 2:10-14)*
39. b *(Romans 16:23)*
40. d *(John 3:3-13; Titus 3:5)*
41. c *(Numbers 10:29)*
42. a *(Nehemiah 2:10, 19)*
43. c *(2 Kings 15:13)*
44. d *(Judges 3:31)*
45. a *(Numbers 13:22)*
46. b *(Genesis 11:28-31)*
47. b *(2 Samuel 6:3-10)*
48. c
49. b *(Esther 1:1)*
50. d *(Genesis 29:24; 30:9-13; 35:26)*

1. c *(Acts 27:2-5)*
2. a *(Acts 17:17)*
3. b
4. b *(Deuteronomy 7:1)*
5. a *(Acts 17:19, 22)*
6. d *(Judges 8:33; 9:4)*
7. c *(Deuteronomy 32:14; Psalm 22:12)*
8. a *(Isaiah 62:4)*
9. c *(Esther 1:10)*
10. c *(Acts 12:20)*
11. a *(Mark 7:11)*
12. d *(1 Samuel 5:1-7)*
13. d *(John 11:16)*
14. d *(Judges 3)*
15. b *(Numbers 11:24-29)*
16. d *(Exodus 16:36; Leviticus 6:20)*
17. a *(2 Kings 25:27; Jeremiah 52:31)*
18. b *(Acts 18:12)*
19. c *(2 Kings 15:30)*
20. c *(Hebrews 4:15)*
21. c *(1 Chronicles 4:9-10)*
22. c *(2 Samuel 23:8; 1 Chronicles 12:6; 27:2)*
23. c *(Joshua 15:8; Judges 19:10)*
24. b *(2 Kings 11–12)*
25. a *(Acts 9:36)*
26. a *(Genesis 4:21)*
27. b *(Romans 3:24)*
28. c *(Judges 1:16; 4:11)*
29. c *(Joshua 10:3-5)*
30. a *(Job 41:1; Psalm 104:26)*
31. b
32. c *(Joshua 15:21-31)*
33. d *(1 Samuel 14:49)*
34. d *(Genesis 46:21)*
35. b *(2 Kings 18:4)*
36. d *(1 Chronicles 27:30)*
37. b *(Matthew 23:5)*
38. d *(Jeremiah 7:18; 44:17-19)*
39. b *(2 Samuel 4:2-12)*
40. d *(Ezra 2:2; 4:8; Nehemiah 3:17; 10:25; 12:3)*
41. b
42. b *(Ezra 8:36; Esther 3:12; 8:9)*
43. c *(Acts 20:4)*
44. c *(Numbers 11:1-3; Deuteronomy 9:22)*
45. c *(Jeremiah 43:7-9; Ezekiel 30:18)*
46. d *(Ezra 5:3, 6)*
47. b *(Ezra 10:34)*
48. c
49. a *(Judges 8:1-21)*
50. a *(Titus 3:13)*

By Any Other Name

Many Bible characters had more than one name. How else were these people known?

---

1. Abram
2. Sarai
3. Jacob
4. Jesus Christ
5. Saul

1. Cephas
2. Beelzebub
3. Matthew
4. Mara
5. Tabitha

1. Didymus
2. Ahasuerus
3. Hadassah

4. Joshua
5. Justus

EXPERT

1. Hananiah
2. Abijah
3. Jehoram
4. Meshach
5. Abednego

By Any Other Name (Answers)

EASY

1. Abraham (Genesis 12–25)
2. Sarah (Genesis 12–25)
3. Israel (Genesis 32:22-28)
4. Alpha and Omega, Immanuel, Judge, Lamb, Shepherd, Son of David, Son of God, Son of Man, and many others (Matthew, Mark, Luke, John, Revelation)
5. Paul (Acts 13:9)

INTERMEDIATE

1. Peter, Simon (John 1:42)
2. Satan (Matthew 10:25; Luke 11:15-19)
3. Levi (Matthew 9:9; Mark 2:14)
4. Naomi (Ruth 1:20)
5. Dorcas (Acts 9:36-41)

ADVANCED

1. Thomas (John 11:16)
2. Xerxes (Ezra 4:6; Esther 1:1)
3. Esther (Esther 2:7)
4. Hoshea (Numbers 13:16)
5. Jesus (not Christ; Colossians 4:11)

EXPERT

1. Shadrach (Daniel 1:7)
2. Abijam (Compare 1 Kings 15:6-8; 1 Chronicles 3:10; 2 Chronicles 12:16 in KJV or NLT with NIV)
3. Joram (2 Kings 11:2)
4. Mishael (Daniel 1:7)
5. Azariah (Daniel 1:7)

That's a Good Question!

Each question below is found somewhere in the Bible. Using the hint provided, determine the person who asked the question. For a bonus, provide the name of the book where the question can be found.

EASY

1. "Doesn't life consist of more than food and clothing?" Hint: He said we should look to the birds and flowers.
2. "My God, my God! Why have you forsaken me?" Hint: This was originally asked by someone in the Old Testament.
3. "Did God really say you must not eat any of the fruit in the garden?" Hint: This was not asked by a human.
4. "Have you noticed my servant Job?" Hint: This conversation took place in heaven.
5. "Where is the newborn king of the Jews?" Hint: They were very wise men.
6. "What did you go out into the desert to see?" Hint: They didn't go to see a reed swayed by the wind.
7. "But you, lazybones, how long will you sleep? When will you wake up?" Hint: The wise man who asked this also advised learning from the ant.
8. "What's more, who can say but that you have been elevated to the palace for just such a time as this?" Hint: The queen he questioned was his niece.

9. "Who is this pagan Philistine anyway, that he is allowed to defy the armies of the living God?" Hint: The Philistine stood head and shoulders above the rest.

10. "Why did you bring us out here to die in the wilderness? Weren't there enough graves for us in Egypt? Why did you make us leave?" Hint: The people who asked this stood between a giant body of water and a large army.

11. "Who are these who are clothed in white? Where do they come from?" Hint: The one he questioned could only have dreamed the answer.

12. "Were you not afraid to kill the Lord's anointed one?" Hint: The Lord's anointed had actually committed suicide.

13. "Do you not realize that a great leader and a great man has fallen today in Israel?" Hint: The great man was once his enemy.

14. "Are you really my son Esau?" Hint: The answer to this question was a lie.

15. "Have I sinned? What have I done to you, O watcher of all humanity? Why have you made me your target? Am I a burden to you?" Hint: The answer proved a point to Satan.

16. "Tell me what you want, Queen Esther. What is your request?" Hint: She didn't want half of the kingdom.

17. "Can all your worries add a single moment to your life?" Hint: Seek first God's kingdom instead.

18. "Son of man, can these bones become living people again?" Hint: Only God could answer this question.

19. "Do you know when the mountain goats give birth? Have you watched as the wild deer are born?" Hint: No one would know better than him.

20. "Judas, how can you betray me, the Son of Man, with a kiss?" Hint: Judas hung himself soon after this.

21. "How could I become a father at the age of one hundred?" Hint: His wife wasn't much younger.

22. "Why, then, did you bring me out of my mother's womb? Why didn't you let me die at birth?" Hint: His children had died, his fortune was lost, and his health was gone.

23. "If a shepherd has one hundred sheep, and one wanders away and is lost, what will he do? Won't he leave the ninety-nine others and go out into the hills to search for the lost one?" Hint: He was the ultimate shepherd.

24. "Saul! Saul! Why are you persecuting me?" Hint: He was the last person Saul expected to see.

25. "And why worry about a speck in your friend's eye when you have a log in your own?" Hint: He was speaking to hypocrites.

26. "Are you the one to build me a temple to live in?" Hint: He was saving that job for Solomon.

27. "But who am I to appear before Pharaoh? How can you expect me to lead the Israelites out of Egypt?" Hint: The man who asked this was an eighty-year-old shepherd.

28. "What good is it for one blind person to lead another?" Hint: He was really speaking of spiritual blindness.

29. "Does Job fear God for nothing? Have you not put a hedge around him and his household and everything he has?" Hint: They would soon find out.

30. "The Lord is my light and my salvation—so why should I be afraid?" Hint: He was probably in tune.

31. "Am I my brother's keeper?" Hint: He was his brother's murderer.

32. "Why should my face not look sad when the city where my fathers are buried lies in ruins, and its gates have been destroyed by fire?" Hint: He was cupbearer to the king.

33. "My own people won't listen to me anymore. How can I expect Pharaoh to listen?" Hint: He had already tried to get out of this task.

34. "For who can remain innocent after attacking the Lord's anointed one?" Hint: He took his water jug instead.

35. "What do people get for all their hard work?" Hint: He thought that everything was meaningless.

36. "Where were you when I laid the foundations of the earth?" Hint: He spoke out of the storm.

37. "Was your God, whom you worship continually, able to rescue you from the lions?" Hint: He should never have passed the decree requiring people to pray only to him.

38. "What is your advice? How should I answer these people who want me to lighten the burdens imposed by my father?" Hint: He should have listened to his elders.

39. "Can you tell me what my dream was and what it means?" Hint: He promoted the interpreter to ruler over Babylon.

40. "Suppose the whole body were an eye—then how would you hear? Or if your whole body were just one big ear, how could you smell anything?" Hint: He often traveled with a doctor.

41. "And how do you benefit if you gain the whole world but lose your own soul in the process? Is anything worth more than your soul?" Hint: He knew more about people's souls than anyone else.

42. "Simon son of John, do you love me more than these?" Hint: He asked this question three times.

43. "Why hasn't the son of Jesse been here for dinner either yesterday or today?" Hint: He asked this but was not really interested in the man's company.

44. "How can an old man go back into his mother's womb and be born again?" Hint: Jesus was disappointed that this man didn't know the answer.

45. "Can you hold back the movements of the stars? Are you able to restrain the Pleiades or Orion?" Hint: This was a rhetorical question.

INTERMEDIATE

1. "But am I not a Benjamite, from the smallest tribe of Israel, and is not my clan the least of all the clans of the tribe of Benjamin?" Hint: A humble remark from a future king.

2. "If I want him to remain alive until I return, what is that to you?" Hint: A rumor began as a result of this question.

3. "Who is the king of Israel trying to catch anyway? Should he spend his time chasing one who is as worthless as a dead dog or a flea?" Hint: A scrap of cloth proved he wouldn't harm the Lord's anointed.

4. "Should you hit a man for telling the truth?" Hint: He was on trial.

5. "How could I go home to wine and dine and sleep with my wife?" Hint: David wished he would.

6. "If you love only those who love you, what good is that?" Hint: Even the tax collectors do that!

7. "Why are you treating me, your servant, so miserably? What did I do to deserve the burden of a people like this?

Are they my children? Am I their father? Is that why you have told me to carry them in my arms—like a nurse carries a baby—to the land you swore to give their ancestors?" Hint: God gave a meaty answer.

8. "But how can I curse those whom God has not cursed? How can I condemn those whom the Lord has not condemned?" Hint: He had just had a conversation with an animal.

9. "What have I done to you that deserves your beating me these three times?" Hint: He had just taken his master for a ride.

10. "Why didn't you tell me she was your wife?" Hint: He had said she was his sister.

11. "Will he even assault the queen right here in the palace, before my very eyes?" Hint: He hung Haman on the gallows as punishment.

12. "I am unworthy—how can I reply to you?" Hint: He placed his hand over his mouth.

13. "Should I drink the blood of these men who went at the risk of their lives?" Hint: He poured it out onto the ground instead.

14. "Has any nation ever heard the voice of God speaking from fire—as you did—and survived? Has any other god taken one nation for himself by rescuing it from another by means of trials, miraculous signs, wonders, war, awesome power, and terrifying acts?" Hint: He was 120 years old.

15. "Must we bring you water from this rock?" Hint: He was about to hit rock bottom.

16. "What are mortals that you should think of us, mere humans that you should care for us?" Hint: This was asked according to the "gittith."

17. "What are you doing around here anyway? What about those few sheep you're supposed to be taking care of?" Hint: He was speaking to his brother—and a future king.

18. "Is there no one still left of the house of Saul to whom I can show God's kindness?" Hint: His best friend's son was still left.

19. "What have I done? What is my crime? How have I offended your father that he is so determined to kill me?" Hint: His best friend did not have an answer to this question.

20. "But what good is salt if it has lost its flavor?" Hint: It's only good for being thrown out and trampled on.

21. "If you had one sheep, and it fell into a well on the Sabbath, wouldn't you get to work and pull it out?" Hint: It was better to do good on the Sabbath rather than do evil.

22. "Can anything ever separate us from Christ's love?" Hint: It won't be trouble or hardship or persecution or famine or nakedness or danger or sword.

23. "Teacher, what good things must I do to have eternal life?" Hint: It would have been easier for a camel to go through the eye of a needle.

24. "Why are you so sad? You aren't sick, are you?" Hint: Jerusalem lay in ruins.

25. "Lord, doesn't it seem unfair to you that my sister just sits here while I do all the work?" Hint: She needed to learn to take a seat.

26. "Are you still trying to maintain your integrity?" Hint: She told him to curse God and die.

27. "Why have you done this? Why have you allowed the boys to live?" Hint: Someone wanted babies killed.

28. "Where are you?" Hint: Someone was trying to hide from God.

29. "What does this bunch of poor, feeble Jews think they are doing? Do they think they can build the wall in a day if they offer enough sacrifices?" Hint: The building project continued anyway.

30. "Who has bewitched you?" Hint: The Judaizers had captivated them.

31. "Well, whose spirit do you want me to call up?" Hint: The king of Israel was participating in a seance.

32. "You parents—if your children ask for a loaf of bread, do you give them a stone instead?" Hint: The same people wouldn't give their sons a snake if their sons wanted fish instead.

33. "What should we do to you to stop this storm?" Hint: The man who answered was in for a whale of a time.

34. "Lord, how often should I forgive someone who sins against me? Seven times?" Hint: The person he asked answered this question with a math equation.

35. "Is it right for you to be angry because the plant died?" Hint: The person he asked this of was so angry he wanted to wither up and die himself.

36. "What is more pleasing to the Lord: your burnt offerings and sacrifices or your obedience to his voice?" Hint: The king was in a lot of trouble.

37. "For if a man cannot manage his own household, how can he take care of God's church?" Hint: This question showed a church leader the importance of choosing elders wisely.

38. "What should I do to honor a man who truly pleases me?" Hint: There was a misunderstanding about which man this person wanted to honor.

39. "Why haven't you met your quotas either yesterday or today?" Hint: The people couldn't meet the quota because their supplies were withheld.

40. "Would you like the shadow on the sundial to go forward ten steps or backward ten steps?" Hint: This became a sign that God would heal Hezekiah.

41. "Dear brothers and sisters, what's the use of saying you have faith if you don't prove it by your actions?" Hint: This was asked by the leader of the church in Jerusalem.

42. "Was this the price you and your husband received for your land?" Hint: He'd already seen the consequences of lying.

43. "For who by himself is able to govern this great nation of yours?" Hint: There was wisdom found in the answer.

44. "Do you think it is a small matter to become the king's son-in-law?" Hint: Two hundred Philistines had paid for this marriage with their lives.

45. "Dear woman, why do you involve me?" Hint: This was a wedding no one would ever forget.

ADVANCED

1. "When I go to bed, I think, 'When will it be morning?'" Hint: Worms and scabs covered his body.

2. "Has anyone just built a new house but not yet dedicated it? . . . Has anyone just planted a vineyard but not yet eaten any of its fruit? . . . Has anyone just become engaged?" Hint: Whoever answered yes was allowed to go home instead of fight in the upcoming battle.

3. "After all, God is not the God of the Jews only, is he? Isn't he also the God of the Gentiles?" Hint: Though a Jew, he knew that God is not only the God of the Jews.

4. "Will a man rob God?" Hint: Those questioned had failed to pay their dues.

5. "After all, what gives us hope and joy, and what is our proud reward and crown?" Hint: Those he asked were the answer to his question.

6. "Has not God made foolish the wisdom of the world?" Hint: This was asked by a man who claimed to be the chief of sinners.

7. "Don't you fear God even when you are dying?" Hint: This man was dying as he asked the question.

8. "Men of Galilee, why are you standing here staring at the sky?" Hint: They weren't watching birds.

9. "What crime have I committed? What have I done against you, your officials, or the people that I should be imprisoned like this?" Hint: They thought he was deserting to the Babylonians.

10. "Snakes! Sons of vipers! How will you escape the judgment of hell?" Hint: These vipers were the leaders of the people.

11. "Isn't there one woman in our tribe or among all the Israelites you could marry? Why must you go to the pagan Philistines to find a wife?" Hint: Their son got into a hairy mess.

12. "O man of God, what have you done to me? Have you come here to punish my sins by killing my son?" Hint: The widow believed because of the answer.

13. "How long will you wander, my wayward daughter?" Hint: The unfaithful daughter was a nation.

14. "What are you doing, hitting your neighbor like that?" Hint: The two who were fighting were slaves.

15. "Why are you looking in a tomb for someone who is alive?" Hint: The tomb was empty.

16. "Isn't killing Naboth bad enough? Must you rob him, too?" Hint: The story would end with bloodthirsty dogs.

17. "Why have you disturbed me by calling me back?" Hint: The person who asked this was already dead.

18. "Why are you arguing with me? And why are you testing the Lord?" Hint: The people he asked were thirsty.

19. "I know Jesus, and I know Paul. But who are you?" Hint: The people being asked were about to lose their shirts.

20. "Why are you bothering us, Son of God?" Hint: The ones speaking would soon be driven over the edge.

21. "Are these all the sons you have?" Hint: The missing son was a shepherd.

22. "Has the Lord spoken only through Moses? Hasn't he spoken through us, too?" Hint: The answer made one of them sick.

23. "Who is that man walking through the fields to meet us?" Hint: That man was about to become her husband.

24. "How can you say you love me when you don't confide in me?" Hint: She wanted to sap his strength.

25. "Why should you go on with me? Can I still give birth to other sons who could grow up to be your husbands?" Hint: She called herself "Mara."

26. "Does a jar ever say, 'The potter who made me is stupid'?" Hint: Paul quotes the essence of this question in Romans 9.

27. "Can an Ethiopian change the color of his skin? Can a leopard take away its spots?" Hint: Neither can you do good who are accustomed to doing evil.

28. "Don't you realize that friendship with this world makes you an enemy of God?" Hint: Jesus' half brother asked this.

29. "Is there no balm in Gilead? Is there no physician there? Why then is there no healing for the wound of my people?" Hint: It was a metaphorical wound.

30. "Does a spring of water bubble out with both fresh water and bitter water?" Hint: It all depends on what you say.

31. "Why aren't you eating? Why be so sad just because you have no children? You have me—isn't that better than having ten sons?" Hint: His wife was mistaken for a drunk.

32. "If I can thank God for the food and enjoy it, why should I be condemned for eating it?" Hint: His question dealt with a meaty issue.

33. "But if someone sins against the Lord, who can intercede?" Hint: His sons were failing to follow in his footsteps.

34. "Was I crucified for you?" Hint: He was thankful he hadn't even baptized many of them.

35. "Do you not realize that Christ Jesus is in you—unless, of course, you fail the test?" Hint: He was talking about a self-examination.

36. "Am I now trying to win the approval of men, or of God? Or am I trying to please men?" Hint: He was not concerned with the approval of the Judaizers.

37. "Am I a dog that you come at me with a stick?" Hint: He was about to lose his head.

38. "Will you then boast, 'I am a god!' to those who kill you?" Hint: He was "tyred" of their pride.

39. "Am I God? Can I kill and bring back to life? Why does this fellow send someone to me to be cured of his leprosy?" Hint: The man then went to Elisha.

40. "Why did you lie to us? Why did you say that you live in a distant land when you live right here among us?" Hint: He was fooled by their moldy bread and worn-out clothes.

41. "Do you not know that in a race all the runners run, but only one gets the prize?" Hint: He buffeted his own body.

42. "Should we accept only good things from the hand of God and never anything bad?" Hint: He accepted a lot of trouble.

43. "How could evil men like you speak what is good and right?" Hint: For out of the overflow of the heart the mouth speaks.

44. "Well then, should we keep on sinning so that God can show us more and more kindness and forgiveness?" Hint: By no means!

45. "Ananias, why has Satan filled your heart?" Hint: Ananias didn't have time to answer.

EXPERT

1. "And don't you know that if a man joins himself to a prostitute, he becomes one body with her?" Hint: But he who unites himself with the Lord is one with him in spirit.

2. "Then what is all the bleating of sheep and lowing of cattle I hear?" Hint: Dead sheep don't bleat.

3. "O Lord my God, why have you brought tragedy on this widow who has opened her home to me, causing her son

to die?" Hint: God answered this prayer by raising him from the dead.

4. "How could your servant, a mere dog, accomplish such a feat?" Hint: He assassinated the king of Aram after receiving the answer.

5. "How can a mere mortal stand before God and claim to be righteous? Who in all the earth is pure?" Hint: He believed people were no more than maggots to God.

6. "Should I come with punishment and scolding, or should I come with quiet love and gentleness?" Hint: He came to them the first time on his second missionary journey.

7. "How long before you stop talking?" Hint: He believed that Job suffered the consequences of his sins.

8. "And if the bugler doesn't sound a clear call, how will the soldiers know they are being called to battle?" Hint: He cared more for spiritual gifts than for musical instruments.

9. "How can I, when there is no one to instruct me?" Hint: He didn't understand Isaiah's writing.

10. "What will a man get for killing this Philistine and putting an end to his abuse of Israel?" Hint: He gave it his best shot.

11. "Don't you realize how kind, tolerant, and patient God is with you? Or don't you care? Can't you see how kind he has been in giving you time to turn from your sin?" Hint: He had repented on the road to Damascus.

12. "Why should we, mere humans, complain when we are punished for our sins?" Hint: He is known for his weeping.

13. "And what value was there in fighting wild beasts—those men of Ephesus—if there will be no resurrection from the dead?" Hint: He once caused a riot in Ephesus.

14. "Can a mortal be just and upright before God? Can a person be pure before the Creator?" Hint: He originally heard this question in a vision.

15. "Why are you living in luxurious houses while my house lies in ruins?" Hint: He proposed a major building program.

16. "Can you solve the mysteries of God? Can you discover everything there is to know about the Almighty?" Hint: He thought Job hadn't received all he had deserved.

17. "What do you mean by crushing my people and grinding the faces of the poor?" Hint: He was pronouncing judgment on their deeds.

18. "Does God twist justice? Does the Almighty twist what is right?" Hint: He wasn't a very encouraging friend.

19. "You say it is wrong to commit adultery, but do you do it? You condemn idolatry, but do you steal from pagan temples?" Hint: He wrote this to a church he had never visited.

20. "Was it only to your master and you that my master sent me to say these things, and not to the men sitting on the wall—who, like you, will have to eat their own filth and drink their own urine?" Hint: Hezekiah's men wished he had said this in Aramaic.

21. "I tasted a little honey. It was only a little bit on the end of a stick. Does that deserve death?" Hint: His dad made the rules.

22. "But why should I fast when he is dead? Can I bring him back again?" Hint: His son, conceived during an affair, had just died.

23. "Why are you trying to do all this alone?" Hint: His son-in-law was the only judge for the entire nation.

24. "Why spend your money on food that does not give you strength? Why pay for food that does you no good?" Hint: Listen, instead, and "get food that is good for the soul."

25. "I have taken off my robe—must I put it on again? I have washed my feet—must I soil them again?" Hint: She told her story to the daughters of Jerusalem.

26. "What did that crazy fellow want? Is everything all right?" Hint: The alleged madman had come to anoint Jehu king.

27. "Why bring him to me? Am I so short of madmen that you have to bring this fellow here to carry on like this in front of me? Must this man come into my house?" Hint: The alleged madman would become a king.

28. "Did you know that the Lord is going to take your master away from you today?" Hint: The chariots of fire took the master away.

29. "Who do you think you are, distracting the people from their tasks?" Hint: The king of Egypt felt cheated.

30. "For the Lord Almighty has purposed, and who can thwart him?" Hint: The Lord had purposed to crush Assyria.

31. "Didn't I tell you that he never prophesies anything good about me, but only bad?" Hint: The lying spirit of other prophets had enticed him.

32. "Was I too weak to save you? Is that why the house is silent and empty when I come home? Is it because I have no power to rescue?" Hint: The one who asked this was omnipotent.

33. "So it's you, is it—Israel's troublemaker?" Hint: The person who asked the question was the real troublemaker of Israel.

34. "Of what value is an idol, since a man has carved it? Or an image that teaches lies?" Hint: The person who was asked this had two big questions to ask God.

35. "Must we always solve our differences with swords? Don't you realize the only thing we will gain is bitterness toward each other? When will you call off your men from chasing their Israelite brothers?" Hint: The question brought about a truce.

36. "Don't you realize the Philistines rule over us? What are you doing to us?" Hint: Their enemies had been outfoxed.

37. "Has no one told you, my lord, about the time when Jezebel was trying to kill the Lord's prophets?" Hint: There is a book of the Bible with the same name as the person who asked this question.

38. "What benefit did you reap at that time from the things you are now ashamed of?" Hint: These things result in death!

39. "Why didn't you eat the sin offering in the sanctuary area?" Hint: The people he asked had just watched their brothers die.

40. "Is the Lord's arm too short?" Hint: They quailed at his answer.

41. "Should the king show such kindness to a dead dog like me?" Hint: This "dead dog" was in the royal line.

42. "What is sweeter than honey? What is stronger than a lion?" Hint: This question was the answer to a riddle.

43. "But how is it to your credit if you receive a beating for doing wrong and endure it?" Hint: This was a question he had to master.

44. "What do you lack here? How have we disappointed you that you want to go home?" Hint: This was asked of an archenemy of David.

45. "Don't you know that a little yeast works through the whole batch of dough?" Hint: This wasn't asked by a baker. It was asked by a tentmaker.

That's a Good Question! (Answers)

1. Jesus asked this during his Sermon on the Mount. (Matthew 6:25)

2. David first asked this in a psalm; Jesus quoted this psalm while he was on the cross. (Psalm 22:1; see also Matthew 27:46; Mark 15:34)

3. Satan asked Eve this question as he convinced her to disobey God. (Genesis 3:1)

4. God asked Satan this question. (Job 1:8)

5. The magi asked this in Jerusalem when they were looking for Jesus. (Matthew 2:2)

6. Jesus asked this of the Jewish leaders. (Matthew 11:7, NIV; see also Luke 7:24)

7. Solomon, the author of Proverbs, asked this. (Proverbs 6:9)

8. Mordecai asked Queen Esther this question to encourage her to use her influence to save the Jewish people. (Esther 4:14)

9. David asked this about Goliath. (1 Samuel 17:26)

10. The Hebrews complained to Moses after he led them out of Egypt. (Exodus 14:11)

11. The elders in heaven asked John this in his vision about the end times. (Revelation 7:13)

12. David asked this of the man who claimed to have killed Saul. (2 Samuel 1:14)

13. David asked his men this question when Abner was killed. (2 Samuel 3:38)

14. Isaac asked Jacob this question when Jacob wore a disguise in order to trick his father. (Genesis 27:24)

15. Job asked God this while Job suffered. (Job 7:20)

16. King Xerxes asked Esther this question after she invited the king to a banquet. (Esther 7:2)

17. Jesus asked this during his Sermon on the Mount. (Matthew 6:27; see also Luke 12:25)

18. God asked this of Ezekiel before he turned the bones into living flesh. (Ezekiel 37:3)

19. God asked Job this question to teach Job of God's power. (Job 39:1)

20. Jesus asked Judas this question when Judas led the chief priests to arrest him. (Luke 22:48)

21. Abraham asked God this question after God promised he would father a son. (Genesis 17:16)

22. Job asked this of God while Job suffered. (Job 10:18)

23. Jesus asked this while sharing his concern for the spiritually lost.

(Matthew 18:12; see also Luke 15:3-4)

24. Jesus asked Saul this when he confronted Saul on the road to Damascus. (Acts 9:4)

25. Jesus asked this during his Sermon on the Mount. (Matthew 7:3; see also Luke 6:41)

26. God asked David this when David planned to build a temple for God. (2 Samuel 7:5)

27. Moses asked God this question when God sent him to Pharaoh. (Exodus 3:11)

28. Jesus said this about the Jewish leaders who were leading their followers astray. (Luke 6:39)

29. Satan asked God this question. (Job 1:9-10, NIV)

30. David asked this in a psalm. (Psalm 27:1)

31. Cain asked this question of God after Cain had killed his brother, Abel. (Genesis 4:9, NIV)

32. Nehemiah asked King Artaxerxes this question. (Nehemiah 2:3, NIV)

33. Moses asked God this question after God continued to send him back to Pharaoh. (Exodus 6:12)

34. David asked Abishai this question when the future king passed on a second chance to kill Saul. (1 Samuel 26:9)

35. Solomon asked this at the start of Ecclesiastes. (Ecclesiastes 1:3)

36. God said this to Job when he confronted Job for questioning the divine plan. (Job 38:4)

37. King Darius asked Daniel this after he spent a night in the lions' den. (Daniel 6:20)

38. Rehoboam asked this when the people requested relief. His poor decision sparked a revolution. (1 Kings 12:9)

39. Nebuchadnezzar asked Daniel this

while referring to his dream of a large statue. (Daniel 2:26)

40. Paul wrote this to the church in Corinth describing Christians as the body of Christ. (1 Corinthians 12:17)

41. Jesus asked this while explaining the cost of following him. (Matthew 16:26; see also Mark 8:36; Luke 9:25)

42. Jesus asked Peter this question. (John 21:15)

43. Saul asked Jonathan this because the king wanted to kill David. (1 Samuel 20:27)

44. Nicodemus asked Jesus this question when he visited Jesus by night. (John 3:4)

45. God said this to Job to remind Job that God was still in charge. (Job 38:31)

INTERMEDIATE

1. Saul asked this when he was invited to dinner with Samuel. (1 Samuel 9:21, NIV)

2. Jesus asked this of Peter when Peter had asked what would happen to the apostle John. (John 21:22)

3. David asked this question of Saul after David spared Saul's life. (1 Samuel 24:14)

4. Jesus asked this after one of the high priest's men struck him. (John 18:23)

5. Uriah said this to David when David was trying to cover up for his adultery with Uriah's wife, Bathsheba. (2 Samuel 11:11)

6. Jesus asked this during his Sermon on the Mount. (Matthew 5:46)

7. Moses asked God this when the people continued to complain. (Numbers 11:11-13)

8. Balaam refused to curse the Hebrews for Balak and delivered a blessing instead. (Numbers 23:8)

9. Balaam's donkey asked this after saving Balaam's life. (Numbers 22:28)

10. Pharaoh asked Abram this after Pharaoh had brought Sarai into his harem. (Genesis 12:18)

11. King Xerxes asked this question when he saw Haman fall at Queen Esther to beg for mercy. (Esther 7:8)

12. Job asked this in response to God's questions. (Job 40:4, NIV)

13. David asked this after his men risked their lives in order to draw water from a well near Bethlehem. (1 Chronicles 11:19, NIV)

14. Moses asked this to encourage the people before they went into the Promised Land. (Deuteronomy 4:33-34)

15. Moses asked this question and dishonored God in the account of his striking the rock at Kadesh. (Numbers 20:10)

16. David asked this of God in a psalm. (Psalm 8:4)

17. David's brother Eliab asked David this when David visited the front lines and asked questions about Goliath. (1 Samuel 17:28)

18. David wanted to show kindness on account of his friendship with Jonathan. (2 Samuel 9:3, NIV)

19. David asked Jonathan this when Saul planned to kill him. (1 Samuel 20:1)

20. Jesus asked this rhetorical question in his Sermon on the Mount. (Matthew 5:13)

21. Jesus asked this of the Pharisees when they questioned his healing on the Sabbath. (Matthew 12:11)

22. Paul wrote this in his epistle to the Romans. (Romans 8:35)

23. A wealthy man asked Jesus this question. (Matthew 19:16; see also Mark 10:17; Luke 18:18)

24. King Artaxerxes asked this after Nehemiah heard that the walls of Jerusalem were in ruins. (Nehemiah 2:2)

25. Martha asked Jesus this question when her sister, Mary, sat at Jesus' feet rather than helping in the kitchen. (Luke 10:40)

26. Job's wife asked Job this after Job was struck by Satan but refused to dishonor God. (Job 2:9)

27. Pharaoh said this to the Hebrew midwives when they disobeyed his order. (Exodus 1:18)

28. God asked Adam this question after Adam had sinned. (Genesis 3:9)

29. Sanballat asked this to ridicule Nehemiah's efforts at rebuilding Jerusalem's walls. (Nehemiah 4:2)

30. Paul wrote this to the church in Galatia. (Galatians 3:1, NIV)

31. The witch of Endor asked Saul this when the king went to her in order to bring Samuel's spirit back from the dead. (1 Samuel 28:11)

32. Jesus asked this during his Sermon on the Mount. (Matthew 7:9)

33. The sailors on the boat asked Jonah this question. (Jonah 1:11)

34. Peter asked Jesus this question. (Matthew 18:21)

35. God asked this of Jonah after he withered the vine. God had created the vine as an object lesson to teach Jonah compassion for Nineveh. (Jonah 4:9)

36. Samuel confronted Saul when the king disobeyed God's command. (1 Samuel 15:22)

37. Paul wrote this to Timothy when he was giving the qualifications

for a leader in the church. (1 Timothy 3:5)

38. King Xerxes asked Haman this when the king wanted to honor Mordecai. (Esther 6:6)

39. Pharaoh's foreman asked the Hebrew slaves this question. (Exodus 5:14)

40. Isaiah asked this of Hezekiah so that the miracle would convince the king of God's promise. (2 Kings 20:9)

41. James wrote this in the book named after him. (James 2:14)

42. Peter asked Sapphira this before God killed her for sharing in her husband's lie. (Acts 5:8)

43. Solomon asked this when he asked God for wisdom. (1 Kings 3:9)

44. David asked this when he was invited to marry Saul's daughter. (1 Samuel 18:23, NIV)

45. Jesus asked this to his mother at the wedding in Cana. (John 2:4, NIV)

ADVANCED

1. Job asked this to demonstrate how miserable he was. (Job 7:4)

2. Moses instructed the people about future battles. (Deuteronomy 20:5-8)

3. Paul wrote this in his epistle to the Romans. (Romans 3:29)

4. God asked Israel this through Malachi because they were not bringing the tithes and offerings they owed. (Malachi 3:8, NIV)

5. Paul wrote to the church of Thessalonica expressing his desire to be with them again. (1 Thessalonians 2:19)

6. Paul wrote this to the church at Corinth. (1 Corinthians 1:20, NIV)

7. One of the crucified thieves rebuked the dying criminal who was insulting Jesus. (Luke 23:40)

8. Two angels asked the disciples this after Jesus ascended into heaven. (Acts 1:11)

9. Jeremiah asked this of King Zedekiah after giving him God's message that the Babylonians would destroy Jerusalem. (Jeremiah 37:18)

10. Jesus asked this of the Jewish leaders. (Matthew 23:33)

11. Samson's parents asked him this when he wanted to get married. (Judges 14:3)

12. The widow of Zarephath asked this of Elijah, who responded by bringing the boy back to life. (1 Kings 17:18)

13. Through Jeremiah, the Lord asked this of Israel. (Jeremiah 31:22)

14. Moses asked this question when he saw two Hebrew slaves fighting. (Exodus 2:13)

15. An angel asked this question of the woman who came to Jesus' tomb. (Luke 24:5)

16. Elijah, on behalf of God, asked Ahab this after the king had killed Naboth. (1 Kings 21:19)

17. Samuel's spirit asked Saul this when the king brought forth his spirit in a seance. (1 Samuel 28:15)

18. Moses asked this while he urged the Hebrews to remain faithful to God. (Exodus 17:2)

19. An evil spirit asked this of the seven sons of Sceva when they commanded him to come out. (Acts 19:15)

20. The demons of two possessed men asked this of Jesus before he cast them into a herd of pigs. (Matthew 8:29)

21. Samuel asked Jesse when the prophet came to anoint a new king. (1 Samuel 16:11)

22. Miriam and Aaron asked this to challenge Moses' authority. (Numbers 12:2)

23. Rebekah asked this question when she saw Isaac for the first time. (Genesis 24:65)

24. Delilah asked Samson this to trick him into giving her the secret of his strength. (Judges 16:15)

25. Naomi asked her daughters-in-law this after their husbands died. (Ruth 1:11)

26. Isaiah used this metaphor to point out the foolishness of those in Judah who thought God couldn't see what they did. (Isaiah 29:16)

27. Jeremiah asked this as part of his warning of coming judgment on Judah. (Jeremiah 13:23)

28. James wrote this in the book named after him. (James 4:4)

29. Jeremiah asked this as he lamented the prophecy of judgment against the Israelites. (Jeremiah 8:22, NIV)

30. James wrote this as part of his teaching on the tongue. (James 3:11)

31. Elkanah, Hannah's husband, asked this when she was discouraged because she had no children. (1 Samuel 1:8)

32. Paul wrote this to the church in Corinth discussing with them eating meat and sacrificed idols. (1 Corinthians 10:30)

33. Eli asked his sons this after he heard that they were corrupt priests. (1 Samuel 2:25)

34. Paul wrote this to the church at Corinth to urge them to be united. (1 Corinthians 1:13)

35. Paul wrote this to the church in Corinth. (2 Corinthians 13:5, NIV)

36. Paul wrote this to the church in Galatia. (Galatians 1:10, NIV)

37. Goliath asked David this question before David killed him. (1 Samuel 17:43)

38. God asked this through Ezekiel to the ruler of Tyre as he pronounced coming judgment. (Ezekiel 28:9)

39. King Jehoram (Joram) asked this when Naaman sent a letter asking to have his leprosy healed. (2 Kings 5:7, NIV)

40. Joshua asked this after he realized that the men from Gibeon had tricked him. (Joshua 9:22)

41. Paul wrote this to the church at Corinth. (1 Corinthians 9:24, NIV)

42. Job asked his wife this after she urged him to curse God. (Job 2:10)

43. Jesus asked this of the Pharisees when they accused him of driving out demons by Beelzebub. (Matthew 12:34)

44. Paul wrote this in his epistle to the Romans. (Romans 6:1)

45. Peter asked Ananias this before God killed him for his deception. (Acts 5:3)

EXPERT

1. Paul wrote this to the church at Corinth while warning them to flee from sexual immorality. (1 Corinthians 6:16)

2. Samuel asked this to confront Saul. Saul had lied to Samuel and said that he had killed all the animals. (1 Samuel 15:14)

3. Elijah asked this question when the son of his host had died. (1 Kings 17:20)

4. Hazael asked Elisha this after Elisha prophesied that Hazael would bring great destruction to Israel. (2 Kings 8:13, NIV)

5. Bildad asked this to remind Job of his sin. (Job 25:4)

6. Paul wrote this to the church at

Corinth when he told them that he planned to see them soon. (1 Corinthians 4:21)

7. Bildad asked this during his second speech while accusing Job of not being responsible. (Job 18:2)

8. Paul wrote this as part of a discussion on tongues. (1 Corinthians 14:8)

9. The Ethiopian eunuch asked Philip this when Philip asked if he understood what he was reading. (Acts 8:31)

10. David asked this about Goliath. (1 Samuel 17:26)

11. Paul asked this of the church in Rome while urging them not to pass judgment on others. (Romans 2:4)

12. Jeremiah asked this in Lamentations while reflecting on the fall of Jerusalem. (Lamentations 3:39)

13. Paul wrote this to the church in Corinth encouraging them with the hope of the Resurrection. (1 Corinthians 15:32)

14. Eliphaz asked Job this question when Job claimed he was innocent of any wrongdoing. (Job 4:17)

15. Haggai prophesied this when the exiled Jews had returned to Jerusalem but had not completed reconstruction of the temple. (Haggai 1:4)

16. Zophar asked Job this question. (Job 11:7)

17. God asked this of the elders and leaders of Israel. (Isaiah 3:15, NIV)

18. Bildad asked this to confront Job's righteous attitude. (Job 8:3)

19. Paul wrote this in his epistle to the Romans. (Romans 2:22)

20. The Assyrian field commander asked this when Hezekiah's officials requested that he speak in Aramaic. (2 Kings 18:27, NIV)

21. Jonathan asked this when he was told that he had disobeyed his father's new law. (1 Samuel 14:43)

22. David asked this when his illegitimate son with Bathsheba had died. (2 Samuel 12:23)

23. Jethro asked this to urge Moses to appoint assistants for himself. (Exodus 18:14)

24. God asked this through the prophet Isaiah as part of an invitation to salvation. (Isaiah 55:2)

25. Solomon's wife asked him this when he knocked on her door. (Song of Songs 5:3, NIV)

26. One of Jehu's officers asked Jehu this question after Elisha anointed Jehu king to succeed Ahab. (2 Kings 9:11)

27. King Achish asked this when David feigned insanity. (1 Samuel 21:14-15, NIV)

28. The prophets at Bethel asked this on the day that Elijah was taken to heaven. (2 Kings 2:3)

29. Pharaoh asked Moses and Aaron this question soon after they arrived in Egypt and began talking to the people about leaving Egypt. (Exodus 5:4)

30. Isaiah asked this rhetorical question regarding the coming judgment on Assyria. (Isaiah 14:27, NIV)

31. Ahab asked Jehoshaphat this when, over Ahab's protests, Jehoshaphat insisted that the two kings ask one of God's prophets about an upcoming battle. (1 Kings 22:18, NIV)

32. God asked Israel this question through Isaiah. (Isaiah 50:2)

33. Ahab asked this question when Elijah came out of hiding to meet the king. (1 Kings 18:17)

34. God asked Habakkuk this as part

of his response to Habakkuk's question. (Habakkuk 2:18, NIV)

35. Abner asked David's general, Joash, this question when David's men were fighting Saul's men. (2 Samuel 2:26)

36. Men from Judah asked Samson this after he tied three hundred foxes together, tied torches to their tails, and destroyed their fields. (Judges 15:11)

37. Obadiah asked Elijah this question while the prophet was hiding from Jezebel, who was killing the prophets. (1 Kings 18:13)

38. Paul wrote this in his epistle to the Romans. (Romans 6:21, NIV)

39. Moses asked Eleazer and Ithamar this when they failed to complete their priestly duty. (Leviticus 10:17)

40. God asked Moses this before a miraculous provision of food. (Numbers 11:23, NIV)

41. Mephibosheth asked this when David showed kindness to him on account of Jonathan. (2 Samuel 9:8)

42. The Philistines got this answer to Samson's riddle from Samson's wife. (Judges 14:18)

43. Peter asked this to encourage slaves to continue to do good and to submit to their masters. (1 Peter 2:20, NIV)

44. Pharaoh asked this question of Hadad when Hadad wanted to leave his exile in Egypt and return to Israel. (1 Kings 11:22)

45. Paul wrote this to the church at Corinth. (1 Corinthians 5:6, NIV)

Quizzes

These multiple-choice holiday quizzes are based on facts found in the Bible. Choose the letter that best answers each question.

Valentine's Day

EASY

1. According to Genesis 2:18, why did God create woman?
   a. God was still lonely after he had created Adam.
   b. He'd made two of every other creature, and he wanted to keep the trend going.
   c. Adam had a spare rib that needed to be used.
   d. It was not good for man to be alone.

2. According to Genesis 2:24, what happens when a man is united to his wife?
   a. They have a child.
   b. They are drawn closer to the Lord.
   c. They become one flesh.
   d. They start arguing about money.

3. How did Samson prove his love for Delilah?
   a. He told her the secret of his strength.
   b. He had her name tattooed on his arm.

c. He killed thirty men to save her honor.

d. He became a Philistine.

4. Who loved his wife so much that he married her even though she was pregnant with a baby that wasn't his?

a. Abraham

b. David

c. Solomon

d. Joseph

5. According to 1 Corinthians 13, the "Love Chapter," love is . . . ?

a. patient

b. kind

c. not proud

d. All of the above

INTERMEDIATE

1. What did Abram do when Pharaoh started eying Sarai, Abram's wife?

a. He started eying Pharaoh's wife, just to show him how it felt.

b. He told Pharaoh that Sarai was his sister.

c. He cursed Pharaoh in a jealous rage.

d. He prayed that God would kill Pharaoh and all of Pharaoh's men.

2. What did Isaac do when the Philistine king Abimelech started eying Rebekah, Isaac's wife?

a. He laughed it off because he could tell that Abimelech was drunk.

b. He killed Abimelech's second-in-command.

c. He told Abimelech that Rebekah was his sister.

d. He called down curses from God on Abimelech and the entire Philistine nation.

3. What did Jacob do in order to marry his beloved Rachel?

a. He chose to marry Rachel's older sister first, saving the best for last.

b. He worked for fourteen years.

c. He presented her father with the foreskins of two

hundred Philistines so her father would allow the marriage.

d. All of the above

4. How did Ruth meet her future husband Boaz?
   a. She was picking up leftover grain in his field.
   b. She was a friend of Boaz's brother.
   c. She was drawing water from a well when he stopped by to water his camels.
   d. She was taken as a captive when Boaz invaded her village.

5. Which of the following statements comes from 1 Corinthians 13, the "Love Chapter"?
   a. Love means never having to say you're sorry.
   b. If you love something, set it free.
   c. Love never fails.
   d. All you need is love.

ADVANCED

1. Why didn't Samson's marriage work out?
   a. His wife cut his hair.
   b. Samson killed his brothers-in-law with the jawbone of a donkey.
   c. His wife got tired of Samson's riddles.
   d. His father-in-law gave Samson's bride to the best man.

2. What did the beloved wives of Abraham, Jacob, and Elkanah have in common?
   a. They were all visited by an angel (or visitor) from the Lord.
   b. They all had difficulty bearing children.
   c. They are all listed in Matthew's genealogy of Jesus.
   d. All of the above

3. What did Michal do to save her husband, David?
   a. She put an idol in her bed, covered it with goatskins, and told her father that David was ill.
   b. She stepped in front of a spear that her father, Saul, had thrown at David.

    c. She smuggled David into Philistine territory, where he would be safe from Saul.

    d. She divorced him.

4. What secret did Esther keep from her husband, King Xerxes?

    a. Her first husband was Xerxes' brother.

    b. She had been in love with Haman when she agreed to marry the king.

    c. She was Jewish.

    d. She was involved in Haman's plot against Mordecai.

5. Why did God command Hosea to marry Gomer, an adulterous wife?

    a. She was the daughter of a Levite.

    b. Their relationship would show Israel how it had neglected its love for God.

    c. God was punishing Hosea for worshiping idols.

    d. Gomer's children needed a godly influence in their lives.

EXPERT

1. What did Jacob do when his beloved wife Rachel died?

    a. He buried her in the tomb of his fathers near Mamre in Canaan.

    b. He lost his will to live and died himself less than a year later.

    c. He erected a pillar to mark her tomb near Bethlehem.

    d. He consoled himself with Bilhah, Rachel's maidservant.

2. What did David do to earn the right to marry the king's daughter?

    a. He killed Goliath and brought the giant's sword to Saul.

    b. He was anointed by Samuel to be the successor to Saul.

    c. He killed one hundred Philistines, melted down their armor, and built an altar to the Lord.

    d. He brought Saul the foreskins of two hundred Philistine warriors.

3. To what does Solomon compare his lover's hair in his epic love letter, the Song of Songs?

a. Flocks of goats
b. The ravens that nest in the trees
c. The golden grain of the first harvest
d. The mane of a lion that lies in wait

4. In Paul's opinion, what is the best course of action for a woman who loses her husband?
   a. To remarry as soon as possible so that she will be cared for in her later years
   b. To wait awhile before she remarries, in order to preserve the memory of her husband
   c. To respect her children's wishes as to whether she should remarry
   d. To remain a widow for the rest of her life

5. According to Ephesians 5:28, he who loves his wife . . . ?
   a. Loves himself
   b. Loves the one from whom all love comes
   c. Understands what the will of the Lord is
   d. Will not be corrupted by sinful desires

Good Friday/Easter

EASY

1. Who betrayed Jesus?
   a. Malchus, the high priest's servant
   b. The chief priests and elders
   c. Judas Iscariot
   d. His younger brother

2. Where was Jesus arrested?
   a. In an olive grove called Gethsemane
   b. On the shore near the Sea of Galilee
   c. In the temple at Jerusalem
   d. Outside his father's house in Nazareth

3. What did Peter do three times while Jesus was on trial?
   a. Cut off someone's ear
   b. Denied knowing Jesus
   c. Encouraged the other disciples to hold fast to their faith
   d. Fell asleep

4. Why did the Jewish leaders want Jesus dead?
   a. He claimed to be the Son of God.
   b. He had made them look like fools when they tried to question his teachings.
   c. It was part of the Passover ceremony to execute false teachers.
   d. They were afraid that he was planning to overthrow the Roman government.

5. Who was the governor who offered to release Jesus?
   a. Pilate
   b. Centurius
   c. Abimelech
   d. Augustus

6. How was Jesus executed?
   a. Stoning
   b. Flogging
   c. With swords
   d. Crucifixion

7. On what day of the week was Jesus crucified?
   a. The Sabbath
   b. Sunday
   c. Friday
   d. Monday

8. Who was crucified with Jesus?
   a. Two robbers
   b. Four of his disciples
   c. Three false prophets
   d. No one

9. What did the centurion say after Jesus died?
   a. "You have crucified an innocent man!"
   b. "I wash my hands of this man's blood!"
   c. "Truly, this was the Son of God!"
   d. Nothing—he was not able to speak.

10. On what day of the week did Jesus rise from the dead?
    a. Sunday
    b. The Sabbath

c. Friday

d. Wednesday

11. Why did Pilate order Jesus' tomb to be guarded?
    a. He wanted to show the Pharisees that he took their concerns seriously.
    b. The recent earthquake had brought out looters.
    c. He wanted to prevent the disciples from stealing Jesus' body.
    d. He wasn't convinced that Jesus was actually dead.

12. What did Mary Magdalene and her companion see when they visited Jesus' tomb the day after the Sabbath?
    a. A large rock that had been moved
    b. An empty tomb
    c. An angel wearing snow-white clothes
    d. All of the above

13. How many of Jesus' twelve disciples saw him after his resurrection?
    a. Two—Peter and John
    b. Three—Peter, John, and Thomas
    c. Eleven—all but Judas Iscariot
    d. All twelve of them

14. How did Jesus convince Thomas that he had risen from the dead?
    a. A voice from heaven proclaimed the good news.
    b. He let Thomas touch his crucifixion scars.
    c. He showed Thomas his graveclothes.
    d. He brought a legion of angels to testify on his behalf.

15. How did the legend of the Easter bunny get started?
    a. According to Mark, a small rabbit sat in front of the empty tomb.
    b. The traditional Easter meal of first-century Christians was rabbit.
    c. The Greek word for "resurrection" resembles the word for "rabbit."
    d. The legend of the Easter bunny has nothing to do with the Bible.

INTERMEDIATE

1. What did Peter do when the guards tried to arrest Jesus?
   a. He drew his sword and cut off a servant's ear.
   b. He helped the soldiers put chains on Jesus.
   c. He demanded that he be arrested too.
   d. Nothing—he was still asleep in Gethsemane.

2. What did Judas Iscariot do after he betrayed Jesus?
   a. He betrayed Peter and the rest of the disciples.
   b. He fled to Egypt and lived in obscurity.
   c. He was eventually reconciled with the apostles and
      worked in the Jerusalem church.
   d. He hanged himself.

3. How did Jesus respond to the false witnesses' accusa-
   tions against him?
   a. He quoted Old Testament prophecies.
   b. He remained silent.
   c. He warned them of the coming judgment.
   d. He denied the false charges and explained the truth.

4. Whom did the crowd outside of Pilate's palace demand
   that Pilate release?
   a. Jesus
   b. A murderer named Barabbas
   c. The two robbers who were crucified with Christ
   d. Jesus' disciples

5. Who helped Jesus carry his cross to Golgotha?
   a. Joseph of Arimathea
   b. His disciples
   c. Simon of Cyrene
   d. Cyrus of Simene

6. What was written on the sign that hung above Jesus' head
   while he was on the cross?
   a. "The Son of God"
   b. "The Son of Joseph"
   c. "Blasphemer"
   d. "The King of the Jews"

7. Why did the soldiers cast lots?
   a. To pass the time while they waited for Jesus to die
   b. To see which one of them would have to take Jesus' body down from the cross
   c. To see who would get Jesus' undergarment
   d. To see whether the robbers or Jesus would die first

8. What was offered to Jesus while he hung on the cross?
   a. A pardon, if he would take back his claim of being the Son of God
   b. A chance to see his parents one last time
   c. Wine mixed with myrrh to deaden his pain
   d. A cloak to cover his nakedness

9. What did Joseph of Arimathea ask Pilate for?
   a. Thirty pieces of silver
   b. A day of mourning for all of Jerusalem
   c. Guards to be posted around Jesus' tomb
   d. Jesus' body

10. What did the angel at Jesus' tomb say to Mary Magdalene and the other Mary?
    a. "He has been raised from the dead."
    b. "Come, see where his body was lying."
    c. "You will see him."
    d. All of the above

11. Why did the guards at the tomb say that Jesus' disciples had stolen his body in the middle of the night?
    a. They were bribed.
    b. They were drunk and didn't know what they were saying.
    c. That's what they actually believed happened.
    d. They had fallen asleep and were covering up their incompetence.

12. Who was the first disciple to enter Jesus' tomb after his resurrection?
    a. John
    b. Peter
    c. Judas Iscariot
    d. The Bible doesn't say.

13. Why were the disciples startled and frightened when Jesus appeared to them?
   a. He looked nothing like his former self.
   b. An incredible brightness had filled the room.
   c. They thought he was a ghost.
   d. They were afraid that he had been followed by the Jewish leaders.

14. What did Jesus do after he blessed his disciples for the final time?
   a. He disappeared.
   b. He ascended to heaven.
   c. He appeared to those who had persecuted him.
   d. The Bible doesn't say.

15. How many people actually saw the resurrected Jesus?
   a. None
   b. Three
   c. Fifteen, counting the four women at the tomb
   d. Over five hundred

ADVANCED

1. How did Judas know where to find Jesus on the night of his arrest?
   a. He overheard Peter and Jesus discussing it in the upper room.
   b. He had an accomplice follow Jesus.
   c. The Pharisees knew the path Jesus took to walk to the temple.
   d. Jesus had often met with his disciples at that site.

2. How did the arresting soldiers react when Jesus identified himself?
   a. They fled in terror.
   b. They struck him repeatedly.
   c. They fell down.
   d. They cursed Judas for involving them in a religious dispute.

3. Where was Jesus taken first after he was arrested?
   a. To a cell in Capernaum

b. To Caiaphas, the high priest

c. To Annas, Caiaphas's father-in-law

d. To Pilate's palace

4. What happened when Jesus suggested that the high priest question people who had heard his teachings?

a. Jesus was slapped in the face.

b. Some Pharisees demanded that Jesus be released.

c. Barabbas was brought in to refute everything Jesus had said.

d. The high priest demanded that Jesus be executed for his disrespect.

5. When Jesus told Pilate that he "came to bring the truth to the world," Pilate replied with what famous statement?

a. "The truth shall set you free."

b. "Great is Truth, and mighty above all things."

c. "[Fight] the never ending battle for truth, justice, and the American Way."

d. "What is truth?"

6. If Pilate found no basis for a charge against Jesus (John 18:38), why did he have Jesus flogged? (John 19:1)

a. He hoped that the flogging would appease the Jewish leaders.

b. Every person who was accused in a Roman court of law received a flogging.

c. Pilate remembered that Jesus had spoken harsh words against Herod.

d. Only Roman citizens were exempt from flogging.

7. What arrangements did Jesus make for his mother while he hung on the cross?

a. He sold his clothes and gave her the money.

b. He asked Joseph of Arimathea to reserve a burial plot for her.

c. He gave her permission to remarry.

d. He instructed John, one of his disciples, to take her into his home.

8. What was the day before the Sabbath—the day of Jesus' crucifixion—known as?

a. Sabbath Eve
b. Maundy Friday
c. Preparation Day
d. The Day of Atonement

9. Why were the soldiers going to break Jesus' legs?
   a. Pilate had commanded them to do so.
   b. The Jewish leaders were in a hurry to take down the dead bodies.
   c. The soldiers enjoyed torturing their prisoners.
   d. It was a typical punishment for Jewish rebels.

10. Why was Pilate surprised to hear that Jesus was dead? (Mark 15:44)
    a. Crucified men often lived two or three days before dying.
    b. Pilate hadn't given permission to begin the crucifixion.
    c. Pilate believed that the Son of God could not be killed.
    d. Pilate had expected that the disciples would try to rescue Jesus.

11. Why didn't Peter and John realize that Jesus had risen from the dead even after they saw the empty tomb?
    a. They thought the Roman soldiers had moved the body.
    b. They didn't realize that the Scriptures had predicted Christ's resurrection.
    c. Thomas had convinced them that Jesus' resurrection was impossible.
    d. They believed that they had run to the wrong tomb.

12. What mistake did Mary Magdalene make at Jesus' tomb?
    a. She mistook the angel for one of the disciples.
    b. She addressed the soldiers harshly, a serious social offense in Palestine.
    c. She placed incense on Jesus' burial clothes, not realizing that they were empty.
    d. She mistook the risen Jesus for a gardener.

13. Why did the resurrected Jesus tell Mary not to hold on to him?
    a. Women were not allowed to touch dead bodies.
    b. He had not yet returned to the Father.

c. He had work to accomplish in Jerusalem.

d. He wanted her to repent for her lack of faith.

14. When did the two men on the road to Emmaus recognize Jesus?
    a. When he broke bread with them
    b. When they saw the scars on his hands, feet, and side
    c. When he told them that his Father was God
    d. When he told them details of their lives that no one else knew

15. How did Jesus prove to his disciples that he was not a ghost?
    a. He passed his hand through a flame.
    b. He washed their feet.
    c. He ate some fish.
    d. He embraced each of them.

EXPERT

1. What happened to the young man wearing nothing but a linen garment who followed Jesus after his arrest?
   a. Peter cut off his ear in the Garden of Gethsemane.
   b. He ended up comforting Peter after the disciple had denied Jesus for the third time.
   c. He ended up running away naked.
   d. He received Jesus' cloak and undergarment at the Crucifixion.

2. Why did the chief priests and elders hand Jesus over to Pilate?
   a. All Jewish legal matters were turned over to Pilate.
   b. Jesus' crimes were against Rome, not against Jewish law.
   c. The Jewish leaders were not allowed to execute prisoners and needed the authority of the Roman government to do so.
   d. Pilate was known for his ruthless treatment of prisoners.

3. What was done with the thirty silver coins that Judas returned to the chief priests?

a. They were used to buy a plot of land that became a burial site for foreigners.

b. They were used to pay for Jesus' burial.

c. They were used to buy a new curtain for the temple after the old one was torn in two.

d. They were given to Mary, the mother of Jesus.

4. Why didn't the Jewish leaders enter Pilate's palace to attend Jesus' trial?

a. They weren't invited.

b. They didn't want to become ceremonially unclean by entering the house of a Gentile.

c. They secretly hoped to avoid any blame for Jesus' death.

d. They were too busy inciting the crowd to call for Jesus' crucifixion.

5. Why was Herod pleased when Jesus was brought before him?

a. He wanted to see Jesus perform a miracle.

b. He was relieved that Jesus was not John the Baptist come back to life.

c. He had many questions to ask Jesus about eternal life.

d. He wanted to embarrass Pilate in front of the Jewish leaders.

6. Who persuaded Pilate to wash his hands of the conviction and execution of Jesus?

a. The Jewish leaders

b. The crowd outside his palace

c. His mother

d. His wife

7. What shape was the cross used in many Roman executions?

a. T

b. X

c. Y

d. All of the above

8. Why did Jesus refuse the wine mixed with gall that was offered to him by the soldiers? (Matthew 27:34)

a. He had taken the Nazirite vow, which meant he could have no wine or strong drink.

b. He wanted to be fully conscious until his death.

c. The wine had been made by Gentiles.

d. He gave his portion of the wine to ease the suffering of the criminals being crucified on either side of him.

9. When Jesus cried out, "Eli, Eli, lema sabachthani?" who did the people think he was talking to?

a. God, his father in heaven

b. Abraham, the father of the Jewish nation

c. Joseph, his earthly father

d. The prophet Elijah

10. What did the tearing of the temple curtain at the moment of Christ's death (Matthew 27:51) symbolize?

a. The division of the Jewish nation

b. The eventual destruction of the temple in A.D. 70

c. Christ had made it possible for a believer to enter into God's presence directly.

d. The moral bankruptcy of the high priest

11. What unusual event following Jesus' death is described only in Matthew's Gospel?

a. The sudden death of Pontius Pilate

b. The words *Eli, Eli, lema sabachthani?* suddenly appeared on the altar of the temple of Jerusalem.

c. Tombs broke open and dead people started walking around Jerusalem.

d. The Jewish leaders who had instigated Jesus' crucifixion were stricken with painful boils.

12. The man who accompanied Joseph of Arimathea to ask Pilate for Jesus' body was a key figure in one of the most famous passages in all of Scripture. Who was he?

a. The man who had asked Jesus if he could bury his father first

b. Nicodemus, to whom Jesus was speaking when he proclaimed the famous John 3:16 passage

c. The tax collector who had invited Jesus to eat in his home

d. Saul, who would later change his name and become the apostle Paul

13. What news did the Jewish leaders want to suppress at all costs? (Matthew 27:64)
    a. That Jesus had risen from the dead
    b. That Jesus had raised Lazarus from the dead
    c. That Jesus was born of a virgin
    d. That Jesus had written the Sermon on the Mount himself

14. Why did the women visit Jesus' tomb early Sunday morning?
    a. They wanted to get there in time to see Jesus' resurrection.
    b. They were going to anoint Jesus' corpse with spices.
    c. They were plotting to steal Jesus' body.
    d. They had heard a rumor that the body was going to be moved.

15. In 1 Corinthians 15, Paul says that if Christ was not raised from the dead . . .
    a. the apostles were false witnesses.
    b. those who have hope in him are the most miserable people in the world.
    c. the Christian faith is useless.
    d. All of the above

Mother's Day

EASY

1. Who is the mother of the human race?
   a. Mother Nature
   b. Ishtar
   c. Eve
   d. Mary

2. Why did Sarah laugh when the visitor from the Lord told her she'd have a child?
   a. Abraham was laughing also.
   b. Her name meant "childless."
   c. She had just given birth to her tenth child and was not planning on having any more.
   d. She was ninety years old.

3. What were the names of Rebekah's battling twin sons?
   a. Peter and Paul
   b. Esau and Jacob
   c. Joseph and Benjamin
   d. Abner and Judas

4. Who was the mother of Joseph, Jacob's favorite son?
   a. Leah
   b. Bilhah
   c. Rachel
   d. The Bible doesn't say.

5. What did Moses' mother do to protect her three-month-old son?
   a. She changed his name to Moses, which means "May God curse anyone who harms me."
   b. She killed an Egyptian servant who was staying in her house.
   c. She put him in a basket and placed it in the Nile River.
   d. She fled to the desert.

6. In Solomon's great test of wisdom, how did he determine which of the quarreling women was actually the baby's mother?
   a. She was the one who was willing to give up the baby in order to spare its life.
   b. She was the one who would not renounce her motherhood, even if it meant that the child would die.
   c. She was the one who had a "motherly glow" about her.
   d. She was the one who most closely resembled the baby.

7. What was the name of John the Baptist's mother?
   a. Brittany
   b. Shiprah
   c. Mary Magdalene
   d. Elizabeth

8. What was unusual about Jesus' mother?
   a. She was a relative of the Roman emperor, Caesar Augustus.
   b. She was a carpenter.

c. She had been a priest in the temple.

d. She was a virgin when Jesus was born.

9. Where was Jesus' mother during his crucifixion?
   a. She had died a few years before.
   b. She had been imprisoned for criticizing the governor.
   c. She was present at the Crucifixion.
   d. She remained in Nazareth, refusing to leave her house.

10. According to Ephesians 6:2, what is the first commandment with a promise?
    a. Honor your father and mother.
    b. Love your neighbor as yourself.
    c. Remember the Sabbath day by keeping it holy.
    d. You shall not murder.

INTERMEDIATE

1. Who was the mother of Abram's first child?
   a. Sarai
   b. Sarah
   c. An Egyptian maidservant named Hagar
   d. The Bible doesn't say.

2. What did Rebekah do for her favorite son, Jacob?
   a. She made him a brightly colored coat to wear.
   b. She gave him a nickname that literally meant "my favorite."
   c. She chose a wife for him.
   d. She helped him trick his father into giving him the blessing that was meant for his brother, Esau.

3. What did Rachel do when she saw that she was not bearing her husband, Jacob, any children?
   a. She demanded that Jacob father a child with her maidservant.
   b. She trusted that God would one day open her womb.
   c. She asked Jacob to stop fathering children with her sister, Leah.
   d. She returned to her father, Laban.

4. What instructions did the angel of the Lord give to Samson's mother?

a. Don't drink wine or beer.
b. Eat right.
c. Don't cut your boy's hair.
d. All of the above

5. Why was Hannah almost forced to leave the temple as she prayed for a son?
   a. The other mothers in the temple were uncomfortable around her.
   b. She touched implements intended for the priest's use.
   c. The priest thought she was drunk.
   d. She was a Moabite.

6. According to Proverbs 31:28, what will the wife of noble character be called by her children?
   a. The Queen of Heaven
   b. Healer of the Nations
   c. Bride of the Holy One
   d. Blessed

7. To what did Jesus compare his concern for his people?
   a. A mother hen gathering her chicks under her wing
   b. A mother watching her child die
   c. A mother giving instructions to her children
   d. A mother in labor

8. Why were Elizabeth's neighbors and relatives surprised when she named her son John?
   a. No one else in the family was named John.
   b. The angel had told her to name the child Thaddaeus.
   c. She did not consult her husband before making the decision.
   d. She had intended to name the child Malachi.

9. What did the mother of James and John request of Jesus that made the rest of the disciples angry?
   a. She wanted Jesus to give them miraculous healing powers.
   b. She wanted Jesus to dismiss Peter and Andrew.
   c. She wanted Jesus to explain his parables to her sons before he explained them to the rest of the disciples.

    d. She wanted one of her sons to sit on Jesus' right hand and the other to sit on his left hand in his kingdom.

10. What was John instructed to do regarding Jesus' mother?
    a. "Adopt" her as his own mother after Jesus' death
    b. Break the news to her that her son was dead
    c. Take her with him to the isle of Patmos
    d. Not trouble her with the work of the church

ADVANCED

1. Which of the following was not part of the Lord's promise to Hagar regarding her son, Ishmael?
    a. "He will be free and untamed as a wild donkey."
    b. "He will be against everyone, and everyone will be against him."
    c. "His descendants will roam the deserts."
    d. "He will live at odds with the rest of his brothers."

2. What timetable did the Lord give Abraham when he promised that ninety-year-old Sarah would have a child?
    a. "In nine months"
    b. "By this time next year"
    c. "When Sarah is ninety-nine years old"
    d. "Before she dies"

3. Which of the following is described as a source of grief to Rebekah?
    a. Her son Esau's taste in women
    b. Her son Jacob's tendency to take advantage of his brother
    c. The conflict between Jacob and Esau
    d. The strained relationship between her husband, Isaac, and his sons

4. What did Rachel name the son she gave birth to as she was dying?
    a. Benjamin
    b. Ben-oni
    c. Ben-hur
    d. Ben-gai

5. Which judge is described as "a mother in Israel"?
   a. Leah
   b. Samson
   c. Jael
   d. Deborah

6. Which of the following was included in Hannah's vow to the Lord?
   a. She would raise her son according to God's covenants with his people.
   b. Her son would never drink alcohol.
   c. He would never get a haircut.
   d. All of the above

7. According to Proverbs 15:20, what does a foolish son do?
   a. Calls his mother by her first name
   b. Despises his mother
   c. Scorns the tradition of his mother
   d. Considers not the feelings of his mother

8. What did Elizabeth do when she found out that she was pregnant?
   a. She went into seclusion for five months.
   b. She notified all of her relatives, including Mary.
   c. She laughed at the angel who gave her the news.
   d. She placed an altar in her house so that she could praise God continuously.

9. What did the Syrophoenician mother in Mark 7:24-30 beg Jesus to do?
   a. Rebuke his disciples for failing to give money to her son
   b. Take her and her daughter with him to Jerusalem
   c. Heal her deaf and dumb son
   d. Drive a demon out of her daughter

10. What does the Bible tell us about Timothy's mother?
    a. She was Greek.
    b. Her Christian faith was a source of conflict between her and her mother.
    c. She passed her faith on to her son.
    d. All of the above

EXPERT

1. What was Hagar's name for the Lord?
   a. "He who has heard my cry"
   b. "The God who touches the heart of the faithful"
   c. "The Lord who tastes the bitterness of my tears"
   d. "The One who sees me"

2. Why was Rachel so desperate to get some of the mandrakes that Reuben found? (Genesis 30:14-15)
   a. Mandrakes were superstitiously believed to induce pregnancy when eaten.
   b. Mandrakes were Jacob's favorite food; she was preparing a special meal in order to entice him to lay with her.
   c. She had lost the mandrakes on her way home from the field and would have been punished if she hadn't found them.
   d. Mandrakes were believed to be a cure for the palsy that Rachel's father suffered from.

3. Who was the mother of Joseph's sons Manasseh and Ephraim?
   a. Potiphar's wife
   b. Atsinoph
   c. Asenath
   d. The Bible doesn't say.

4. According to Deborah, what had ceased until she "arose a mother in Israel"?
   a. Laughing and dancing
   b. Respect for women
   c. Miracles
   d. Village life

5. What was the occupation of the mother of Jephthah, the judge of Israel?
   a. Prophetess
   b. High priestess in the cult of Baal
   c. Prostitute
   d. Weaver

6. What did Micah's mother do with the eleven hundred shekels of silver that her son returned to her after he stole it?
    a. She offered it as a reward for the man who brought her son to her—dead or alive.
    b. She consecrated it to the Lord and then used it to make an idol.
    c. She bribed the Philistines to keep them from destroying her family home.
    d. She hurled all of the silver into a canyon.

7. Elijah brought back to life the son of what woman?
    a. The queen of Sheba
    b. Queen Jezebel
    c. Athalia
    d. The widow of Zarepheth

8. What did the mothers of Samaria do during the Aramean siege of their city?
    a. Offered their children as slaves in order to end the siege
    b. Ate their children because there was no food
    c. Sacrificed their children to Molech, hoping that he would protect their city
    d. Sent their children to Jerusalem until the armies had left

9. What did Herodias talk her daughter into doing?
    a. Convincing Herod to kill John the Baptist
    b. Purchasing costly perfume to pour on Jesus' head
    c. Begging the Lord to heal Herodias's illness
    d. Accusing Peter of being one of Jesus' followers

10. According to 1 Timothy 5:4, how should the children or grandchildren of a widow put their religion into practice?
    a. By spreading the message of the Resurrection to all parts of the world
    b. By honoring the wishes of the widow on her deathbed
    c. By caring for their own family
    d. By tithing their money to other widows in the community

Father's Day

1. Who was the first father in the Bible to lose a son to violence?
   a. Abraham
   b. Adam
   c. Abel
   d. Alkaline

2. How did Noah save his family?
   a. He smuggled them out of Sodom and Gomorrah in the middle of the night.
   b. He used a rope and basket to lower them out of the Tower of Babel.
   c. He built an ark to save them from a flood.
   d. He taught them the ways of the Lord.

3. Whom did God choose to be father of a great nation?
   a. Aphrika
   b. Mekziko
   c. Joshua
   d. Abram

4. Which of the following refers to Jacob's offspring?
   a. The twelve tribes of Israel
   b. The Abomination of Desolation
   c. The Sanhedrin
   d. The apostles

5. How is the fifth commandment, "Honor your father and your mother," different from the other nine?
   a. It is the only commandment with a promise attached to it.
   b. It is the only commandment that doesn't begin with "You shall not. . . ."
   c. It is the only commandment that speaks of human relationships.
   d. It is the only commandment that was later overturned in a Jewish court of law.

6. Which of the following begins with the words "Our Father in heaven"?
   a. The Shepherd's Psalm
   b. The Lord's Prayer
   c. The Love Chapter (1 Corinthians 13)
   d. The Song of Songs

7. What was young Jesus referring to when he said, "Didn't you know I had to be in my Father's house"?
   a. The temple
   b. Heaven
   c. Joseph's home in Nazareth
   d. Mount Sinai

8. In the parable of the lost son, what did the father do when his prodigal son returned?
   a. He hired him as a servant.
   b. He had him thrown in prison because he did not recognize his son.
   c. He threw a huge party.
   d. The parable doesn't say.

9. Whom did Jesus call the father of lies?
   a. The devil
   b. Peter
   c. Caiaphas, the high priest
   d. The man who causes one person to stray from the path of righteousness

10. Which of the following words is an affectionate term for "father"?
    a. Abba
    b. Corbin
    c. Nazareth
    d. Petra

INTERMEDIATE

1. According to Genesis 2:24, why will a man leave his father and mother?
   a. Because he is inherently sinful
   b. To give them peace in their later years

c. To be united to his wife

d. To seek the Lord's will for his life

2. What did God command Abraham to do regarding his son Isaac?
   a. Change his name to Isaaccar
   b. Give him to his nephew Lot as a servant
   c. Provide him with priestly training
   d. Offer him as a human sacrifice

3. Which famous father is the nation of Israel named for?
   a. David
   b. Judah
   c. Jacob
   d. Jehoshaphat

4. How did Jacob respond when he got the news that his favorite son Joseph was dead?
   a. He accused Asher of the crime and banished him to Egypt.
   b. He ripped his clothes apart.
   c. He refused to eat for eight days.
   d. He sacrificed a lamb and ate it with bitter herbs.

5. What was the Old Testament penalty for cursing one's father?
   a. Forty lashes with a papyrus reed
   b. A mark on the skin
   c. Separation from one's tribe for four to six weeks, depending on how severe the cursing was
   d. Death

6. What did Samson's father-to-be see that caused him to panic?
   a. A Philistine army burning his crops
   b. A burning bush
   c. An angel of the Lord
   d. A vision of a coming famine

7. According to Proverbs 17:25, what does a foolish son bring to his father?
   a. Ulcers
   b. Grief

c. A bad reputation

d. Sympathy from neighbors

8. What did Jesus say to the disciple who wanted to bury his father?

   a. "Wait until he's dead."

   b. "Go in peace, with God's blessing."

   c. "Let the fathers bury the fathers."

   d. "Let the dead bury their dead."

9. What did God do when his Son was being crucified?

   a. He vowed revenge on all of Jesus' tormentors.

   b. He sent a legion of angels to minister to Jesus' needs.

   c. He turned away as Jesus bore the sins of mankind.

   d. He struck dead the centurion who was in charge of Jesus' crucifixion.

10. How did the Jewish leaders respond at the Feast of Dedication when Jesus said, "I am God's Son"?

   a. They accused Jesus of blasphemy and tried to seize him.

   b. They believed and were baptized by Jesus' disciples.

   c. They brought an expert in the Law to refute his claim.

   d. They agreed with him so as not to anger the crowd.

ADVANCED

1. What is the promise that accompanies the fifth commandment, "Honor your father and your mother"? (Exodus 20:12)

   a. So that you may receive the inheritance of your family

   b. So that you may avoid the slavery your fathers knew in Egypt

   c. So that you may please your heavenly Father

   d. So that you may live long in the land the Lord your God is giving you

2. What role did Aaron and his sons serve in the wilderness?

   a. They stopped the plague that killed hundreds of Israelites.

   b. They gathered the manna for the people to eat.

   c. They fulfilled priestly responsibilities.

   d. They interpreted God's instructions for Moses.

3. What were Aaron's sons killed for?

   a. Laughing while offering sacrifices

   b. Offering unauthorized fire before the Lord

   c. Offering a blemished lamb before the Lord

   d. Warming their dinners on the ashes of a burnt offering

4. What were Israelite fathers to do to teach the Lord's commandments to their children?

   a. Write them on the doorframes of their houses

   b. Sing them before the entire congregation of Israel

   c. Use strict corporal punishment until the child had memorized the law

   d. All of the above

5. Why might it be said that Joshua had no parents?

   a. His mother's name was Nobudi.

   b. He was the son of Nun.

   c. He was "adopted" by the Lord when he became leader of Israel.

   d. He is the only major figure in Scripture whose parents are never mentioned by name.

6. How did David respond when he was told that the child he had conceived with Bathsheba was dead?

   a. He executed the messenger who brought him the news.

   b. He tore his clothes, poured ashes on his head, and mourned for a week.

   c. He worshiped in the house of the Lord.

   d. He blamed the descendants of Saul.

7. Why were Reuben's rights as firstborn given to the sons of Joseph?

   a. Reuben led his brothers in their assault on Joseph.

   b. Reuben defiled his father's marriage bed by sleeping with his concubine.

   c. Reuben had refused a blessing from his father, Jacob.

   d. Reuben was the son of Zilpah, Leah's maid, and thus not a legitimate heir.

8. Name the two fathers who could brag about having a son named James among Jesus' twelve apostles.
   a. Gaius and Gideon
   b. James the Elder and Zechariah
   c. Thaddaeus and Simon
   d. Alphaeus and Zebedee

9. What did the niece/stepdaughter of Herod request of him?
   a. The keys to the chariot
   b. The head of John the Baptist
   c. The crucifixion of Jesus
   d. We don't know. The Bible says only that Herod granted her request.

10. How did Zechariah respond when the angel told him he would have a son?
    a. He laughed.
    b. He asked, "How can I know this will happen?"
    c. He asked, "What shall I call the child?"
    d. He didn't respond; Zechariah couldn't talk.

EXPERT

1. Cain named this city—the first one mentioned in the Bible—after his first son.
   a. Nuiark
   b. Babel
   c. Irad
   d. Enoch

2. Why were Jewish fathers commanded to consecrate their firstborn sons to the Lord?
   a. God had delivered every firstborn among the Israelites during the tenth plague in Egypt.
   b. The consecration was a symbolic atonement for the sin of Cain, the first firstborn son.
   c. Firstborn children tend to be brighter and more attractive than their younger siblings.
   d. God was merely following Hebrew custom in emphasizing the importance of the firstborn son.

3. What did Zelophehad's daughters request of Moses and the leaders of Israel?
   a. Husbands from among the tribe of Manasseh
   b. The right to vote on issues that concerned their family and tribe
   c. Permission to bury their father in the Desert of Zin
   d. The inheritance of land that would have been their father's

4. According to Deuteronomy 21:18-21, what was a father to do with a stubborn and rebellious son who would not respond to discipline?
   a. Deny him an inheritance in the Promised Land
   b. Renounce him in a public ceremony
   c. Let the town elders stone him to death
   d. Bring charges against him in a court of law

5. Why was Jephthah so upset to see his daughter come out to meet him when he returned from battle?
   a. He thought he had been followed by enemy soldiers.
   b. He had to sacrifice her as a burnt offering.
   c. She was carrying a hidden sword.
   d. He knew she had secretly helped the enemy Ammonites.

6. What charge did David give his son Solomon before David died?
   a. Wipe out the last trace of Saul's dynasty.
   b. Abhor the assembly of evildoers and refuse to sit with the wicked.
   c. Be strong, be a man, and observe what the Lord your God requires.
   d. Extol the Lord at all times; let his praise be always on your lips.

7. How were Job's ten children killed?
   a. They were bitten by poisonous serpents.
   b. A wind gust caused a house to fall on them.
   c. They were slaughtered by the Chaldeans.
   d. Lightning struck them as they offered a sacrifice.

8. Name Hosea's three children.
   a. Jotham, Ahaz, and Hezekiah
   b. Shem, Ham, and Japheth
   c. Jehoshaphat, Jotham, and Hilkiah
   d. Jezreel, Lo-ruhamah, and Lo-ammi

9. What does the Bible tell us about Timothy's father?
   a. He was a Greek.
   b. He perished in a shipwreck off the coast of Berea.
   c. He strengthened Timothy in the faith.
   d. He cursed Paul for leading his son to the faith.

10. Who is described in Hebrews 7:1-3 as being without mother or father?
    a. Orphans
    b. Adam
    c. Melchizedek
    d. Jesus Christ, the author and finisher of our faith

Christmas

EASY

1. What was the name of the angel who visited Mary?
   a. Gabriel
   b. Michael
   c. Jehu
   d. The Bible doesn't say.

2. Who was Jesus' earthly father?
   a. Zechariah
   b. Joseph
   c. John the Baptist
   d. The Bible doesn't mention him by name.

3. Where was Joseph living when Caesar Augustus's decree went out?
   a. In Ephesus
   b. In Nazareth
   c. In Egypt
   d. The Bible doesn't say.

4. Who accompanied Joseph to Bethlehem?
   a. Mary, the woman who was pledged to be his wife
   b. Zechariah and Elizabeth
   c. His mother and father
   d. The Bible doesn't say.

5. Where was Jesus born?
   a. Bethel
   b. Bethlehem
   c. Jerusalem
   d. Gaza

6. Why did Mary place her son in a manger?
   a. The angel Gabriel had instructed her to do so.
   b. It was the cleanest place in the stable.
   c. It was Jewish tradition that all firstborn sons be placed in a manger.
   d. There was no room for them in the inn.

7. What is a manger?
   a. A small well
   b. A small wooden basket that served as a bassinet for infants in ancient times
   c. A feeding trough for animals
   d. A stone platform for threshing grain

8. What did Mary use to clothe her newborn son?
   a. Strips of cloth
   b. A large diaper
   c. Sawdust
   d. The saddle blanket from her donkey

9. Who were the first people to visit the baby Jesus?
   a. The innkeeper and his wife
   b. Shepherds
   c. Three wise men
   d. The little drummer boy and his mother

10. How did the shepherds know that Jesus had been born?
    a. An angel delivered the news.
    b. A tribune from Herod's palace had inquired about the event.

c. They could hear the baby crying in the manger.

d. They saw the star above the stable where Jesus lay.

11. What was the shepherds' response when the angel first appeared to them?
    a. They sang a hymn of praise.
    b. They ignored him because they thought he was just a man.
    c. They threw rocks at him, thinking that he was trying to steal their sheep.
    d. They were terrified.

12. What was it that shone around the shepherds when the angel of the Lord appeared to them?
    a. The glow of a brush fire on a hill to the north of their camp
    b. The reflection of the angel's halo
    c. The glory of the Lord
    d. The illumination of the star that the wise men were following

13. What gift(s) did the shepherds bring to Jesus?
    a. Wool blankets
    b. Gold, frankincense, and myrrh
    c. Ten young goats
    d. They probably showed up empty-handed.

14. What gifts did the wise men bring to Jesus?
    a. Gold, incense, and myrrh
    b. Emeralds, rubies, and sapphires
    c. A scroll of the Pentateuch
    d. A seamless robe

15. On what day is Jesus' birth celebrated today?
    a. December 25
    b. The first day of the Jewish Passover
    c. The twenty-fifth day of the Jewish month of Nisan
    d. All of the above

INTERMEDIATE

1. How many of the Gospels describe the events of Jesus' birth?
   a. Two

    b. Three

    c. Four

    d. None

2. Why were Mary and Joseph in Bethlehem when Jesus was born?
    a. A flood had forced them to flee from Nazareth.
    b. They had relatives in Bethlehem.
    c. They were registering for a census.
    d. They had stopped in Bethlehem to water their camels on their way home to Nazareth.

3. Who issued the decree that brought Joseph and Mary to Bethlehem?
    a. Caesar Augustus
    b. Diotrephes
    c. Constantine
    d. Quirinius

4. What was Bethlehem's nickname?
    a. The Heart of the Promised Land
    b. The Jewel of Judea
    c. Birthplace of the Savior
    d. The city of David

5. Why did Joseph go to Bethlehem to register for the census?
    a. Bethlehem was a safer city than those in Galilee.
    b. Joseph was a descendant of David; Bethlehem was the city of David.
    c. Mary had always wanted to see Bethlehem.
    d. Joseph knew the Old Testament prophecies that predicted the Son of God would be born in Bethlehem.

6. How long was Joseph and Mary's trip from Nazareth to Bethlehem?
    a. Five hours
    b. Around three days
    c. Almost two weeks
    d. The Bible doesn't say.

7. What were the shepherds watching for when the angel appeared to them?
    a. The star in the east

b. Thieves and predators that might harm their sheep
c. The wise men
d. A messenger from Jerusalem

8. According to the angel, how would the shepherds recognize the Christ child?
    a. There would be a bright star above the stable where he lay.
    b. There would be an angelic choir surrounding the inn.
    c. The magi would be at the stable.
    d. He would be wrapped in cloths and lying in a manger.

9. What words did the host of angels recite before they left the shepherds? (Luke 2:14)
    a. "Glory to God in the highest heaven."
    b. "Glory, glory! Hallelujah!"
    c. "Go tell it on the mountain."
    d. "Angels we have heard on high."

10. What were the names of the shepherds who visited Jesus?
    a. Misha-el, Hananiah, and Eliphaz
    b. Zadok, Akim, and Eliud
    c. Kenan, Mahalel, and Jared
    d. The Bible doesn't say.

11. Who were the magi?
    a. Astrologers from the East
    b. Kings or princes from the region of Judea
    c. The priestly division that offered sacrifices in the temple
    d. Another name for the Sadducees

12. How many wise men from the East visited Jesus in the stable where he was born?
    a. None
    b. Two
    c. Three
    d. The Bible doesn't say.

13. What were the magi looking for?
    a. They were spying at the behest of Herod.
    b. A place to feed and water their camels
    c. The king of the Jews
    d. Answers to their deep philosophical questions

14. How did Herod's advisors know where Christ was to be born?
    a. They were familiar with Old Testament prophecies.
    b. They saw the star above the stable.
    c. The innkeeper told them.
    d. They followed Joseph and Mary from Nazareth.

15. How did Santa Claus come to be associated with the celebration of Jesus' birth?
    a. One of the wise men who brought gifts to Jesus was named Santicles.
    b. Shepherds—like the ones who visited the baby Jesus—often tended reindeer.
    c. Saint Nicholas, a follower of Jesus, brought gold, incense, and myrrh to the temple every year.
    d. The legend of Santa Claus was not inspired by anything in the Bible.

ADVANCED

1. Which of the following famous Bible characters is not mentioned in Matthew's genealogy of Jesus?
    a. Isaac
    b. Daniel
    c. Ruth
    d. Jacob

2. How is Matthew's genealogy of Jesus (Matthew 1:1-17) different from Luke's? (Luke 3)
    a. Matthew traces the line of Joseph; Luke traces the line of Mary.
    b. Matthew's genealogy moves from past to present; Luke's moves from present to past.
    c. Matthew traces Jesus' ancestors back to Abraham; Luke traces his ancestors all the way back to Adam.
    d. All of the above

3. What do Daniel, Zechariah, and Mary all have in common?
    a. They were all ancestors of Jesus.
    b. They all had children under miraculous circumstances.
    c. They were all visited by the angel Gabriel.
    d. They were all closely related to someone named Joseph.

4. How was Jesus related to John the Baptist?
   a. They were first cousins.
   b. They were second cousins.
   c. John the Baptist was Jesus' uncle.
   d. The Bible doesn't say.

5. What happened when Elizabeth heard Mary's greeting?
   a. She gathered the women of the town to listen to Mary's amazing story.
   b. Her baby leaped in her womb.
   c. She stared at Mary because she didn't recognize her.
   d. She called for her husband, Zechariah.

6. How did Elizabeth refer to Mary?
   a. Mother of my Lord
   b. Fruit of my sister's womb
   c. The blessed mother
   d. The chosen one

7. How long did Mary stay with Elizabeth?
   a. Through Passover
   b. Several hours
   c. About three weeks
   d. About three months

8. What was Joseph's initial response when he discovered that Mary was pregnant?
   a. He praised God that his betrothed would be the mother of the Messiah.
   b. He wanted to divorce her.
   c. He felt overwhelmed at the prospect of raising God's Son.
   d. He planned to flee to Egypt.

9. What caused Joseph to reconsider his plan to divorce Mary?
   a. A voice from heaven told him he would be honored.
   b. Divorcing a pregnant wife was forbidden by Jewish law.
   c. An angel in a dream convinced him to marry Mary.
   d. The Bible doesn't say.

10. What does *Immanuel* mean?
    a. Lord of the humble

b. Savior
c. Prince of peace
d. God with us

11. Why was Joseph instructed to give his son the name Jesus?
    a. Because his son would save his people from their sins
    b. As a tribute to the Old Testament leader Joshua
    c. Because the name means "God with us"
    d. He wasn't; the name *Jesus* was Joseph's idea.

12. Who was required to register for the census ordered by Caesar Augustus?
    a. The citizens of Bethlehem and the surrounding communities
    b. All non-Roman citizens
    c. All males over twenty-one years of age
    d. The entire Roman Empire

13. Who was governor of Syria when Jesus was born?
    a. Sennacherib
    b. Xerxes
    c. Quirinius
    d. The Bible doesn't say.

14. What did the shepherds do after they'd seen the Christ child?
    a. They journeyed to the temple and made a wave offering of thanksgiving.
    b. They "went public," spreading the word about what they'd seen and heard.
    c. They "treasured up" all that they had seen and pondered those things in their hearts.
    d. They abandoned their jobs and became wandering messengers of the Good News.

15. What did King Herod request of the magi?
    a. That they prophesy concerning the future events of his reign
    b. Gifts similar to the ones they presented the Christ child
    c. That they tell him the location of the Christ child when they found him
    d. That they never return to his land again

1. What Old Testament prophet predicted the virgin birth of the Messiah?
   a. Amos
   b. Obadiah
   c. Isaiah
   d. Ezekiel

2. Who is the first person mentioned in Matthew's genealogy of Jesus?
   a. Adam
   b. Abraham
   c. David
   d. Jeconiah

3. What landmark event in Jewish history took place fourteen generations before the birth of Christ?
   a. The exodus from Egypt
   b. David's reign as king
   c. The exile to Babylon
   d. God's covenant with Abraham

4. What famous song derives its title from the angel Gabriel's first word to Mary?
   a. "Ave Maria"
   b. "Great Is Thy Faithfulness"
   c. "Angels We Have Heard on High"
   d. "Stille Nacht (Silent Night)"

5. What was Mary's Magnificat?
   a. The song of praise she sang when she was with Elizabeth
   b. Her visitation from the angel Gabriel
   c. Her virgin conception
   d. The letter of thanks she wrote to Elizabeth

6. Which of the following lines comes from Mary's song in Luke 1?
   a. "Mine eyes have seen the glory of the coming of the Lord."
   b. "Now generation after generation will call me blessed."

    c. "For thine is the kingdom and the power and the glory forever."

    d. "Put on your garments of splendor, O Jerusalem."

7. What is the name of Zechariah's hymn in Luke 1:68-79?
    a. "Just As I Am"
    b. "Magnificat"
    c. "Benedictus"
    d. "Idumea"

8. Why did Joseph consider divorcing Mary quietly when he discovered that she was pregnant?
    a. Under Jewish law, the penalty for adultery was death.
    b. He was under pressure from his friends and family.
    c. He didn't want to publicly disgrace her.
    d. The Bible doesn't say.

9. *Jesus* is the Greek form of what Hebrew name?
    a. Yahweh
    b. Josiah
    c. Jeroboam
    d. Joshua

10. How did people respond to the incredible story the shepherds were telling about what they had seen and heard?
    a. They assumed that the shepherds were drunk or delirious.
    b. They were amazed at what the shepherds said.
    c. They praised God.
    d. They paid no attention because shepherds were considered second-class citizens.

11. What did Herod learn from the magi?
    a. The fickleness of his own subjects
    b. The location of Jesus' birthplace
    c. The exact time that the star appeared
    d. The name of Jesus' mother

12. Where were Joseph, Mary, and Jesus living when the magi found them?
    a. The stable where Jesus was born
    b. A house in Bethlehem

c. With Joseph's family in Nazareth

d. Egypt

13. Which Old Testament prophet did Herod's advisors quote when they told Herod that Christ would be born in Bethlehem?

   a. Micah

   b. Amos

   c. Obadiah

   d. Ezekiel

14. Where does myrrh come from?

   a. The resin ducts in the bark of various flowering trees

   b. The poppies that grow on the banks of the river Jordan

   c. The fertile soil of the Myrrhic Valley

   d. The residue from the walls of the Cave of Adullam

15. Why didn't the magi return to Herod after they'd found the Christ child?

   a. To show their contempt for a foreign king

   b. The star that they followed led them in the opposite direction.

   c. Joseph and Mary pleaded with them not to return.

   d. They were told in a dream not to return.

Quizzes (Answers)

Valentine's Day	Good Friday/Easter

Valentine's Day

EASY

1. d
2. c
3. a *(Judges 16)*
4. d *(Matthew 1:18-25)*
5. d

INTERMEDIATE

1. b *(Genesis 12:10-20)*
2. c *(Genesis 26:1-11)*
3. b *(Genesis 29:14-30)*
4. a *(Ruth 2)*
5. c *(1 Corinthians 13:8)*

ADVANCED

1. d *(Judges 14:1–15:2)*
2. b *(Genesis 16:1; 30:1; 1 Samuel 1:2)*
3. a *(1 Samuel 19:13-14)*
4. c *(Esther 2:20)*
5. b *(Hosea 1–14)*

EXPERT

1. c *(Genesis 35:19-20)*
2. d *(1 Samuel 18:20-27)*
3. a *(Song of Songs 4:1)*
4. d *(1 Corinthians 7:40)*
5. a

Good Friday/Easter

EASY

1. c *(Matthew 26:14-16)*
2. a *(Matthew 26:36-50; John 18:1-12)*
3. b *(Luke 22:54-62)*
4. a *(Matthew 26:63-66)*
5. a *(Matthew 27:11-26)*
6. d *(Matthew 27:31)*
7. c *(Luke 23:54)*
8. a *(Matthew 27:38)*
9. c *(Mark 15:39)*
10. a *(Mark 16:1-7)*
11. c *(Matthew 27:62-66)*
12. d *(Matthew 28:1-7)*
13. c *(John 20:19-31)*
14. b *(John 20:26-28)*
15. d

INTERMEDIATE

1. a *(John 18:10)*
2. d *(Matthew 27:3-10)*
3. b *(Mark 14:55-61)*
4. b *(Mark 15:6-15)*
5. c *(Matthew 27:32)*
6. d *(Matthew 27:37)*
7. c *(John 19:23-24)*
8. c *(Mark 15:23)*
9. d *(Mark 15:43)*
10. d *(Matthew 28:5-7)*
11. a *(Matthew 28:11-15)*
12. b *(John 20:3-8)*
13. c *(Luke 24:37)*

14. b *(Luke 24:50-51)*
15. d *(1 Corinthians 15:6)*

ADVANCED

1. d *(John 18:2)*
2. c *(John 18:6)*
3. c *(John 18:13)*
4. a *(John 18:19-23)*
5. d
6. a
7. d *(John 19:26-27)*
8. c *(Mark 15:42)*
9. a *(John 19:31-33)*
10. a
11. b *(John 20:9)*
12. d *(John 20:15)*
13. b *(John 20:17)*
14. a *(Luke 24:30-31)*
15. c *(Luke 24:41-43)*

EXPERT

1. c *(Mark 14:51-52)*
2. c *(Matthew 27:2)*
3. a *(Matthew 27:6-8)*
4. b *(John 18:28)*
5. a *(Luke 23:8)*
6. d *(Matthew 27:19)*
7. d
8. b
9. d *(Matthew 27:47)*
10. c
11. c *(Matthew 27:52-53)*
12. b *(John 19:38-39)*
13. a
14. b *(Mark 16:1)*
15. d

Mother's Day

EASY

1. c *(Genesis 3:20)*
2. d *(Genesis 18:9-15)*
3. b *(Genesis 25:24-26)*
4. c *(Genesis 30:22-24)*
5. c *(Exodus 2:1-3)*
6. a *(1 Kings 3:16-28)*
7. d *(Luke 1:57-66)*
8. d *(Luke 1:26-38)*

9. c *(John 19:25)*
10. a

INTERMEDIATE

1. c *(Genesis 16)*
2. d *(Genesis 27:1-40)*
3. a *(Genesis 30:1-8)*
4. d *(Judges 13:4-5)*
5. c *(1 Samuel 1:12-14)*
6. d
7. a *(Matthew 23:37)*
8. a *(Luke 1:57-66)*
9. d *(Matthew 20:20-28)*
10. a *(John 19:25-27)*

ADVANCED

1. c *(Genesis 16:11-12)*
2. b *(Genesis 17:21)*
3. a *(Genesis 26:35)*
4. b *(Genesis 35:18)*
5. d *(Judges 5:7)*
6. c *(1 Samuel 1:11)*
7. b
8. a *(Luke 1:24)*
9. d
10. c *(Acts 16:1; 2 Timothy 1:5)*

EXPERT

1. d *(Genesis 16:13)*
2. a
3. c *(Genesis 41:50)*
4. d *(Judges 5:7)*
5. c *(Judges 11:1)*
6. b *(Judges 17)*
7. d *(1 Kings 17:7-24)*
8. b *(Kings 6:24-29)*
9. a *(Matthew 14:6-12)*
10. c

Father's Day

EASY

1. b *(Genesis 4:1-8)*
2. c *(Genesis 6:9–7:23)*
3. d *(Genesis 12:1-2)*
4. a *(Genesis 49:1-28)*
5. a
6. b *(Matthew 6:9)*

7. a *(Luke 2:41-50)*
8. c *(Luke 15:11-32)*
9. a *(John 8:44)*
10. a *(Galatians 4:6)*

INTERMEDIATE

1. c
2. d *(Genesis 22:1-10)*
3. c *(Genesis 32:28)*
4. b *(Genesis 37:31-35)*
5. d *(Leviticus 20:9)*
6. c *(Judges 13)*
7. b
8. d *(Matthew 8:21-22, KJV)*
9. c *(Mark 15:34)*
10. a *(John 10:22-39)*

ADVANCED

1. d
2. c *(Exodus 28:1)*
3. b *(Leviticus 10:1-2)*
4. a *(Deuteronomy 6:9)*
5. b *(Joshua 1:1—Get it?)*
6. c *(2 Samuel 12:19-20)*
7. b *(1 Chronicles 5:1)*
8. d *(Matthew 10:2-4)*
9. b *(Matthew 14:6-12)*
10. b *(Luke 1:18)*

EXPERT

1. d *(Genesis 4:17)*
2. a *(Exodus 12:12-13; 13:1-2)*
3. d *(Numbers 27:1-11)*
4. c
5. b *(Judges 11:30-40)*
6. c *(1 Kings 2:2-3)*
7. b *(Job 1:18-19)*
8. d *(Hosea 1)*
9. a *(Acts 16:1)*
10. c

Christmas

EASY

1. a *(Luke 1:26-28)*
2. b *(Matthew 1:20-21)*
3. b *(Luke 2:1-5)*

4. a *(Luke 2:4-5)*
5. b *(Luke 2:4-7)*
6. d *(Luke 2:7)*
7. c
8. a *(Luke 2:7)*
9. b *(Luke 2:15-16)*
10. a *(Luke 2:8-11)*
11. d *(Luke 2:9)*
12. c *(Luke 2:9)*
13. d *(Luke 2:15-17)*
14. a *(Matthew 2:11)*
15. a

INTERMEDIATE

1. a *(Matthew 1:1–2:12; Luke 1:1–2:20)*
2. c *(Luke 2:1-5)*
3. a *(Luke 2:1)*
4. d *(Luke 2:4)*
5. b *(Luke 2:4)*
6. d
7. b *(Luke 2:8)*
8. d *(Luke 2:12)*
9. a *(Luke 2:14)*
10. d
11. a *(Matthew 2:1-2)*
12. d
13. c *(Matthew 2:2)*
14. a *(Matthew 2:2-6)*
15. d

ADVANCED

1. b *(Matthew 1:1-17)*
2. d
3. c *(Daniel 8:16-17; 9:21; Luke 1:11-20, 26-38)*
4. d *(Luke 1:36)*
5. b *(Luke 1:41)*
6. a *(Luke 1:43)*
7. d *(Luke 1:56)*
8. b *(Matthew 1:19)*
9. c *(Matthew 1:20)*
10. d *(Matthew 1:23)*
11. a *(Matthew 1:21)*
12. d *(Luke 2:1-3)*
13. c *(Luke 2:2)*
14. b *(Luke 2:17)*
15. c *(Matthew 2:8)*

1. c *(Isaiah 7:14)*
2. b *(Matthew 1:2)*
3. c *(Matthew 1:17)*
4. a *(Luke 1:28)*
5. a *(Luke 1:46-55)*
6. b *(Luke 1:46-55)*
7. c

8. c *(Matthew 1:19)*
9. d
10. b *(Luke 2:17-18)*
11. c *(Matthew 2:7)*
12. b *(Matthew 2:11)*
13. a *(Matthew 2:6, quoting Micah 5:2)*
14. a
15. d *(Matthew 2:12)*

By the Numbers

For each group of ten statements, fill in the blank with the correct number from the column on the right.

1. The people of Israel lived in Egypt for ____ years before God sent Moses to bring them to the Promised Land.
2. The mark of the beast that John saw as recorded in the book of Revelation was ____
3. The good shepherd, Jesus said, would leave ____ sheep in the open field to search for the one sheep that was missing.
4. The age of Anna, the prophetess who blessed Jesus' parents in the temple was ____.
5. Noah was ____ years old when he climbed on board the ark.
6. Methuselah, the oldest man who ever lived, died at the age of ____.
7. John saw a vision that God would save ____ of his people.
8. Jesus said that Peter must forgive his brother, not seven times, but ____ times seven.
9. Israel wandered for ____ years total in the desert.
10. Gideon defeated the Midianite army with only ____ men.

40
70
84
99
300
430
600
666
969
144,000

INTERMEDIATE

1. Abimelech killed ____ of his half brothers.
2. All the sheets used to build the tabernacle were ____ cubits wide.
3. Each pillar from the temple Solomon built was ____ feet high.
4. Every ____ years Israel was to celebrate the Year of Jubilee.
5. It took ____ years for Herod to build the temple that stood in Jesus' day.
6. Josiah became king of Judah at age ____.
7. Noah had ____ sons.
8. Rehoboam had ____ sons.
9. The man Jesus healed at the pool of Bethesda had been a cripple for ____ years.
10. Zedekiah became king of Judah at age ____.

3
8
21
27
28
28
38
46
50
69

ADVANCED

1. Aaron was ____ years old when he traveled to Egypt with Moses.
2. Abraham lived ____ years before he died.
3. Abram was ____ years old when Hagar gave birth to Ishmael.
4. Doeg the Edomite killed ____ priests at Nob.
5. Jesus sent out ____ followers to preach about the kingdom of God.
6. Manasseh reigned in Judah for ____ years.
7. Nehemiah and the Israelites took ____ days to rebuild the wall.
8. Sarah lived to age ____ before she died.
9. The priest Eli was ____ years old when he died.
10. There are ____ "sevens" in Daniel's visions.

52
55
62
72
83
85
86
98
127
175

1. Abram took ____ men with him to rescue Lot.
2. Ezekiel lay on his side for ____ days as a symbol of God's message to Israel.
3. Ezra returned to Jerusalem with____ Israelites.
4. Haman offered to donate ____ pounds of silver to the king's treasury.
5. Israel had ____ men available for military duty after the people wandered in the desert for forty years.
6. Joshua defeated ____ kings west of the Jordan River.
7. ____ sheep were sacrificed for the dedication of Solomon's temple.
8. Revelation says that two witnesses will speak on God's behalf for ____ days before they are killed.
9. Each side of the temple area Ezekiel measured was ___ feet in length.
10. The Lord's angel killed ____ Assyrian soldiers when they threatened Jerusalem.

50,000
601,730
185,000
120,000
42,360
1,260
875
390
318
31

By the Numbers (Answers)

EASY

1. 430
2. 666
3. 99
4. 84
5. 600
6. 969
7. 144,000
8. 70
9. 40
10. 300

EXPERT

1. 318
2. 390
3. 42,360
4. 750,000
5. 601,730
6. 31
7. 120,000
8. 1,260
9. 875
10. 185,000

INTERMEDIATE

1. 69
2. 28
3. 27
4. 50
5. 46
6. 8
7. 3
8. 28
9. 38
10. 21

ADVANCED

1. 83
2. 175
3. 86
4. 85
5. 72
6. 55
7. 52
8. 127
9. 98
10. 62

Name That Book

(PART 2)

In which book of the Bible will you find . . . (Extra credit if you can name the chapter and verse, too!)

1. The lions whose mouths were shut by an angel
2. The light that blinded Saul
3. The king whom God made eat grass like a cow for seven years
4. Four Jewish captives who are given the Babylonian names Belteshazzar, Shadrach, Meshach, and Abednego
5. Joseph's interpretation of Pharaoh's dreams
6. The huge crowd of witnesses that surrounds us
7. The grapes the scouts brought back from Israel
8. The gold statue that King Nebuchadnezzar ordered the people to worship
9. God giving Satan permission to test one of his servants
10. Jesus giving the Beatitudes
11. The gallows that Haman built
12. Manna for God's people
13. Instructions for the choir director
14. A floating ax head
15. The flames or tongues of fire that appeared and settled on the believers

16. The fish that housed a prophet for three days and nights
17. The first rainbow
18. The first census of the Israelites
19. Peter's first recorded sermon
20. A father being asked to sacrifice his son
21. John exiled to the island of Patmos
22. Pharaoh's entire army drowned in Red Sea
23. The donkey that spoke to Balaam
24. Jesus described as the Word who in the beginning was with God and who was God
25. The definition of faith as the confident assurance that what we hope for is going to happen
26. Christ declared worthy of more glory than Moses
27. Mordecai's cousin who became the queen of Persia
28. Joseph considering breaking his engagement to Mary
29. Christ compared to Melchizedek
30. David committing adultery and murder
31. A command to kill all of Israel's baby boys
32. The clay jars and torches used in battle against the Midianites
33. The chariot of fire that Elijah rode in
34. Four captives who refuse to defile themselves by eating the food and wine of King Nebuchadnezzar
35. God calling himself the Alpha and the Omega
36. The bronze snake that Moses held up
37. The bow and arrows Jonathan used to warn David of Saul's rage
38. The blazing furnace that couldn't destroy Shadrach, Meshach, and Abednego
39. The belt of truth
40. God's armor for resisting the enemy

INTERMEDIATE

1. The Lion of Judah, who is worthy to open the scroll and break its seven seals
2. Joshua's commission to lead the Israelites into Canaan
3. The baby that leapt within his mother
4. A man who lived 969 years
5. Martha worrying while Mary sits at Jesus' feet

6. Samuel receiving a message from God for Eli
7. The first group of exiles to return to Jerusalem
8. Seventy-two disciples being sent out to proclaim the kingdom of God
9. The boxer that Paul compares himself to
10. The thorn in Paul's flesh
11. Jesus giving Simon Peter the charge to take care of his sheep
12. Moses being commanded to put the Ten Commandments into the ark
13. King Artaxerxes' cupbearer requesting permission to return to Judah and rebuild the city
14. A pillar of salt
15. Absalom raping Tamar
16. A prophet who sees a vision in which the train of the Lord's robe fills the temple
17. The storm that shipwrecked an apostle
18. The broom tree that Elijah sat under
19. The donkey's jawbone that was used to kill a thousand Philistines
20. The burning coal that was touched to the prophet's lips
21. The sycamore tree that Zacchaeus climbed to get a better view
22. The head covering that acted as a sign of authority
23. The roaring lion that Satan is compared to
24. The four angels that held back the four winds from blowing upon the earth
25. The twelve pearls that make up the twelve gates of Jerusalem
26. Solomon concluding that the duty of every person is to fear God and obey his commands
27. The angel of the Lord telling Zechariah that he will give birth to a son and name him John
28. Herod imprisoning John the Baptist
29. The illustration of the Good Samaritan
30. The altar with the inscription "To an Unknown God"
31. The river with the water of life that flows from the throne of God and of the Lamb
32. King Artaxerxes' command to stop rebuilding the temple
33. Twenty-four thrones with twenty-four elders seated on them

34. The ground opening up to swallow the families of Korah, Dathan, and Abiram
35. The lukewarm water used to describe the church at Laodicea
36. Hagar and Sarah being used to illustrate God's two covenants
37. Moses' hand turning white with leprosy
38. The twelve scouts who explored Israel
39. The righteous man who lost his family, possessions, and health because he was a man of integrity
40. The Ethiopian eunuch who desired baptism

ADVANCED

1. The pearl that Jesus compared to the kingdom of heaven
2. The pale green horse with the rider named Death
3. The palace that took Solomon thirteen years to build
4. The ox yoke worn by the prophet to tell Edom, Moab, Ammon, Tyre, and Sidon that they would be controlled by Babylon
5. The olive oil that anointed Saul as king
6. The olive oil that a widow sold to get out of debt
7. The oath and the honeycomb that almost resulted in Jonathan's death
8. The Nile turning to blood
9. The man of lawlessness who will precede Christ's second coming
10. The long robe with the gold sash worn by the Son of Man
11. The letter written to Gaius
12. Ezra leading the people in celebrating the Festival of Shelters
13. The large sheet with the animals, reptiles, and birds that left its viewer perplexed
14. A king who orders that a baby be cut in half
15. King Jehoiakim burning the scroll that Baruch had written on
16. The jar the prophet smashed as a demonstration of God's shattering the people of Judah
17. A jar of flour and jug of oil
18. Mephibosheth inheriting Saul's land

19. Judas hanging himself
20. A hairy baby twin
21. The golden calf that Aaron made
22. The first gatekeepers who were appointed for the temple
23. The first foreign language
24. The fig tree that Jesus saw Nathaniel sitting under
25. Gabriel explaining the vision of the two-horned ram and the goat
26. A dream with angels on a stairway
27. The dragon who waited to devour a baby boy at his birth
28. The door at which Christ stands and knocks
29. Paul describing himself and his preaching as timid, trembling, and plain
30. Pharaoh's daughter who adopts a Hebrew baby
31. King Cyrus who gave back the items taken from the Lord's temple
32. The concubine whose body was cut into twelve pieces
33. The coat, books, and papers that Paul wanted brought to him
34. The cistern that imprisoned a prophet
35. The chains that fell off Peter's wrists
36. The caves that hid God's prophets
37. The cart and calves that returned the ark of the Lord
38. The carriage whose interior was a gift of love from the young women of Jerusalem
39. Two believers who are mistaken for the Greek gods Zeus and Hermes
40. Elihu becoming angry with Eliphaz, Bildad, and Zophar

EXPERT

1. The man in linen clothing who marked the foreheads of those who wept and sighed because of the sins around them
2. The locusts that looked like horses armed for battle
3. Instructions for killing mildew
4. The pure spiritual milk we must crave
5. The first celebration of Purim
6. The fifteen pieces of silver, five bushels of barley, and measure of wine used to buy back the wayward wife of a prophet

7. The large letters of Paul's own handwriting
8. The bitter root of unbelief that can corrupt many
9. The story of Oholah and her sister Oholibah
10. A man hung on his own gallows
11. Aristarchus imprisoned with Paul
12. A wife who pays for her husband with mandrake roots
13. Midwives who disobey Pharaoh
14. Paul stating his plans to go to Spain
15. God forbidding his prophet to marry or have children because of the difficult times that lay ahead
16. God commanding a prophet to lie on his left side for 390 days, then on his right side for 40 days
17. God commanding a prophet to marry a prostitute
18. God forbidding his prophet to pray for the people of Judah
19. The woman who renamed herself "Mara"
20. The basket of ripe fruit that represented Israel's being ripe for punishment
21. John eating a scroll that makes his stomach sour
22. Onesimus and Tychicus being sent to encourage the believers and give them the latest news
23. The son of Shelomith stoned for blasphemy
24. The staff that sprouted, blossomed, and produced almonds
25. The hair that symbolized the coming judgment on Jerusalem
26. The tent peg that was hammered into Sisera's temple
27. The earthly tent that will be taken down
28. The cooking pot that symbolized Jerusalem
29. The perishable containers that contain a precious treasure of light and power
30. The coin in the mouth of a fish used to pay the temple tax
31. Cornelius's obedience to the command of an angel
32. Twelve stones from the Jordan River used in a memorial
33. The prophecy that the Christ would be put in a rich man's grave
34. God declaring that the men of Anathoth who plotted against the prophet would all die as their punishment
35. The oracle taught to King Lemuel by his mother
36. The sandal used to validate a legal transaction
37. The nets that tore because they were so full of fish

38. God's promise to treat Zerubbabel like a signet ring on his finger
39. The illustration of tree grafting
40. The staff that turned into a snake

Name That Book (Part 2, Answers)

EASY

1. Daniel (6:22)
2. Acts (9:3)
3. Daniel (4:32-33)
4. Daniel (1:7)
5. Genesis (41:25-36)
6. Hebrews (12:1, referring to Hebrews 11)
7. Numbers (13:23)
8. Daniel (3:1)
9. Job (1:12)
10. Matthew (5:1-12)
11. Esther (5:14)
12. Exodus (16)
13. Psalms
14. 2 Kings (6:1-6)
15. Acts (2:1-3)
16. Jonah (1:17)
17. Genesis (9:13)
18. Numbers (1:17-19)
19. Acts (2:14-40)
20. Genesis (22:2)
21. Revelation (1:9)
22. Exodus (14:28)
23. Numbers (22:28)
24. John (1:1)
25. Hebrews (11:1)
26. Hebrews (3:3)
27. Esther (2:17)
28. Matthew (1:19)
29. Hebrews (7:15-17)
30. 2 Samuel (11)
31. Exodus (1:16)
32. Judges (7:16-22)
33. 2 Kings (2:11)
34. Daniel (1:8)
35. Revelation (1:8)
36. Numbers (21:9)
37. 1 Samuel (20:35-40)
38. Daniel (3:19-27)
39. Ephesians (6:14)
40. Ephesians (6:13)

INTERMEDIATE

1. Revelation (5:5)
2. Deuteronomy (31:23)
3. Luke (1:41)
4. Genesis (5:27)
5. Luke (10:39-40)
6. 1 Samuel (3:11-14)
7. Ezra (3:8)
8. Luke (10:9)
9. 1 Corinthians (9:26)
10. 2 Corinthians (12:7)
11. John (21:15-18)
12. Exodus (25:16)
13. Nehemiah (2:5)
14. Genesis (19:26)
15. 2 Samuel (13:14)
16. Isaiah (6:1)
17. Acts (27:13)
18. 1 Kings (19:5)
19. Judges (15:15)
20. Isaiah (6:6)
21. Luke (19:4)
22. 1 Corinthians (11:10)
23. 1 Peter (5:8)
24. Revelation (7:1)
25. Revelation (21:21)
26. Ecclesiastes (12:13)
27. Luke (1:13)
28. Luke (3:20)
29. Luke (10:30-37)

30. Acts (17:23)
31. Revelation (22:1)
32. Ezra (4:21)
33. Revelation (4:4)
34. Numbers (16:32)
35. Revelation (3:16)
36. Galatians (4:24)
37. Exodus (4:6)
38. Numbers (13:3)
39. Job (1–2)
40. Acts (8:27)

ADVANCED

1. Matthew (13:46)
2. Revelation (6:8)
3. 1 Kings (7:1)
4. Jeremiah (27:2-8)
5. 1 Samuel (10:1)
6. 2 Kings (4:1-7)
7. 1 Samuel (14:24-27, 38-46)
8. Exodus (7:20)
9. 2 Thessalonians (2:3)
10. Revelation (1:13)
11. 3 John
12. Nehemiah (8:13-18)
13. Acts (10:11-17)
14. 1 Kings (3:16-28)
15. Jeremiah (36:23)
16. Jeremiah (19:11)
17. 1 Kings (17:13-16)
18. 2 Samuel (9:7)
19. Matthew (27:5)
20. Genesis (25:25)
21. Exodus (32:4)
22. 1 Chronicles (26)
23. Genesis (11:1-9)
24. John (1:48)
25. Daniel (8:15-26)
26. Genesis (28:12)
27. Revelation (12:3-4)
28. Revelation (3:20)
29. 1 Corinthians (2:3-4)
30. Exodus (2:10)
31. Ezra (1:7)
32. Judges (19:29)
33. 2 Timothy (4:13)
34. Jeremiah (38:6)
35. Acts (12:7)

36. 1 Kings (18:13)
37. 1 Samuel (6:10-12)
38. Song of Songs (3:9-10)
39. Acts (14:11-12)
40. Job (32)

EXPERT

1. Ezekiel (9:3-4)
2. Revelation (9:7)
3. Leviticus (14:34-53)
4. 1 Peter (2:2)
5. Esther (9:20-23)
6. Hosea (3:1-2)
7. Galatians (6:11)
8. Hebrews (12:15)
9. Ezekiel (23)
10. Esther (7:9-10)
11. Colossians (4:10)
12. Genesis (30:16)
13. Exodus (1:17)
14. Romans (15:24)
15. Jeremiah (16:2-4)
16. Ezekiel (4:4-6)
17. Hosea (1:2)
18. Jeremiah (14:11)
19. Ruth (1:20)
20. Amos (8:1-2)
21. Revelation (10:10)
22. Colossians (4:7-9)
23. Leviticus (24:10-23)
24. Numbers (17:8)
25. Ezekiel (5:1-4)
26. Judges (4:21)
27. 2 Corinthians (5:1)
28. Ezekiel (24:3-8)
29. 2 Corinthians (4:7)
30. Matthew (17:27)
31. Acts (10:1-8)
32. Joshua (4:8)
33. Isaiah (53:9)
34. Jeremiah (11:21-23)
35. Proverbs (31:1)
36. Ruth (4:7)
37. Luke (5:6)
38. Haggai (2:23)
39. Romans (11:17)
40. Exodus (4:3)

Timelines

Place the statements below in their correct chronological order (earliest event or person first).

1. _____
   a. Jesus cleared the temple.
   b. Jesus tempted in the wilderness
   c. Sermon on the Mount
   d. Jesus baptized by John
   e. Jesus cleared the temple—second time.

2. _____
   a. Jesus rode into Jerusalem on a donkey.
   b. Jesus was baptized.
   c. Jesus turned water into wine.
   d. Jesus was crucified.
   e. Jesus rose from the dead.

3. _____
   a. Peter denies Christ when a servant girl tells him, "You were with Jesus."
   b. Jesus predicts Peter will deny him three times.
   c. Peter weeps bitterly.
   d. Peter denies it when a servant girl tells others, "He is one of them."

e. Peter swears he doesn't know Jesus when others say, "You must be one of them" and "You're a Galilean!"

4. _____

a. Paul and Silas
b. David and Jonathan
c. Jesus and Lazarus
d. Paul and Barnabas
e. Moses and Joshua

5. _____

a. A widow's grown son was raised from the dead.
b. Eutychus was raised from the dead.
c. Jesus rose from the dead.
d. Samuel came back from the dead.
e. Elijah escaped death.

6. _____

a. Sword of the Spirit
b. Breastplate of righteousness
c. Belt of truth
d. Shield of faith
e. Helmet of salvation

7. _____

a. Sermon on the Mount
b. Sermon on Pentecost
c. Sermon on Mars Hill
d. Moses' third sermon
e. "The Preacher" of Ecclesiastes shared his thoughts on life.

8. _____

a. God created the world.
b. God created Adam and Eve.
c. God made clothes for Adam and Eve.
d. Adam ate from the tree of knowledge of good and evil.
e. Eve ate from the tree of knowledge of good and evil.

9. _____

a. Joseph was sent to check on his brothers.
b. Joseph was sold into slavery by his brothers.
c. Joseph dreamed his brothers would bow down to him.

d. Joseph's brothers plotted to kill him.

e. Joseph's brothers bowed down to him "with their faces to the ground."

10. _____

a. Joseph ruled Egypt.

b. Jochobed was hired to nurse Moses.

c. Jacob dreamed of a ladder to heaven.

d. Joshua conquered Jericho.

e. Joseph married Mary.

11. _____

a. Eve

b. Abel

c. Seth

d. Cain

e. Adam

12. _____

a. You shall not take the Lord's name in vain.

b. Honor your father and mother.

c. Remember the Sabbath day and keep it holy.

d. You shall not make yourself any idols.

e. You shall have no other gods before me.

13. _____

a. You shall not murder.

b. You shall not give false testimony.

c. You shall not commit adultery.

d. You shall not covet.

e. You shall not steal.

14. _____

a. Plague of frogs on Egypt

b. All the water in Egypt turned to blood

c. Egyptian dust turned into gnats

d. Plague of flies

e. Egyptian livestock struck down

15. _____

a. Hailstorm kills Egyptian livestock and slaves

b. Egypt cloaked in darkness

c. Plague of boils

d. All firstborn Egyptian people and animals die

e. Plague of locusts

16. _____

a. Lot showed two angels hospitality.

b. Lot's family was hurried out of Sodom.

c. Lot's daughters got him drunk in order to have children by him.

d. Abraham interceded on Lot's behalf when the Lord planned to destroy Sodom.

e. Lot's wife died.

17. _____

a. John the Baptist prophesied Jesus' coming.

b. God promised Adam and Eve he would send a Redeemer.

c. Isaiah prophesied how the Messiah would die.

d. Isaiah prophesied the Messiah would be born to a virgin.

e. Jesus began his ministry.

18. _____

a. Jacob stole Esau's blessing.

b. Esau sold his birthright.

c. Jacob was deceived by Laban.

d. Rachel deceived her father.

e. Jacob promised to follow Esau but went a different way.

19. _____

a. Rahab tied a scarlet cord in her window.

b. Rahab married Salmon.

c. Rahab hid the Israelite spies.

d. Rahab became a prostitute.

e. Rahab and her family were rescued.

20. _____

a. Hannah asked God for a son.

b. Hannah left Samuel at the temple.

c. Hannah weaned Samuel.

d. Hannah gave birth to Samuel.

e. Hannah gave birth to three sons and two daughters.

21. _____

a. Jacob deceived his father-in-law.

b. Jacob's wife Rachel lied to her father.

c. Jacob's sons deceived Shechem and his father, Hamor.

d. Jacob's sons lied to their father about Joseph's fate.

e. Jacob lied to his father.

22. _____

a. Jesus sat on a mountain, and his disciples came to hear him teach.

b. Jesus prayed while his friends slept on the Mount of Olives.

c. Aaron died on Mount Hor.

d. Abraham was tested on Mount Moriah.

e. Moses met with God on Mount Sinai.

23. _____

a. God led the Israelites with a pillar of fire by night, to give light in the darkness.

b. The Israelites had light as usual, although the rest of Egypt was cloaked in thick darkness.

c. God called the light "Day."

d. God said, "Let there be light," and there was light.

e. Moses' face shone with a bright light.

24. _____

a. David hurled a stone from his sling and hit Goliath.

b. John declared God could change stones into children of Abraham.

c. The shepherd boy put five smooth stones in his shepherd's bag.

d. Joshua built a memorial of stones in the river Jordan.

e. Satan tempted the Lord to change stones into bread.

25. _____

a. God made the stars, sun, and moon.

b. God made light.

c. God made the sky.

d. God made the birds.

e. God made the fish.

26. _____

a. God gave David instructions for building the temple.

b. God gave instructions for building the tabernacle.

    c. The first temple was destroyed.

    d. Zerubbabel rebuilt the Lord's temple.

    e. The Pharisees stated that their temple had taken forty-six years to build.

27. _____

    a. Jesus confronted Saul, and Saul became blind.

    b. Saul muttered threats against the Lord's followers.

    c. Saul went to Damascus to arrest every follower of Jesus he could find.

    d. Saul guarded the coats of those who stoned Stephen.

    e. Ananias prayed for Saul, and Saul was healed and filled with the Spirit.

28. _____

    a. John sees visions on Patmos.

    b. John the Baptist baptizes in the wilderness.

    c. John leans on Jesus' bosom.

    d. John cares for Jesus' mother.

    e. John the Baptist is beheaded.

29. _____

    a. Man and woman ate forbidden fruit.

    b. People killed God's messengers.

    c. People learned all kinds of sexual immorality.

    d. People built an idolatrous tower.

    e. People learned to kill each other.

30. _____

    a. Sarah trusted that she would conceive.

    b. Abraham offered his heir on a sacrificial altar.

    c. Noah spent more than eighty years building a dry-docked boat.

    d. Moses refused to be called the son of Pharaoh's daughter.

    e. Abraham followed God without knowing where he was going.

INTERMEDIATE

1. _____

    a. Elisha prophesied in Israel.

    b. Ahab became king of Israel.

c. Elijah prophesied in Israel.

d. Joash became king of Israel.

e. Ahijah prophesied against King Jeroboam of Israel.

2. _____

a. Job was stricken with horrible boils.

b. Job's livestock were captured and his servants were killed.

c. Job's children were killed.

d. God gave Job twice as much as he had had before.

e. Job said, "The Lord giveth and the Lord taketh away. Blessed be the name of the Lord."

3. _____

a. Job's three friends told him, "You must be suffering because of some sin you have committed."

b. Job's wife said, "Curse God and die!"

c. Young Elihu accused Job of not listening to God.

d. Job defended himself and asked God to explain himself.

e. God asked Job, "Who do you think you are?" and Job decided God knew what he was doing.

4. _____

a. Ananias of Damascus prayed for a new convert.

b. Aquila of Pontus taught a young preacher.

c. Artaxerxes of Persia reigned.

d. Ahasuerus of Persia reigned.

e. Ahijah of Shiloh prophesied.

5. _____

a. Miriam

b. Mary

c. Matthew

d. Mephibosheth

e. Manoah

6. _____

a. Samson

b. Samuel

c. Sarah

d. Saul, king of Israel

e. Silas

7. _____

   a. David and Michal
   b. Samson and the Philistine girl from Timnah
   c. Jacob and Leah
   d. Abraham and Sarah
   e. Esau and Adah

8. _____

   a. God brought water from the rock at Kadesh.
   b. God opened the spring En Hakkore at Lehi.
   c. God brought water from the rock at Horeb.
   d. God parted the Red Sea.
   e. God stopped the Jordan River so it piled up in a heap.

9. _____

   a. Jesus healed a man who had been unable to speak.
   b. Isaiah prophesied that the mute will speak.
   c. Job said, "I put my hand over my mouth."
   d. Jesus remained silent when mocked.
   e. The prophets of Baal pleaded with him to answer them,
      but there was only silence.

10. _____

   a. Sarai became Sarah.
   b. Abram became Abraham.
   c. Jacob became Israel.
   d. Saul became Paul.
   e. Simon became Peter.

11. _____

   a. God created the earth.
   b. God created the sun.
   c. God created dry land.
   d. God created fish and birds.
   e. God created man.

12. _____

   a. Hannah left Samuel at the temple.
   b. Mary and Joseph left Jesus behind in Jerusalem.
   c. Jesus said to leave your gift at the altar and go be
      reconciled to your brother.

d. Adam and Eve had to leave the Garden of Eden.

e. Moses' mother left him in the Nile.

13. _____

a. Jochobed gave birth to a son.

b. Pharaoh's daughter named the baby Moses.

c. Jochobed placed her son in a basket.

d. Jochobed hid her son three months.

e. Miriam guarded the baby.

14. _____

a. Samson killed Philistines.

b. David killed Goliath.

c. The angel of death killed Pharaoh's son.

d. Nabal died.

e. King Belshazzar was put to death.

15. _____

a. Jesus questioned by Caiaphas.

b. Jesus questioned by Pilate.

c. Jesus questioned by Herod.

d. Jesus condemned by Pilate.

e. Jesus condemned by religious council.

16. _____

a. God promised Abraham a son.

b. Sarah gave birth to Isaac.

c. God told Abraham to sacrifice his only son, Isaac.

d. Hagar gave birth to Ishmael.

e. Abraham sent Hagar and Ishmael away.

17. _____

a. God asked two times, "What are you doing here, Elijah?"

b. Jesus asked three times, "Simon, do you love me?"

c. God called the boy Samuel three times, "Samuel! Samuel!"

d. God called Adam once, "Where are you?"

e. Peter denied Jesus three times.

18. _____

a. God promised to preserve seven thousand in Israel who had never kissed Baal.

b. Orpah kissed her mother-in-law good-bye.

c. Jacob kissed Rachel.

d. Jacob kissed his father, Isaac.

e. Joseph kissed his brothers and wept.

19. _____

a. Peter visited Cornelius and shared the good news of salvation through Jesus.

b. God told Peter, "If God says something is acceptable, don't say it isn't."

c. An angel instructed Cornelius to send for Peter.

d. Peter went up to the housetop to pray.

e. Peter went with the Gentile men, as he had been directed to do.

20. _____

a. Jewish believers criticized Peter for going into a Gentile home and eating there.

b. Peter reported the vision he had had and the Gentiles' response to his message.

c. Cornelius, his relatives, and his friends believed Peter's message and were baptized with the Holy Spirit.

d. Peter gave orders for Cornelius and the others to be baptized with water.

e. Cornelius began to worship Peter, who said, "Stand up! I'm a human being like you!"

21. _____

a. Barnabas was sent to Antioch to investigate rumors of Gentiles becoming followers of Jesus.

b. Barnabas went to Tarsus to find Saul.

c. Barnabas brought a sizable contribution and laid it at the apostles' feet.

d. Barnabas introduced Paul to the apostles.

e. Barnabas sailed for Cyprus with John Mark.

22. _____

a. People worshiped at Mount Sinai.

b. People worshiped in the tent of meeting.

c. People worshiped at private family altars.

d. People worshiped in the temple at Jerusalem.

e. People worshiped in spirit and in truth everywhere.

23. _____

    a. Barnabas took John Mark to Cyprus.

    b. Paul and Barnabas took John Mark to Perga.

    c. John Mark's companionship was a source of dispute for Paul and Barnabas.

    d. John Mark became a useful helper to Paul.

    e. John Mark turned back to Jerusalem at Perga.

24. _____

    a. Jesus selected Judas, called Thaddaeus, to be his disciple.

    b. The council at Jerusalem selected Judas Barsabbas to be their delegate.

    c. Judas of Damascus housed Saul when he was blind.

    d. Jesus had a brother named Judas.

    e. Jesus was betrayed by Judas, called Iscariot.

25. _____

    a. Paul and Silas were beaten and jailed.

    b. A great earthquake shook the prison, opened the doors, and loosed every prisoner's chains.

    c. Paul and Silas were put in the inner dungeon, and their feet were locked in the stocks.

    d. Paul and Silas prayed and sang hymns to God.

    e. Paul stopped the jailer from killing himself.

26. _____

    a. David spared Saul's life as he slept.

    b. Saul tried to kill David with a spear.

    c. Saul sent men to kill David at home.

    d. David spared Saul's life in a cave.

    e. Saul asked David to swear he wouldn't wipe out Saul's descendants.

27. _____

    a. Daniel and his three friends requested a vegetarian diet.

    b. Daniel's friends were thrown into the fiery furnace.

    c. Daniel was thrown into the lions' den.

    d. Daniel interpreted the handwriting on the wall.

    e. Daniel interpreted Nebuchadnezzar's dream.

28. _____
   a. Joshua led the people.
   b. Zerubbabel led the people.
   c. Gideon led the people.
   d. David led the people.
   e. Moses led the people.

29. _____
   a. Rahab forsook her people and was thus spared from death.
   b. Ruth left her homeland and thus became an ancestor to the Messiah.
   c. Deborah led God's army into battle.
   d. Rebekah left her home to marry a husband she had not met.
   e. Abigail interceded for her husband's foolishness, sparing herself and her whole family from death.

30. _____
   a. Manasseh and Ephraim
   b. Jacob and Esau
   c. Perez and Zerah
   d. Ishmael and Isaac
   e. Moses and Aaron

ADVANCED

1. _____
   a. James, the brother of John, was martyred by King Herod Agrippa.
   b. An angel of the Lord struck down Herod Agrippa for allowing people to worship him.
   c. Herod Agrippa had Peter imprisoned, planning to kill him after the Passover.
   d. Herod Agrippa searched for Peter, but could not find him.
   e. Herod Agrippa executed sixteen guards.

2. _____
   a. Jesus was betrayed by Judas.
   b. Delilah betrayed Samson to the Philistines.
   c. Joram was betrayed by Jehu.

d. David was betrayed by Absalom.

e. Jehozabad and Jozabad betrayed and assassinated King Joash.

3. _____

a. Cyrus became king of Persia and allowed the Jewish exiles to return home.

b. Esther became queen of Persia.

c. Zerubbabel rebuilt the temple.

d. Ezra encouraged the people.

e. Nehemiah rebuilt the walls of Jerusalem.

4. _____

a. Stephen preached to the Sanhedrin.

b. The apostles preached in the temple courts after an angel had freed them from jail.

c. Peter preached to the Sanhedrin—the same men who had condemned Jesus.

d. Peter preached at Cornelius's house.

e. Peter preached on the Day of Pentecost.

5. _____

a. A Roman official's wife counseled him to have nothing to do with Jesus.

b. A woman tentmaker instructed Apollos.

c. A businesswoman from Thyatira took care of Paul and Silas.

d. A prophetess led the nation of Israel.

e. A queen interceded on behalf of her nation.

6. _____

a. Ehud escaped after assassinating King Eglah.

b. Spies escaped out a window on a rope.

c. Saul escaped over the wall in a basket.

d. Samson escaped from the city by ripping gates off their hinges.

e. David escaped through a window.

7. _____

a. Miriam became leprous, then was healed.

b. Moses' hand became leprous, then was healed.

    c. Naaman was healed of his leprosy after bathing in the Jordan.

    d. Jesus healed a man of his leprosy.

    e. Jesus healed ten men of their leprosy.

8. _____

    a. Samson and Delilah

    b. Judah and Tamar

    c. David and Bathsheba

    d. Abram and Hagar

    e. Jacob and Zilpah

9. _____

    a. Abraham told the king of Gerar that Sarah was his sister.

    b. Isaac told the king of Gerar that Rebekah was his sister.

    c. Pharaoh took Abraham's wife to be his own wife.

    d. God told Abimelech that Sarah was Abraham's wife.

    e. Abimelech caught Isaac caressing Rebekah.

10. _____

    a. The Shunammite's son was brought back to life.

    b. Lazarus was raised from the dead.

    c. Jairus's daughter was raised from the dead.

    d. A man came back to life after being thrown into Elisha's tomb.

    e. The earth shook, tombs opened, and many holy people who had died came back to life.

11. _____

    a. Joseph ruled Egypt.

    b. Mary and Joseph escaped to Egypt.

    c. Jeremiah was taken to Egypt.

    d. Abraham visited Egypt.

    e. Moses predicted plagues on Egypt.

12. _____

    a. Paul visited Rome.

    b. Paul visited Cyprus.

    c. Paul visited Thessalonica.

    d. Paul visited Corinth.

    e. Paul visited Ephesus.

13. _____

    a. The prophet from Tishbe prophesied a three-year drought.

    b. God sent a prophet to live in a ravine.

    c. God ordered ravens to bring a prophet bread and meat.

    d. The prophet from Tishbe met a widow gathering sticks.

    e. God commanded a woman from Zarephath to supply a prophet with food.

14. _____

    a. Elijah raised a widow's son from the dead.

    b. Elijah repaired the altar of the Lord.

    c. God spoke to Elijah in a gentle whisper.

    d. Elijah promised Obadiah to present himself before the king that day.

    e. Elijah threw his cloak across Elisha's shoulders.

15. _____

    a. Lamech killed a man for wounding him.

    b. Cain killed his brother.

    c. Abner killed Asahel.

    d. Joab killed Abner.

    e. Herod had John the Baptist killed.

16. _____

    a. Paul cast a demon out of a slave girl and was imprisoned for it.

    b. A servant girl accused Peter to other people.

    c. A servant girl accused Peter to his face.

    d. A servant girl told the apostles that Peter was at the door.

    e. A servant girl told a man with leprosy that an Israelite prophet could heal him.

17. _____

    a. A famine in the land sent the father of many nations to Egypt.

    b. A famine sent a family from Bethlehem to Moab.

    c. God gave the king a choice between three years of famine, three months of war, or three days of plague.

    d. A famine in the land sent ten brothers to Egypt.

e. A famine in Samaria resulted in a donkey's head selling for two pounds of silver.

18. _____

a. Pharaoh ordered the midwives to kill all the Hebrew male babies.
b. The midwife tied a scarlet thread around the wrist of the child.
c. The midwife exclaimed, "Don't be afraid—you have another son!"
d. The midwives feared God and allowed the boys to live.
e. God blessed the midwives and gave them families of their own.

19. _____

a. Jesus told the Pharisees that if the people were quiet the stones would cry out.
b. Jesus turned the water in six stone waterpots into wine.
c. Jesus told his friends to roll the stone aside.
d. Jesus said, "Let those who have never sinned throw the first stone."
e. An angel rolled away a sealed tombstone.

20. _____

a. Nicodemus came to Jesus secretly by night.
b. Two of John's disciples became Jesus' disciples.
c. Jesus' disciples forsook him and fled.
d. Nicodemus became known as a follower of Jesus.
e. Jesus healed a man who was born blind, who later was accused of being Jesus' disciple.

21. _____

a. Paul exhorted believers in Asia to be filled with the Spirit.
b. Disciples were filled with the Spirit in Ephesus.
c. Gentiles were filled with the Spirit in Caesarea.
d. Disciples were filled with the Spirit in Samaria.
e. One hundred twenty were filled with the Spirit in Jerusalem.

22. _____

a. The first Feast of Ingathering
b. The first Passover feast
c. The first love-feast

d. The first Feast of Purim

e. The first Feast of Dedication

23. _____

a. Jeroboam II was king of Israel.

b. Jeroboam I was king of Israel.

c. Jehoash was king of Israel.

d. Jehu was king of Israel.

e. Joram was king of Israel.

24. _____

a. Elkanah

b. Ephraim

c. Eleazar

d. Ezra

e. Ezekiel

25. _____

a. The two daughters-in-law of Naomi

b. The three sons of Zeruiah

c. The twelve sons of Israel

d. The two "sons of Thunder"

e. The five daughters of Zelophehad

26. _____

a. Two bears came out of the woods and killed some young men who mocked the bald-headed prophet.

b. God sent a great fish to swallow Jonah for three days.

c. Peter looked for tax money in a fish's mouth and found it.

d. Balaam's donkey spoke.

e. A lion killed a disobedient prophet, then stood still beside him and his donkey.

27. _____

a. Lot left Haran with Abram.

b. Lot was taken captive, then rescued by Abram.

c. Lot moved to the plain of Jordan.

d. Lot became a city official in Sodom.

e. Lot moved into the city of Sodom.

28. _____

a. Elijah taken to heaven in a whirlwind.

b. The Shunammite couple build Elisha a room.

c. Elisha curses some boys who called him a "baldhead."

d. Elisha plowed with twelve yoke of oxen.

e. Naaman is healed of leprosy by Elisha.

29. _____

a. Xerxes and Vashti

b. Ahab and Jezebel

c. Saul and Ahinoam

d. David and Bathsheba

e. Solomon and the Shulamite

30. _____

a. Jacob anointed a stone and named the place "Bethel."

b. Jacob and Laban shared a meal beside a pile of stones.

c. Jacob used a stone for a pillow.

d. Joshua ordered twelve stones gathered from the middle of the Jordan.

e. Joshua trapped five kings in a cave by piling stones in the entranceway.

EXPERT

1. _____

a. Tattenai wrote a letter to King Darius protesting the rebuilding of the temple.

b. King Darius wrote a letter to Tattenai saying, "You are to help rebuild the temple."

c. Zerubbabel led a group of exiles back to Israel.

d. Ezra led a group of exiles back to Israel.

e. King Artaxerxes wrote a letter to Ezra.

2. _____

a. Zebedee

b. Zeruiah

c. Zechariah

d. Zadak

e. Zacchaeus

3. _____

a. Eutychus fell asleep during a sermon.

b. Paul told the Ephesian elders he would never see them again.

c. Paul raised Eutychus from the dead.

d. Paul went to Jerusalem, where the elders tried to protect him.

e. A prophet told Paul he would be imprisoned in Jerusalem.

4. _____

a. Jesus said, "I am the Bread of Life."

b. Jesus broke bread and said, "This is my body."

c. The man of God was invited to come eat bread by a lying prophet.

d. The first Feast of Unleavened Bread was held.

e. A medium constrained the king to eat bread.

5. _____

a. A contest was held at Mount Carmel.

b. An angel fed a prophet of God.

c. God spoke in a still, small voice.

d. A prophet of God traveled for forty days without food.

e. God's prophet made an ax head float.

6. _____

a. God sent quail to feed the Israelite camp.

b. God had a raven deliver food to his prophet.

c. God multiplied oil and flour to feed a family and his prophet.

d. God multiplied five loaves and two fishes to feed a multitude.

e. God sent white honey-flavored bread flakes to feed his people.

7. _____

a. Jehoram was king of Judah.

b. Asa was king of Judah.

c. Jehoshaphat was king of Judah.

d. Joash was king of Judah.

e. Athaliah was queen of Judah.

8. _____

a. God sent the worst hailstorm in Egypt's history.

b. The angel blew his trumpet, and fire, hail, and blood were thrown down.

c. Seventy-five-pound hailstones fell upon the earth.

d. People cursed God because of the hailstorm.

e. In heaven, the temple of God was opened, the ark could be seen, and there was a great hailstorm.

9. _____

   a. Jeremiah called Baruch to record the prophecies of the Lord.

   b. Jeremiah sent Baruch to read a scroll of prophecies in the temple.

   c. God commanded the Judeans to free their Hebrew slaves.

   d. King Jehoiakim burned Jeremiah's scroll.

   e. Jeremiah rewrote the Lord's scroll.

10. _____

   a. Ebed-melech gave Jeremiah some rags and old clothes.

   b. Jeremiah was imprisoned in a muddy cistern.

   c. The captain of the guard gave Jeremiah some food and money and let him go.

   d. Babylon besieged Jerusalem, and Jerusalem fell.

   e. Jeremiah was taken to Egypt.

11. _____

   a. Ezekiel saw a vision of the end times.

   b. Ezekiel was told that people will throw money away like trash.

   c. Ezekiel was lifted up by the hair of his head and shown a vision of Jerusalem.

   d. Ezekiel prophesied the coming Exile.

   e. Ezekiel saw the glory of the Lord leave the temple.

12. _____

   a. Ezekiel saw a vision of a new temple.

   b. Ezekiel received word that Jerusalem had fallen.

   c. Ezekiel saw a vision of the River of Healing, which brought new life to the Dead Sea.

   d. Ezekiel saw the glory of the Lord return.

   e. The Lord told Ezekiel that the Lord would be the Good Shepherd.

13. _____

    a. Barnabas and Paul took John Mark to Antioch.

    b. Paul and Barnabas parted company.

    c. Paul and Barnabas were dedicated for the Lord's "special work."

    d. The governor of Paphos believed Paul and Barnabas's message.

    e. Paul and Barnabas sailed to Cyprus.

14. _____

    a. Paul preached in Iconium and fled for his life.

    b. Paul preached in Lystra, and God healed a man crippled from birth.

    c. Paul was stoned and left for dead by the people of Lystra.

    d. The people of Lystra decided Paul was Zeus and tried to hold a festival in his honor.

    e. Paul preached to and was rejected by the Jews in Antioch of Pisidia, so he began focusing on preaching to the Gentiles.

15. _____

    a. Paul and Barnabas preached in Derbe and made many disciples there.

    b. Paul and Barnabas returned to Lystra, Iconium, and Antioch of Pisidia, strengthening the disciples and appointing elders.

    c. Paul and Barnabas returned to Antioch of Syria.

    d. Paul and Barnabas reported to the church what the Lord had done.

    e. Paul and Barnabas went to Attalia.

16. _____

    a. Paul and Barnabas were sent to Jerusalem to get the apostles' counsel.

    b. Men came to Antioch of Syria and taught that circumcision was necessary for salvation.

    c. Paul and Barnabas visited the believers in Phoenicia and Samaria, where they were told that the Gentiles were following Jesus, too.

d. Peter and Paul declared that God accepts Gentiles without the Jewish law.

e. Former Pharisees declared that all believers must be circumcised and keep the law of Moses.

17. _____

a. Joel predicted judgment on the nations.

b. A severe locust plague devastated Judah.

c. Joel called the people to repentance.

d. Joel predicted the outpouring of God's Spirit.

e. Joel promised relief from the plague.

18. _____

a. Assyria laid siege to Jerusalem.

b. Egypt pursued Israel fleeing from bondage.

c. Philistines warred against Israel.

d. The king of Moab sought to destroy Israel through a curse.

e. Babylonians took residents of Judah and Jerusalem to Babylon.

19. _____

a. Rule by fathers of clans

b. Rule by a single national leader

c. Rule by magistrates and priests

d. Rule by governors and priests

e. Rule by kings and priests

20. _____

a. Isaiah told of God's Servant who would come.

b. Malachi warned the people of the judgment coming in the Day of the Lord.

c. Jeremiah remembered the Lord's great faithfulness.

d. Haggai exhorted the people to continue building the temple.

e. Joel preached repentance and warned of a locust plague.

21. _____

a. The people rebelled against Rehoboam.

b. Ahab corrupted Israel with Baal worship.

    c. Jehu killed Jezebel and established that "might makes right."

    d. Several kings gained the throne through conspiracy and assassination.

    e. Jeroboam I corrupted Israel with calf worship.

22. _____

    a. Vision of four creatures, each with four faces and four wings

    b. Vision of dry bones brought to life

    c. Vision of Joshua being opposed by Satan before the Angel of the Lord

    d. Vision of four creatures, each with a different face and six wings

    e. Vision of victorious ones standing on a sea of glass and fire, singing

23. _____

    a. Vision of a man measuring Jerusalem

    b. Vision of the affliction of God's Servant

    c. Vision of a dragon seeking to devour a child

    d. Vision of a beast speaking great and blasphemous things

    e. Vision of a little horn speaking pompous things

24. _____

    a. Paul was beaten at Philippi.

    b. Paul was pursued by Jews from city to city.

    c. Paul was imprisoned in Caesarea.

    d. Paul was stoned in Lystra.

    e. Paul was shunned by the church in Damascus.

25. _____

    a. Paul was mocked in Athens.

    b. Paul was blinded by a vision.

    c. Paul escaped a murderous plot in Judea.

    d. Paul escaped death by hiding in a basket.

    e. Paul was arrested in the temple.

26. _____

    a. Paul stopped an idolatrous gathering at Lystra.

    b. Paul refused to leave Philippi without an apology from the magistrates.

c. Paul stated his case to Felix, Festus, and King Agrippa.

d. While in Corinth, Paul was taken to court, interrupted before he could defend himself by Gallio the proconsul, and the case was thrown out of court.

e. Paul paid for the purification rites of four Jewish men in order to prove his loyalty to the nation.

27. _____

a. The council at Jerusalem decided that all believers should abstain from sexual immorality and eating certain things, but that circumcision was unnecessary.

b. The church at Antioch rejoiced when they heard the council's decision.

c. Judas Barsabbas and Silas preached in Antioch, then returned to Jerusalem.

d. The council at Jerusalem sent delegates to Antioch to carry a letter reporting their decision.

e. Paul and Barnabas argued with Jews in Antioch regarding the question of circumcision.

28. _____

a. Paul and Silas traveled to Derbe and Lystra, where they met Timothy.

b. Paul and Barnabas disagreed over John Mark's presence on their second missionary journey.

c. Paul had a vision of a man in Macedonia begging him to "come help us."

d. Paul cast a demon out of a slave girl and was thrown in prison, where the jailer was saved.

e. Paul, Silas, and Timothy traveled to Philippi, where Lydia believed the gospel.

29. _____

a. After being rejected in the Corinthian synagogue, Paul preached to the Gentiles.

b. In Corinth, God told Paul not to fear but to preach.

c. Some Jews took Paul to court, but Governor Gallio threw them out.

d. Crispus, the synagogue leader, and his household believed in the Lord.

e. Paul, Priscilla, and Aquila traveled together.

30. _____

    a. Paul went to Ephesus, where twelve men were baptized in the Holy Spirit.

    b. Men who were not believers tried to cast out a demon in the name of "Jesus, whom Paul preaches," and the demon attacked them.

    c. An Ephesian idol maker started a riot, but the mayor calmed everyone down.

    d. Many Ephesians became believers and burned their books of witchcraft.

    e. Priscilla and Aquila taught Apollos.

Timelines (Answers)

EASY

1. d, b, a, c, e
2. b, c, a, d, e
3. b, a, d, e, c
4. e, b, c, d, a
5. d, e, a, c, b
6. c, b, d, e, a
7. d, e, a, b, c
8. a, b, e, d, c
9. c, a, d, b, e
10. c, a, b, d, e
11. e, a, d, b, c
12. e, d, a, c, b
13. a, c, e, b, d
14. b, a, c, d, e
15. c, a, e, b, d
16. d, a, b, e, c
17. b, d, c, a, e
18. b, a, c, d, e
19. d, c, a, e, b
20. a, d, c, b, e
21. e, a, b, c, d
22. d, e, c, a, b
23. d, c, b, a, e
24. d, c, a, b, e
25. b, c, a, e, d
26. b, a, c, d, e
27. d, b, c, a, e
28. b, e, c, d, a
29. a, e, d, c, b
30. c, e, a, b, d

INTERMEDIATE

1. e, c, b, a, d
2. b, c, e, a, d
3. b, a, d, c, e
4. e, d, c, a, b
5. a, e, d, b, c
6. c, a, b, d, e
7. d, e, c, b, a
8. d, c, a, e, b
9. c, e, b, a, d
10. b, a, c, e, d
11. a, c, b, d, e
12. d, e, a, b, c
13. a, d, c, e, b
14. c, a, b, d, e
15. a, e, b, c, d
16. a, d, b, e, c
17. d, c, a, e, b
18. d, c, e, b, a
19. c, d, b, e, a
20. e, c, d, a, b
21. c, a, b, d, e
22. c, a, b, d, e
23. b, e, c, a, d
24. d, a, e, c, b
25. a, c, d, b, e
26. b, c, d, e, a
27. a, e, b, d, c
28. e, a, c, d, b
29. d, a, c, b, e
30. d, b, c, a, e

ADVANCED

1. a, c, d, e, b
2. b, d, c, e, a
3. a, c, b, d, e
4. e, c, b, a, d
5. d, e, a, c, b
6. b, a, d, e, c
7. b, c, a, e, d

8. d, e, b, a, c
9. c, a, d, b, e
10. a, d, c, b, e
11. d, a, e, c, b
12. b, c, d, e, a
13. a, c, b, d, e
14. a, d, b, c, e
15. b, a, c, d, e
16. e, c, b, d, a
17. a, d, b, c, e
18. c, b, a, d, e
19. b, d, c, a, e
20. b, a, e, c, d
21. e, d, c, b, a
22. b, a, d, e, c
23. b, e, d, c, a
24. b, c, a, e, d
25. c, e, a, b, d
26. d, e, a, b, c
27. a, c, e, b, d
28. d, a, c, b, e
29. c, d, e, b, a
30. c, a, b, d, e

EXPERT

1. c, a, b, e, d
2. b, d, c, a, e

3. a, c, b, e, d
4. d, e, c, a, b
5. a, b, d, c, e
6. a, e, b, c, d
7. b, c, a, e, d
8. a, b, e, c, d
9. c, a, b, d, e
10. b, a, c, e, d
11. a, b, c, e, d
12. b, e, a, d, c
13. c, e, d, a, b
14. e, a, b, d, c
15. a, b, e, c, d
16. b, a, c, e, d
17. b, c, e, d, a
18. b, d, c, a, e
19. a, b, c, e, d
20. e, a, c, d, b
21. a, e, b, c, d
22. a, b, c, d, e
23. b, e, a, c, d
24. e, d, b, a, c
25. b, d, a, e, c
26. a, b, d, e, c
27. e, a, d, b, c
28. b, a, c, e, d
29. a, d, b, c, e
30. e, a, b, d, c

Who Am I?

The clues provided will help you identify each of these Bible person-
alities. We've listed the most difficult clues first, so if you're looking
for a real challenge, guess the answer by reading a clue at a time.

EASY

1. **Who am I?**
   a. I died on Mount Pisgah at the ripe age of 120.
   b. I rescued a group of women from some selfish shepherds.
   c. Like Jesus, I once went without food for forty days.
   d. My brother was Israel's first high priest.
   e. My name means "to draw out," for I was taken from the Nile.
   f. God delivered the Ten Commandments to me.

2. **Who am I?**
   a. I spent part of my life in jail.
   b. My brothers visited me, but I pretended not to know them.
   c. I married the daughter of an Egyptian priest.
   d. God helped me interpret dreams.
   e. I went from being a slave to being a ruler of Egypt.
   f. I helped Egypt survive a famine.

3. **Who am I?**
   a. I was a prophet.
   b. My father's name was Amittai.

    c. I was of the tribe of Zebulun.

    d. I got mad at a worm.

    e. A group of sailors threw me into the sea.

    f. I was swallowed by a large fish.

4. **Who am I?**

    a. I was married.

    b. I had three sons mentioned by name in the Bible (and many more besides), one of whom died before I did.

    c. God saw that I was lonely.

    d. I was a gardener.

    e. I named some animals.

    f. I was the first person God created.

5. **Who am I?**

    a. I had three children named in Scripture.

    b. My husband blamed me for his wrongdoing.

    c. I disobeyed God by eating the wrong thing.

    d. I heard a snake talk once.

    e. God cursed me.

    f. I was the second person God created.

6. **Who am I?**

    a. My parents were farmers.

    b. I had two brothers named in the Bible.

    c. My name means "I have created."

    d. I eventually settled in the land of Nod.

    e. God gave me a mark so that people wouldn't kill me.

    f. I killed my brother.

7. **Who am I?**

    a. I was a shepherd.

    b. I wanted to please God.

    c. My dad was in agriculture.

    d. I offered my best sheep as a sacrifice to God.

    e. I was killed by my brother.

    f. I was the youngest of my family when I died.

8. **Who am I?**

    a. My name means "relief."

    b. My dad was a farmer.

    c. I had three sons, one of whom I cursed.

d. I obeyed God even when my neighbors said I was crazy.

e. I lived through a major flood.

f. My boat-building skills were second to none.

9. **Who am I?**

   a. I began life in Ur of the Chaldeans.

   b. My father, Terah, was supposed to go to Canaan but stopped at Haran instead.

   c. Three heavenly visitors once came to my tent.

   d. My wife had only one son, but not until I was very old.

   e. Lot was my nephew.

   f. I am the father of the Jewish nation.

10. **Who am I?**

    a. I was an only child.

    b. My parents were old when I was born.

    c. I had twin boys.

    d. I was almost a human sacrifice.

    e. My name means "laughter."

    f. My father was the father of the Jewish nation.

11. **Who are we?**

    a. There were twelve of us.

    b. One of us came from each tribe of Israel.

    c. We left camp for forty days.

    d. Among our group was Moses' successor.

    e. We did reconnaissance work.

    f. Only two of us brought back a good report.

12. **Who am I?**

    a. Before I died, I made the people of Israel take an oath of loyalty.

    b. I was of the tribe of Ephraim.

    c. My name appears in the first verse in the book of Judges.

    d. I bowed down to the commander of the Lord's army.

    e. I succeeded Moses as leader of the Israelites.

    f. I made sure the walls of Jericho came tumbling down.

13. **Who am I?**

    a. I'm counted as a hero of faith in Hebrews 11.

    b. I used flax to hide a couple of strangers.

c. When asked what happened to the strangers, I said they ran to the hills.

d. I was a prostitute, but God saw what was in my heart.

e. I lived in Jericho.

f. I hung a scarlet rope out my window in order to be saved.

14. **Who am I?**

a. Among the crimes I could have been arrested for were arson and murder.

b. My parents learned of my coming birth from an angel.

c. My last act of violence claimed more lives than anything I had done before.

d. I took the vow of a Nazirite at a very early age.

e. Philistine women always got me into trouble.

f. I am legendary for my strength and my long hair.

15. **Who am I?**

a. I was a wheat farmer.

b. I was kind to people who came to pick up my leftovers.

c. My son was Obed, the grandfather of King David.

d. I met my wife in my own fields.

e. I was distantly related to Naomi.

f. I married Ruth.

16. **Who am I?**

a. My sons' names were Joel and Abijah.

b. I put to death Agag, king of Amalek.

c. Some say I came back from the dead to rebuke a disobedient king.

d. As a young boy, God spoke to me in the night.

e. I saw a young man looking for donkeys and made him king of Israel.

f. After God rejected Saul, I anointed David as king of Israel.

17. **Who am I?**

a. I was a tall, good-looking young man.

b. My sons and I were killed in a battle with the Philistines.

c. I showed my bravery by destroying the Ammonite army of King Nahash.

d. Once I ordered my son be put to death because he tasted honey.

e. My son's best friend was David.

f. I was the first God-appointed king of Israel.

18. **Who am I?**

a. I made sure my son became the next king of Israel.

b. My first husband died in battle.

c. I was unusually beautiful.

d. The prophet Nathan told me and my husband that our first child would die.

e. My first husband was Uriah.

f. I had an affair with King David.

19. **Who am I?**

a. I built altars for the pagan gods Ashtoreth, Chemosh, and Molech.

b. I was very, very rich.

c. I had my half brother killed because he had asked to marry Abishag the Shunammite.

d. When I prayed in the temple, fire came from heaven to burn up the offering.

e. My mother was Bathsheba.

f. I succeeded King David to the throne.

20. **Who am I?**

a. I was a Hebrew prophet.

b. Ahab and Jezebel were my constant foes.

c. Fifty men who tried to seize me were burned by fire from heaven.

d. I foretold a drought that would last three years.

e. I won a great contest with the priests of Baal on Mount Carmel.

f. I was taken to heaven in a whirlwind.

21. **Who am I?**

a. I had three daughters named Jemimah, Keziah, and Keren-happuch.

b. I would always make a burnt offering on behalf of my children.

c. I had three friends who made me miserable.

d. The book of the Bible that talks about me has a conversation between Satan and God.

e. I lost my children, livestock, and health in a short amount of time.

f. I am famous for suffering a lot.

22. **Who am I?**

a. I was a prophet and minister in Babylon.

b. I was taken captive as a young man.

c. I could interpret dreams.

d. I was given the name Belteshazzar.

e. I prayed facing east three times a day.

f. I was delivered from a lions' den.

23. **Who am I?**

a. I was a Pharisee.

b. My name appears only in John's Gospel.

c. I had at least one conversation with Jesus.

d. I believed that Jesus' miracles were proof that God had sent him.

e. I accompanied Joseph of Arimathea when he buried Jesus.

f. The famous words of John 3:16 were spoken to me.

24. **Who am I?**

a. I left everything to follow Jesus.

b. My father's name was Alphaeus.

c. I invited many people to my home to meet Jesus.

d. I lived in Capernaum.

e. I was a tax collector.

f. I wrote one of the Gospels.

25. **Who am I?**

a. My husband once saw an angel.

b. My husband wanted to give our son a name we had never talked about.

c. A close relative and I were pregnant at the same time.

d. My husband was a priest who served in the temple.

e. I could feel my baby jump inside of me when my relative came to my house.

f. I was the mother of John the Baptist.

26. **Who am I?**
    a. I lived in Bethany.
    b. I had a brother.
    c. My sister complained about me once.
    d. I took the time to hear Jesus teach.
    e. I sat at Jesus' feet.
    f. I'm not known for doing housework.

27. **Who am I?**
    a. I didn't enjoy a favorable reputation in my town.
    b. Eventually I gave back a lot more that I took.
    c. I lived in Jericho.
    d. I was one of the country's richest tax collectors.
    e. I was excited when Jesus came to my home.
    f. I climbed a tree so I could have a better look at Jesus.

28. **Who am I?**
    a. I was a disciple.
    b. I was the only disciple that wasn't from Galilee.
    c. I kept the money for the disciples.
    d. I once protested because someone purchased expensive perfume.
    e. The devil Jesus talked about was me.
    f. I betrayed Jesus.

29. **Who am I?**
    a. I spoke up in support when Jesus wanted to make a dangerous trip to Bethany.
    b. I could be pessimistic.
    c. I was one of the twelve disciples.
    d. When I saw the evidence, I exclaimed, "My Lord and my God!"
    e. My nickname was "the twin."
    f. Most people know my name because I doubted.

30. **Who am I?**
    a. I was very religious before I became a believer.
    b. After my conversion, I went to Arabia and then to Damascus.
    c. I wrote several books of the Bible.
    d. I spent my last days in a Roman jail.

e. I was born in Tarsus.

f. I was converted on the road to Damascus.

INTERMEDIATE

1. **Who am I?**
   a. I was the captain of the king's bodyguard.
   b. I lived in Egypt.
   c. I was chief executioner.
   d. I bought a young Hebrew slave from Ishmaelite merchants.
   e. After my wife accused him of attempted rape, I had him put into prison.
   f. This slave, whose name was Joseph, later became a great man.

2. **Who are we?**
   a. We are first mentioned in the book of Exodus.
   b. God put us to work when we were between the ages of thirty and fifty.
   c. Of all Israel's tribes that entered Canaan, only our group did not receive land.
   d. A member of our group became the personal priest of Micah's household shrine.
   e. We sang magnificently in Solomon's temple.
   f. We carried the ark of the covenant from place to place.

3. **Who am I?**
   a. My job was to gather food for my family.
   b. I was hiding in a winepress when an angel visited me.
   c. I defeated the Midianite army under the cover of darkness.
   d. The ephod I made from the gold I captured became a snare to the Israelites.
   e. I chose my soldiers by how they drank water.
   f. I asked God to make a fleece wet.

4. **Who am I?**
   a. My sons were evil.
   b. A prophet told me that our line of family priests would come to an end.

c. Once I accused a woman near the tabernacle of being drunk.

d. I died the day the ark of the covenant was captured.

e. I was Samuel's mentor.

f. When Samuel thought I was calling, it was the Lord.

5. **Who am I?**

a. I am not human.

b. I carry messages for God.

c. I talked to the Virgin Mary.

d. I talked to John the Baptist's father.

e. I am one of the archangels.

f. I explained visions to Daniel.

6. **Who am I?**

a. My father was Haran.

b. My children became the ancestors of Israel's enemies Moab and Ammon.

c. My uncle had to rescue me from a raiding party.

d. I settled in Sodom because I thought the land was good.

e. My uncle was the father of the Jewish nation.

f. My wife turned into a pillar of salt.

7. **Who am I?**

a. I was buried in a cave in the field of Machpelah, near Mamre in Canaan.

b. Abimelech was furious with my husband for lying about me.

c. I met my husband because of the faith of his servant.

d. My brother Laban welcomed my son to his home.

e. I deceived my husband as he lay dying.

f. Abraham was my father-in-law.

8. **Who am I?**

a. My wives and I had quite a tribe.

b. My only daughter was violated by a prince.

c. I moved to Egypt late in life.

d. I had to spend fourteen years of my life working for a relative.

e. My name means "grabber."

f. God changed my name after I wrestled him for a blessing.

9. **Who am I?**
   a. I lived in Haran.
   b. I once stole idols and hid them under my saddle.
   c. I died giving birth to my second son.
   d. One of my sons saved both Egypt and Israel from famine.
   e. My first son was my husband's favorite.
   f. My sister was Leah.

10. **Who am I?**
    a. My mother named me "son of my sorrow," but my father changed it.
    b. I was a shepherd.
    c. My father wouldn't let my brothers take me to Egypt for fear that something would happen to me.
    d. My next oldest brother once framed me for stealing.
    e. We moved to Egypt to survive a famine.
    f. My father's name was changed to Israel.

11. **Who am I?**
    a. I once received a case of leprosy for my rebellious behavior.
    b. I started rumors about my brother because he had married a foreigner.
    c. I helped a ruler's daughter find a nurse for my baby brother.
    d. I was a singer, and I played tambourine.
    e. My older brother was Israel's high priest.
    f. My song of victory can be found in Exodus 15.

12. **Who am I?**
    a. I lived in Mount Ephraim.
    b. People came to me to settle differences.
    c. My husband's name was Lappidoth.
    d. I predicted that the enemy's leader would be killed by a woman.
    e. I sang a song of victory with Barak in Judges 5.
    f. I was Israel's only female judge.

13. **Who am I?**
    a. I was from the valley of Sorek.
    b. I almost single-handedly ruined a great man.
    c. I took money from the rulers of the Philistine cities.
    d. I was a nag.
    e. I accused my boyfriend of lying to me.
    f. My job was to find out why Samson was so strong.

14. **Who am I?**
    a. I became a widow at a young age.
    b. My mother-in-law treated me kindly even though I was a foreigner.
    c. I left my homeland to settle in the city where Jesus would be born.
    d. I had to beg not to be left behind.
    e. I met my second husband in his wheat field.
    f. I married my kinsman-redeemer, a man named Boaz.

15. **Who am I?**
    a. My husband's other wife constantly humiliated me.
    b. My husband didn't understand why my barrenness bothered me so.
    c. One of my prayers is listed in the Bible.
    d. My husband was Elkanah.
    e. I promised God if he would give me children I would give them back to him.
    f. I was Samuel's mother.

16. **Who are we?**
    a. We were a sea people.
    b. You could find us in Ashdod, Ekron, Ashkelon, Gath, and Gaza.
    c. Samson, Saul, and David fought against us.
    d. Our chief god was called Dagon.
    e. We captured the ark of the covenant, but God made us give it back.
    f. One of us was killed with a slingshot.

17. **Who am I?**
    a. My child was handicapped.
    b. I was the oldest son in my family.
    c. I died in battle.

d. I shot arrows into the air to warn my friend to flee.

e. With my armor bearer, I struck down a whole group of Philistine soldiers.

f. My best friend was King David, before he was king.

18. Who am I?

a. I was sought out by the king of Israel.

b. My kind of services had been officially outlawed.

c. When the king visited me, he was wearing a disguise.

d. The king came to me because God would not answer his questions.

e. The king asked me to bring someone from the dead.

f. Samuel appeared in my home even though he was dead.

19. Who am I?

a. I was a Hebrew prophet.

b. I told a king to make plans for the temple.

c. I assisted at Solomon's inauguration.

d. I gave Solomon the second name of Jedidiah.

e. I told King David a story about a rich man and a poor man.

f. I confronted David about his sin with Bathsheba.

20. Who am I?

a. I killed my oldest brother.

b. I followed the foolish advice of Ahithophel.

c. Joab killed me.

d. My father wept bitterly when he heard of my death.

e. My hair caught in the branches of a tree as I rode a mule.

f. I led a rebellion against my father, King David, that failed.

21. Who am I?

a. I traveled with my brother and sister.

b. I lost two sons because of their improper worship before God's altar.

c. My walking stick was placed in the ark of the covenant.

d. I married Elisheba and had four children.

e. I built the golden calf that brought such grief to Israel.

f. I witnessed the plagues of Egypt firsthand.

22. **Who am I?**
    a. I was a prophet's apprentice.
    b. Before I died, I told a king to shoot an arrow from a window.
    c. I helped anoint Jehu king of Israel.
    d. My servant contracted leprosy because of his greed.
    e. I helped a little boy come back to life.
    f. I told Naaman how he could be cured of leprosy.

23. **Who am I?**
    a. I was appointed governor of the Jews.
    b. I was cupbearer to King Artaxerxes.
    c. There is a book of the Bible that is called by my name.
    d. My enemies were Sanballat and Tobiah.
    e. Ezra was a friend of mine.
    f. I asked to rebuild the wall of Jerusalem.

24. **Who am I?**
    a. I was an orphan.
    b. Sometimes I am known by the name Hadassah.
    c. I was considered beautiful.
    d. I was chosen to be queen by Ahasuerus.
    e. I was raised by my cousin Mordecai.
    f. I kept my people from being killed by pleading with the king.

25. **Who am I?**
    a. My dad was a priest named Buzi.
    b. I was raised by the Kebar River in a foreign colony.
    c. I was captured with King Jehoiachin.
    d. I was married and had a home.
    e. I was a prophet known for fantastic visions.
    f. I saw dry bones come to life.

26. **Who am I?**
    a. My father was Nabopolassar.
    b. I once built a statue ninety feet high on the plain of Dura.
    c. I had a dream about feet of clay.
    d. I went insane for a number of years until I acknowledged God.
    e. I was the king of Babylon.
    f. I threw Shadrach, Meshach, and Abednego into the fiery furnace.

27. **Who am I?**
    a. I was a fisherman.
    b. Jesus saw me while I was preparing my fishing net.
    c. I was with Jesus when he was transfigured on the mountain.
    d. I was the first disciple to die for my faith.
    e. My father's name was Zebedee.
    f. My younger brother, John, was a disciple too.

28. **Who am I?**
    a. I was a Gentile.
    b. I was with Paul when we wrote his last letter.
    c. I was in a shipwreck.
    d. I wrote the early history of the church.
    e. I was a doctor.
    f. I wrote two Bible books to Theophilus.

29. **Who am I?**
    a. I lived in Samaria.
    b. I met Jesus and his disciples.
    c. Marriage wasn't my strong suit.
    d. I brought a lot of my neighbors to meet Jesus.
    e. I believed in the Messiah, even before I knew it was Jesus.
    f. I gave Jesus water from Jacob's well, and he told me about living water.

30. **Who am I?**
    a. I murdered someone.
    b. I was involved in more than one riot.
    c. I started at least one riot myself.
    d. I was granted a reprieve by an angry crowd.
    e. A Roman governor offered me my freedom.
    f. Foolish people chose me over Jesus to be released from prison and death.

ADVANCED

1. **Who am I?**
    a. I knew King Artaxerxes.
    b. I was a descendant of Aaron.
    c. I was called a scribe.

d. There is an Old Testament book with my name.

e. I was very grieved to find that the Israelites had intermarried.

f. I ordered the men of Judah to send away their foreign wives.

2. **Who am I?**

a. My father's name was Jepphuneh.

b. I gave my daughter Acsah as a bride to Othniel because of his bravery.

c. When I was an old man, I received the land of Hebron as my inheritance.

d. I was one of the two Israelites of my generation who entered the Promised Land.

e. I carried fruit back from the Promised Land.

f. I gave a favorable report of my travels to Moses, Aaron, and the people.

3. **Who am I?**

a. I was a queen.

b. Once I covered a statue with blankets in order to fool my father.

c. My husband had to kill a hundred Philistines before he could marry me.

d. Jonathan was my brother.

e. I despised my husband for dancing in front of the ark of the covenant.

f. I was King David's first wife.

4. **Who am I?**

a. I lived in Lo-debar.

b. My servant lied so that he could have the land the king had given me.

c. I was a descendant of royalty but never became a king.

d. I was crippled from a fall in childhood.

e. My servants were the household of Ziba.

f. I was given a place of honor at King David's table.

5. **Who are we?**

a. Paul started a fight between us and another religious group.

b. We helped arrest Peter and John for preaching that
   Jesus had risen from the dead.
c. We believed the Pentateuch (first five books of the OT)
   was the complete Word of God.
d. We asked Jesus a question about marriage in heaven.
e. We did not believe in angels or demons.
f. We did not believe in eternal life.

6. **Who am I?**
   a. I waited for the consolation of Israel.
   b. I was an old man who lived in Jerusalem.
   c. The Holy Spirit led me to the temple.
   d. I told a young mother that a sword would pierce her
      soul.
   e. I was one of the first to meet baby Jesus.
   f. The Lord told me I would not die before I saw the Christ.

7. **Who am I?**
   a. I was present the night Jesus was arrested.
   b. All four of the Gospels talk about me, but only John
      mentions my name.
   c. One of my relatives questioned Peter in the courtyard.
   d. Only Luke describes how I was healed.
   e. I was the servant of the high priest.
   f. Peter slashed off my ear with a sword.

8. **Who am I?**
   a. My name appears only once in the Bible.
   b. I was a friend of Paul's.
   c. Paul wrote me a letter once.
   d. I had a guest room ready for Paul to stay in.
   e. The New Testament book with my name is one of the
      shortest.
   f. I had a slave named Onesimus.

9. **Who am I?**
   a. My son's name was Enosh.
   b. I had my first son when I was 105 years old.
   c. I died at 912 years of age.
   d. I am grandfather to Kenan.
   e. I was like my dad in every way.
   f. I never knew my two older brothers.

10. Who am I?

a. Adam was my great-great-great-great-great-grandfather.

b. I was very close to God.

c. I lived to be 365 years old.

d. I am the son of Jared.

e. My son's name is Methuselah.

f. I didn't die; I just disappeared one day.

11. Who am I?

a. My wives' names were Adah, Basemath, and Oholibamah.

b. My mother favored my younger brother.

c. I was very skilled with a bow and arrow.

d. My people were called Edomites.

e. My name means "hair," for I was covered with red hair at birth.

f. I traded my birthright for stew.

12. Who am I?

a. My oldest son's name meant "God noticed my trouble."

b. My son once found mandrake roots that I wouldn't share with my sister.

c. My last son's name was Zebulun.

d. I had lovely eyes.

e. One of my sons is the father of the tribe of Judah.

f. My father tricked my husband into marrying me.

13. Who am I?

a. My father was king of Tyre and Sidon.

b. I introduced Phoenician worship on a grand scale.

c. My own servants threw me from a window.

d. I conspired to take a vineyard and give it to my husband.

e. I couldn't be buried because my remains could not be found.

f. I hated Elijah and wanted him dead.

14. Who am I?

a. I was a descendant of Levi.

b. Most of my story appears in Numbers 16.

c. I was angry because Moses thought he was better than the rest of us.

d. I conspired with Dathan and Abiram and On.

e. Because of my rebellion, more than 250 people died.

f. I was killed in an earthquake.

15. **Who am I?**

a. My father was Caleb's younger brother.

b. Caleb gave me a bride for capturing Kiriath Sepher.

c. My wife received springs of water as a gift from her father.

d. Israel had forty years of rest under my rule.

e. I rescued Israel from Chushan-rishathaim of Aram.

f. I was Israel's first judge.

16. **Who am I?**

a. I was a Benjamite.

b. I rescued Israel from Moab.

c. Israel had eighty years of rest under my rule.

d. I owned an eighteen-inch, double-edged dagger.

e. I killed a fat king, then escaped.

f. I may have been Israel's only left-handed judge.

17. **Who am I?**

a. I was the illegitimate son of Gilead.

b. I conquered the Ammonites.

c. I was a judge of Israel.

d. I ruled six years.

e. I promised God I would sacrifice what came out of my front door.

f. My daughter never married because of my vow.

18. **Who am I?**

a. My name is not given in the Bible, so I'm identified with my husband.

b. I was of the tribe of Dan.

c. The angel of the Lord appeared to me.

d. My son was a Nazirite.

e. I didn't drink alcohol while I was pregnant.

f. I'm one mother who never cut her son's hair.

19. **Who am I?**

a. My husband was Elimelech.

b. When we were young, we left our land because of a famine.

c. After my husband died, I wanted people to call me Mara, which means "bitter."

d. I traveled from Moab to return to Bethlehem.

e. I helped my daughter-in-law, who was also a widow, find a husband.

f. My daughter-in-law Ruth was my best friend.

20. **Who am I?**

a. I was married to David.

b. David rescued me and his other wife from the Amalekites.

c. I bore David a son named Kileab.

d. I kept David from killing my first husband.

e. I gave David and his men bread, wine, sheep, grain, and cakes.

f. My husband Nabal died after I told him of his foolishness.

21. **Who am I?**

a. I was accused of having blasphemed God and the king.

b. I owned a piece of land that had been in my family for years.

c. I lived in the valley of Jezreel.

d. I was stoned to death.

e. Ahab wanted my vineyard.

f. Jezebel arranged to have me falsely accused and sentenced to death.

22. **Who am I?**

a. I was a Hebrew prophet.

b. I wrote a biography of kings Uzziah and Hezekiah.

c. My father was Amoz.

d. There is a book in the Old Testament called by my name.

e. My book is the longest prophetic book of the Bible—sixty-six chapters.

f. I was known as the evangelical prophet.

23. **Who am I?**

a. I was probably from Beth-horon.

b. I was a friend of Tobiah.

c. I had a civil or military command in Samaria.

d. I was a contemporary of Nehemiah.

e. I gave the Jews a very difficult time.

f. I was angry when they rebuilt the walls of Jerusalem.

24. Who am I?

a. I was son of Jair, descendant of Kish the Benjamite.

b. I lived in Shushan in Persia.

c. I refused to bow down to a high official.

d. I foiled an assassination plot against the king and was later rewarded.

e. I adopted my orphaned cousin.

f. You can read about me in the book of Esther.

25. Who am I?

a. I was a priest.

b. My father was Hilkiah.

c. I was a prophet.

d. I was very young when the word of God came to me.

e. I prophesied during the reign of Jehoiakim, Zedekiah, and Nebuchadnezzar.

f. I wrote a sorrowful dirge about the fall of Jerusalem.

26. Who am I?

a. I was a prophet.

b. My father was Beeri.

c. I used examples from daily life to teach Israel about God.

d. I prophesied under the reign of Jeroboam in Israel.

e. My name means "salvation."

f. I am the prophet who married a prostitute.

27. Who am I?

a. My second husband was the brother of my first husband.

b. My second husband arrested a great prophet but didn't want to kill him.

c. I gave my daughter evil advice.

d. My daughter danced magnificently for our dinner guests.

e. I hated John the Baptist.

f. My daughter requested a prophet's head as her reward.

28. **Who am I?**
    a. My father's name was Timaeus.
    b. I lived in Jericho.
    c. When asked what I wanted, I said, "Rabbi, I want to see!"
    d. I kept on asking for help even after people told me to stop asking.
    e. After I was healed, I followed the Rabbi along the road.
    f. I was blind until Jesus healed me.

29. **Who am I?**
    a. I lived in Capernaum.
    b. Jesus came to my home.
    c. I saw many miracles performed in my own home.
    d. My daughter was married to a disciple.
    e. I once prepared a meal after being very sick.
    f. Jesus healed me of a high fever.

30. **Who am I?**
    a. In the Gospels, I'm often associated with Bartholomew.
    b. I asked Jesus to show us the Father.
    c. An ex-sorcerer traveled with me for a while.
    d. I invited Nathaniel to "come and see."
    e. I was miraculously transported to Azotus after a baptism.
    f. I led an Ethiopian eunuch to Christ and baptized him.

EXPERT

1. **Who are we?**
   a. We worked for Pharaoh.
   b. We shared living quarters with Joseph, in a manner of speaking.
   c. We had household jobs.
   d. Joseph interpreted our dreams for us.
   e. One of us lived, and one of us died.
   f. The one of us that lived forgot all about Joseph.

2. **Who are we?**
   a. We were the first people in the Bible to practice passive resistance.

b. Because we feared God, we disobeyed Pharaoh's commands.

c. God blessed us and gave us our own children.

d. We told Pharaoh that Hebrew women delivered their children very quickly.

e. Pharaoh had instructed us to kill all Hebrew boys when they were born.

f. Because of us, the Israelites continued to multiply.

3. **Who am I?**

a. I had a grandchild whose name means "foreigner."

b. I tended flocks in the desert with the help of my daughters.

c. I was the priest of Midian.

d. I gave my daughter as a bride to a refugee from Egypt.

e. My other name is Jethro.

f. I became Moses' father-in-law.

4. **Who am I?**

a. My story appears in the book of Exodus.

b. My dad was Uri.

c. God gave me great wisdom and ability.

d. I was an artistic designer of gold and silver.

e. I was skilled as a jeweler and wood-carver in the days of Moses.

f. I was general superintendent in the construction of the tabernacle.

5. **Who am I?**

a. I was of the tribe of Dan.

b. My father was Ahisamach.

c. I helped build an ark, but it wasn't Noah's.

d. I was a skilled craftsman.

e. Moses appointed me and my boss.

f. I helped Bezalel complete the tabernacle furnishings.

6. **Who are we?**

a. We were buried by Mishael and Elzaphon.

b. When we died, our father lost half of his sons.

c. Our father was not allowed to grieve our deaths publicly.

d. You can read about our short lives in the book of Leviticus.

e. We did not please God with our actions before his altar.

f. We were burned to death by fire from heaven.

7. **Who am I?**

a. I could be a man or woman.

b. Everything you'd want to know about me can be found in Numbers 6.

c. I took a vow that I wouldn't drink wine or have anything to do with grapes.

d. I didn't go near dead bodies of any kind.

e. I didn't cut my hair.

f. Samson was one.

8. **Who am I?**

a. I knew the ways of the wilderness.

b. The wife of one of my descendants killed the Canaanite general Sisera.

c. I really wanted to return to my people.

d. Moses promised me that I would share the good things of the land if I went with him.

e. I was Moses' brother-in-law.

f. I was Jethro's son.

9. **Who are we?**

a. We were Hebrews.

b. We wandered with Moses in the desert.

c. We were among the seventy elders.

d. We did not gather around the tabernacle, but God gave us his Spirit also.

e. We prophesied in the camp at the same time as the other elders.

f. Joshua told us to stop, but Moses rebuked him.

10. **Who am I?**

a. I was a king in the days of Moses.

b. I teamed up with the Midianites against the Israelites.

c. If I couldn't get the Israelites cursed, I tried to get them to sin.

d. My kingdom was Moab.

e. I tried to get a well-known diviner to curse Israel.

f. My plan backfired, and Israel was blessed instead.

11. **Who am I?**
    a. I burned a temple and over a thousand people in it.
    b. I wanted to be king of Shechem.
    c. My half brother placed a curse on me.
    d. I was the son of Gideon and one of his concubines.
    e. I killed all my sixty-nine brothers except Jotham.
    f. A woman killed me by dropping a millstone on my head.

12. **Who am I?**
    a. Don't confuse me with an Old Testament prophet who wrote a book.
    b. I lived in the hill country of Ephraim.
    c. I stole silver from my own mother.
    d. I hired a Levite to serve as my own personal priest.
    e. Later on, the priest left me when he got a better offer.
    f. My idols were stolen and worshiped by the tribe of Dan.

13. **Who am I?**
    a. I was an Edomite.
    b. I kept Saul's mules.
    c. I was the chief of Saul's herdsmen.
    d. I told Saul that Ahimelech had helped David.
    e. I killed Ahimelech because Saul's guards wouldn't kill a priest.
    f. I also killed eighty-four priests in the city of Nob.

14. **Who am I?**
    a. I was a Philistine.
    b. I ruled the city of Gath.
    c. I gave David the city of Ziklag.
    d. I made David my bodyguard for life.
    e. David acted like a madman in front of me.
    f. Even though I trusted David, the other Philistines made me send him away.

15. **Who am I?**
    a. I was crowned king in Shechem.
    b. My mother was Naamah.
    c. I traded the temple treasures for peace.
    d. The people asked me to treat them more kindly, but I said no.

    e. Ten of the tribes chose their own king rather than accept me.

    f. My father was Solomon.

16. **Who am I?**

    a. I am a Hebrew princess.

    b. I share the same name of the woman who gave twin sons to Judah.

    c. My mother was Maacah.

    d. I never married.

    e. I was raped by my half brother.

    f. My brother Absalom killed the man who raped me.

17. **Who am I?**

    a. I was beheaded.

    b. I was considered a worthless scoundrel.

    c. I refused to let the soldiers of Judah boss us around.

    d. I came from the tribe of Benjamin.

    e. Joab pursued me all the way across Palestine.

    f. A woman saved her city by having her people throw my head over the walls.

18. **Who am I?**

    a. I destroyed the bronze serpent of Moses.

    b. I got rid of the false gods in Israel.

    c. I was the twelfth king of Judah.

    d. My father was Ahaz.

    e. I summoned Judah and Israel to the Passover celebration.

    f. I repaired and reopened the temple.

19. **Who am I?**

    a. I was from Moresheth, south of Jerusalem.

    b. I prophesied of judgment and forgiveness.

    c. I prophesied during the reign of Hezekiah.

    d. I was a contemporary of Hosea and Isaiah.

    e. I could not find an honest man.

    f. I predicted that the Messiah would be born in Bethlehem.

20. **Who am I?**

    a. I was an expert on religious law.

    b. I was very popular with the people.

c. I was a member of the high council.

d. I was a Pharisee.

e. I talked the high council out of killing Peter and John.

f. I knew if Jesus wasn't the Messiah, his story would soon be forgotten.

21. **Who are we?**

a. We lived in Athens.

b. We heard Paul speak at Mars Hill.

c. One of us was a member of the city council.

d. We wanted to hear about a new religion preached of in the town square.

e. We became believers.

f. We joined Paul and Silas.

22. **Who am I?**

a. I took no notice when Sosthenes was beaten by a mob.

b. I ruled in Achaia.

c. I was not a Jew.

d. I ran a bunch of Jews out of my courtroom.

e. I couldn't have cared less what the Jews did to each other.

f. I had Paul in my courtroom once.

23. **Who am I?**

a. I was an Israelite in Joshua's army.

b. My sin caused Israel to lose to the Canaanites at Ai.

c. I helped with the attack on Jericho.

d. I stole gold and silver that belonged to God.

e. I hid the loot under my tent, as if God couldn't see it there.

f. Joshua had me stoned to death and buried under rocks.

24. **Who am I?**

a. I had two brothers.

b. One of my descendants built the ancient city of Babylon.

c. I am the ancestor of the Canaanites.

d. My lineage was cursed because of my wrongdoing.

e. I did something evil while my father was drunk.

f. I lived through the Flood.

25. **Who am I?**

a. I broke a promise to my daughter-in-law, Tamar.

b. I was a natural leader.

c. I lived in Canaan, then Egypt.

d. I am the fourth son of twelve.

e. My mother was Leah.

f. I am the brother that suggested we sell Joseph as a slave.

26. **Who am I?**

a. I was royalty.

b. I fought the Israelites at Edrei.

c. My army was wiped out; not a single man survived.

d. I suffered the same fate as King Sihon.

e. I was the last of the Rephaites left alive.

f. I am best known for the huge iron bed I slept in.

27. **Who am I?**

a. I carried trumpets for signaling during Moses' last campaign against the Midianites.

b. My mother's name was Putiel.

c. I helped resolve a dispute over an altar built by Israel's eastern tribes.

d. My descendants were to always be priests because of my zeal for God.

e. I ended a plague by killing an immoral Israelite with a spear.

f. I was Eleazar's son and Aaron's grandson.

28. **Who am I?**

a. I was a high priest in the time before the judges.

b. I was the chief leader of the Levites in my lifetime and cared for the sanctuary.

c. When my father died, Moses took his garments and placed them on me.

d. I collected the censers that were held by those who were burned up and hammered them into a sheet to cover the altar.

e. Two of my brothers were killed by fire from heaven.

f. I helped with the inauguration of Joshua.

29. **Who are we?**

a. We traveled in pairs.

b. We didn't take any money with us.

c. We received explicit instructions before we left on our journeys.
d. We stayed in one home in each town we visited.
e. We went to villages Jesus was going to visit.
f. We preached, healed, and cast out demons, and reported our success.

30. **Who are we?**
a. We liked people to see the good things we did.
b. When we gave money, we told people about it.
c. We liked our rewards on earth instead of in heaven.
d. You could really tell when we were fasting.
e. We liked to pray on street corners.
f. Jesus often called us hypocrites.

Who Am I? (Answers)

EASY

1. Moses
2. Joseph
3. Jonah
4. Adam
5. Eve
6. Cain
7. Abel
8. Noah
9. Abram/Abraham
10. Isaac
11. The twelve spies
12. Joshua
13. Rahab
14. Samson
15. Boaz
16. Samuel
17. Saul
18. Bathsheba
19. Solomon
20. Elijah
21. Job
22. Daniel
23. Nicodemus
24. Matthew
25. Elizabeth
26. Mary, the sister of Martha
27. Zacchaeus
28. Judas Iscariot
29. Thomas
30. Paul

INTERMEDIATE

1. Potiphar
2. The Levites
3. Gideon
4. Eli
5. Gabriel
6. Lot
7. Rebekah
8. Jacob/Israel
9. Rachel
10. Benjamin
11. Miriam
12. Deborah
13. Delilah
14. Ruth
15. Hannah
16. Philistines
17. Jonathan
18. Witch of Endor
19. Nathan
20. Absalom
21. Aaron
22. Elisha
23. Nehemiah
24. Esther
25. Ezekiel
26. Nebuchadnezzar
27. James
28. Luke
29. The Samaritan woman at the well
30. Barabbas

ADVANCED

1. Ezra
2. Caleb
3. Michal
4. Mephibosheth
5. Sadducees
6. Simeon
7. Malchus

8. Philemon
9. Seth
10. Enoch
11. Esau
12. Leah
13. Jezebel
14. Korah
15. Othniel
16. Ehud
17. Jephthah
18. Wife of Manoah, Samson's mother
19. Naomi
20. Abigail
21. Naboth
22. Isaiah
23. Sanballat
24. Mordecai
25. Jeremiah
26. Hosea
27. Herodias
28. Bartimaeus
29. Peter's mother-in-law
30. Philip

EXPERT

1. Pharaoh's baker and butler
2. Shiphrah and Puah, Hebrew midwives
3. Reuel

4. Bezalel
5. Oholiab
6. Nadab and Abihu
7. A Nazirite
8. Hobab
9. Eldad and Medad
10. King Balak
11. Abimelech
12. Micah (not the prophet)
13. Doeg
14. King Achish
15. Rehoboam
16. Tamar
17. Sheba
18. Hezekiah
19. Micah
20. Gamaliel
21. Dionysius and Damaris
22. Gallio
23. Achan
24. Ham
25. Judah
26. King Og of Bashan
27. Phinehas
28. Eleazar
29. The seventy disciples Jesus sent out
30. Pharisees

They Said What?

(PART 2)

Guess the identity of the speaker from the statements or questions below.

EASY

1. "I will sing to the Lord, for he has triumphed gloriously; he has thrown both horse and rider into the sea."
2. "If another believer sins against you, go privately and point out the fault. If the other person listens and confesses it, you have won that person back."
3. "Throw me into the sea, and it will become calm again. For I know that this terrible storm is all my fault."
4. "If you are the Son of God, change this stone into a loaf of bread."
5. "It is finished!"
6. "It was the woman you gave me who brought me the fruit, and I ate it."
7. "Just kill me now, Lord! I'd rather be dead than alive because nothing I predicted is going to happen."
8. "Let's build a great city with a tower that reaches to the skies—a monument to our greatness! This will bring us together and keep us from scattering all over the world."
9. "Lord, doesn't it seem unfair to you that my sister just sits here while I do all the work? Tell her to come and help me."

10. "O my son Absalom! O Absalom, my son, my son!"

11. "Should I go and find one of the Hebrew women to nurse the baby for you?"

12. "So don't worry about tomorrow, for tomorrow will bring its own worries. Today's trouble is enough for today."

13. "Son! Why have you done this to us? Your father and I have been frantic, searching for you everywhere."

14. "Find a woman who is a medium, so I can go and ask her what to do."

15. "Tell your wives and sons and daughters to take off their gold earrings, and then bring them to me."

16. "Long live the king! Why shouldn't I be sad? For the city where my ancestors are buried is in ruins, and the gates have been burned down."

17. "That is not true. You did laugh."

18. "The serpent tricked me. That's why I ate it."

19. "They have no more wine."

20. "What's more, who can say but that you have been elevated to the palace for just such a time as this?"

21. "When you help the Hebrew women give birth, kill all the boys as soon as they are born. Allow only the baby girls to live."

22. "Are you still trying to maintain your integrity? Curse God and die."

23. "Where is the newborn king of the Jews? We have seen his star as it arose, and we have come to worship him."

24. "Who could do it better than Joseph?"

25. "Why isn't that bush burning up?"

26. "You are the salt of the earth. But what good is salt if it has lost its flavor? Can you make it useful again? It will be thrown out and trampled underfoot as worthless."

27. "I will go wherever you go and live wherever you live. Your people will be my people, and your God will be my God. I will die where you die and will be buried there."

28. "You come to me with sword, spear, and javelin, but I come to you in the name of the Lord Almighty—the God of the armies of Israel, whom you have defied."

29. "You won't die!"

30. "You'll have to shout louder, for surely he is a god! Perhaps he is deep in thought, or he is relieving himself.

Or maybe he is away on a trip, or he is asleep and needs to be wakened!"

1. "Do you understand what you are reading?"
2. "God has sent me here to keep you and your families alive so that you will become a great nation. Yes, it was God who sent me here, not you!"
3. "Come, let's get him drunk with wine, and then we will sleep with him. That way we will preserve our family line through our father."
4. "Should the king show such kindness to a dead dog like me?"
5. "Are you the Messiah we've been expecting, or should we keep looking for someone else?"
6. "O Lord Almighty, if you will look down upon my sorrow and answer my prayer and give me a son, then I will give him back to you."
7. "I will not let you go unless you bless me."
8. "For I am not ashamed of this Good News about Christ. It is the power of God at work, saving everyone who believes—Jews first and also Gentiles."
9. "Wherever we go, have the kindness to say that you are my sister."
10. "There's a young boy here with five barley loaves and two fish. But what good is that with this huge crowd?"
11. "Let's go at once to take the land. We can certainly conquer it!"
12. "If I am a man of God, let fire come down from heaven and destroy you and your fifty men!"
13. "Do not be afraid to return to Egypt, for all those who wanted to kill you are dead."
14. "How can I know this will happen? I'm an old man now, and my wife is also well along in years."
15. "What is truth?"
16. "I will give to the Lord the first thing coming out of my house to greet me when I return in triumph. I will sacrifice it as a burnt offering."
17. "My father! My father! The chariots and charioteers of Israel!"

18. "Take your sword and kill me before these pagan Philistines run me through and humiliate me."
19. "So if you are standing before the altar in the Temple, offering a sacrifice to God, and you suddenly remember that someone has something against you, leave your sacrifice there beside the altar. Go and be reconciled to that person. Then come and offer your sacrifice to God."
20. "Save yourselves from this generation that has gone astray!"
21. "Don't be afraid. Just stand where you are and watch the Lord rescue you."
22. "Look! There is the Lamb of God who takes away the sin of the world!"
23. "Shout! For the Lord has given you the city!"
24. "What do you mean? How can an old man go back into his mother's womb and be born again?"
25. "Give me an understanding mind so that I can govern your people well and know the difference between right and wrong. For who by himself is able to govern this great nation of yours?"
26. "Is it legal for you to whip a Roman citizen who hasn't even been tried?"
27. "You are a better man than I am, for you have repaid me good for evil."
28. "My lords, come to my home to wash your feet, and be my guests for the night. You may then get up in the morning as early as you like and be on your way again."
29. "I'll draw water for your camels, too, until they have had enough!"
30. "Call me Mara, for the Almighty has made life very bitter for me. I went away full, but the Lord has brought me home empty."

ADVANCED

1. "Has the Lord spoken only through Moses? Hasn't he spoken through us, too?"
2. "O Lord, you have said that you would live in thick darkness. But I have built a glorious Temple for you, where you can live forever!"
3. "Look! There's some water! Why can't I be baptized?"

4. "The Lord, the God of heaven, has given me all the kingdoms of the earth. He has appointed me to build him a Temple at Jerusalem in the land of Judah. All of you who are the Lord's people may return to Israel for this task. May the Lord your God be with you!"

5. "Your blood be upon your own heads—I am innocent. From now on I will go to the Gentiles."

6. "Blessed be Abram by God Most High, Creator of heaven and earth."

7. "I have sinned greatly and shouldn't have taken the census. Please forgive me for doing this foolish thing."

8. "May the gods also kill me if by this time tomorrow I have failed to take your life like those whom you killed."

9. "Hear, O Israel! The Lord is our God, the Lord alone. And you must love the Lord your God with all your heart, all your soul, and all your strength."

10. "Now let me die, for I have seen you with my own eyes and know you are still alive."

11. "You brood of snakes! Who warned you to flee God's coming judgment? Prove by the way you live that you have really turned from your sins and turned to God. Don't just say, 'We're safe—we're the descendants of Abraham.' That proves nothing. God can change these stones here into children of Abraham."

12. "But how can I curse those whom God has not cursed?"

13. "God has brought me laughter! All who hear about this will laugh with me."

14. "If my sadness could be weighed and my troubles be put on the scales, they would be heavier than all the sands of the sea. That is why I spoke so rashly."

15. "Then wash my hands and head as well, Lord, not just my feet!"

16. "O Lord, God of Israel, there is no God like you in all of heaven and earth. You keep your promises and show unfailing love to all who obey you and are eager to do your will."

17. "How glorious the king of Israel looked today! He exposed himself to the servant girls like any indecent person might do!"

18. "Lord, this is wonderful! If you want me to, I'll make three shrines, one for you, one for Moses, and one for Elijah."

19. "Please let me see your glorious presence."

20. "Am I God? He is the only one able to give you children!"

21. "I am the Lord's servant, and I am willing to accept whatever he wants. May everything you have said come true."

22. "Remember, O my God, all that I have done for these people, and bless me for it."

23. "When God comes to lead us back to Canaan, you must take my body back with you."

24. "This is the man the Lord has chosen as your king. No one in all Israel is his equal!"

25. "Lord, now I can die in peace! As you promised me, I have seen the Savior you have given to all people."

26. "I know what I'm doing, my son. Manasseh, too, will become a great people, but his younger brother will become even greater. His descendants will become a multitude of nations!"

27. "The day will come, when I will make a new covenant with the people of Israel and Judah."

28. "For the Lord's victory over Sisera will be at the hands of a woman."

29. "Do you think God wants us to obey you rather than him? We cannot stop telling about the wonderful things we have seen and heard."

30. "Everything I heard in my country about your achievements and wisdom is true!"

EXPERT

1. "For nothing is impossible with God."

2. "I vow by the Lord and by your own life that I will go wherever you go, no matter what happens—whether it means life or death."

3. "Today you have been ordained for the service of the Lord, for you obeyed him even though it meant killing your own sons and brothers. Because of this, he will now give you a great blessing."

4. "Make your confession and tell me what you have done. Don't hide it from me."
5. "Come into my tent, sir. Come in. Don't be afraid."
6. "All of you who are on the Lord's side, come over here and join me."
7. "My son Shechem is truly in love with your daughter, and he longs for her to be his wife. Please let him marry her."
8. "Look, I see the heavens opened and the Son of Man standing in the place of honor at God's right hand!"
9. "Awake, O sword, against my shepherd, the man who is my partner, says the Lord Almighty. Strike down the shepherd, and the sheep will be scattered, and I will turn against the lambs."
10. "Don't you hear their many charges against you?"
11. "Haman has set up a gallows that stands seventy-five feet tall in his own courtyard."
12. "If they sin against you—and who has never sinned?—you may become angry with them and let their enemies conquer them and take them captive to a foreign land far or near."
13. "You may not see me again unless your youngest brother is with you."
14. "What am I going to do with you sons of Zeruiah! If the Lord has told him to curse me, who am I to stop him?"
15. "So shall the owner of this belt be bound by the Jewish leaders in Jerusalem and turned over to the Romans."
16. "Once upon a time the trees decided to elect a king. First they said to the olive tree, 'Be our king!'"
17. "I have found the Book of the Law in the Lord's Temple!"
18. "What do you want with me, king of Judah? I have no quarrel with you today! I only want to fight the nation with which I am at war. And God has told me to hurry! Do not interfere with God, who is with me, or he will destroy you."
19. "Throw her down!"
20. "No one will be executed today, for today the Lord has rescued Israel!"
21. "You and I are brothers, and my troops are yours to command. We will certainly join you in battle."
22. "I demand in the name of the living God that you tell us whether you are the Messiah, the Son of God."

23. "Whoever leads the attack against the Jebusites will become the commander of my armies!"

24. "Come in, wife of Jeroboam! Why are you pretending to be someone else? I have bad news for you."

25. "A warrior still dressing for battle should not boast like a warrior who has already won."

26. "Get out of here, you murderer, you scoundrel! The Lord is paying you back for murdering Saul and his family. You stole his throne, and now the Lord has given it to your son Absalom. At last you will taste some of your own medicine, you murderer!"

27. "I have a secret message for you."

28. "Why couldn't we cast out that demon?"

29. "The unfailing love of the Lord never ends! By his mercies we have been kept from complete destruction."

30. "Our father died in the wilderness without leaving any sons. But he was not among Korah's followers, who rebelled against the Lord. He died because of his own sin. Why should the name of our father disappear just because he had no sons? Give us property along with the rest of our relatives."

They Said What? (Part 2, Answers)

EASY

1. Moses and the people of Israel (Exodus 15:1)
2. Jesus (Matthew 18:15)
3. Jonah (Jonah 1:12)
4. Satan (Luke 4:3)
5. Jesus (John 19:30)
6. Adam (Genesis 3:12)
7. Jonah (Jonah 4:3)
8. The people of Babel (Genesis 11:4)
9. Martha (Luke 10:40)
10. David (2 Samuel 19:4)
11. Miriam (Exodus 2:7)
12. Jesus (Matthew 6:34)
13. Mary (Luke 2:48)
14. Saul (1 Samuel 28:7)
15. Aaron (Exodus 32:2)
16. Nehemiah (Nehemiah 2:3)
17. An angel (Genesis 18:15)
18. Eve (Genesis 3:13)
19. Mary (John 2:3)
20. Mordecai (Esther 4:14)
21. Pharaoh (Exodus 1:16)
22. Job's wife (Job 2:9)
23. The magi (Matthew 2:2)
24. Pharaoh (Genesis 41:38)
25. Moses (Exodus 3:3)
26. Jesus (Matthew 5:13)
27. Ruth (Ruth 1:16-17)
28. David (1 Samuel 17:45)
29. Satan (Genesis 3:4)
30. Elijah (1 Kings 18:27)

INTERMEDIATE

1. Philip (Acts 8:30)
2. Joseph (Genesis 45:7-8)
3. Lot's daughters (Genesis 19:32)
4. Mephibosheth (2 Samuel 9:8)
5. John the Baptist (Luke 7:19)
6. Hannah (1 Samuel 1:11)
7. Jacob (Genesis 32:26)
8. Paul (Romans 1:16)
9. Abraham (Genesis 20:13)
10. Andrew (John 6:9)
11. Caleb (Numbers 13:30)
12. Elijah (2 Kings 1:12)
13. God (Exodus 4:19)
14. Zechariah (Luke 1:18)
15. Pilate (John 18:38)
16. Jephthah (Judges 11:31)
17. Elisha (2 Kings 2:12)
18. Saul (1 Samuel 31:4)
19. Jesus (Matthew 5:23-24)
20. Peter (Acts 2:40)
21. Moses (Exodus 14:13)
22. John the Baptist (John 1:29)
23. Joshua (Joshua 6:16)
24. Nicodemus (John 3:4)
25. Solomon (1 Kings 3:9)
26. Paul (Acts 22:25)
27. Saul (1 Samuel 24:17)
28. Lot (Genesis 19:2)
29. Rebekah (Genesis 24:19)
30. Naomi (Ruth 1:20-21)

ADVANCED

1. Aaron and Miriam (Numbers 12:2)
2. Solomon (2 Chronicles 6:1-2)
3. The Ethiopian eunuch (Acts 8:36)
4. Cyrus, king of Persia (2 Chronicles 36:23)
5. Paul (Acts 18:6)

6. Melchizedek (Genesis 14:19)
7. David (1 Chronicles 21:8)
8. Jezebel (1 Kings 19:2)
9. Moses (Deuteronomy 6:4-5)
10. Jacob (Genesis 46:30)
11. John the Baptist (Luke 3:7-8)
12. Balaam (Numbers 23:8)
13. Sarah (Genesis 21:6)
14. Job (Job 6:2-3)
15. Simon Peter (John 13:9)
16. Solomon (2 Chronicles 6:14)
17. Micah (2 Samuel 6:20)
18. Peter (Matthew 17:4)
19. Moses (Exodus 33:18)
20. Jacob (Genesis 30:2)
21. Mary (Luke 1:38)
22. Nehemiah (Nehemiah 5:19)
23. Joseph (Genesis 50:25)
24. Samuel (1 Samuel 10:24)
25. Simeon (Luke 2:29-31)
26. Jacob (Genesis 48:19)
27. Jeremiah (Jeremiah 31:31)
28. Deborah (Judges 4:9)
29. Peter and John (Acts 4:19-20)
30. Queen of Sheba (1 Kings 10:6)

EXPERT

1. Gabriel (Luke 1:37)
2. Ittai (2 Samuel 15:21)

3. Moses (Exodus 32:29)
4. Joshua (Joshua 7:19)
5. Jael (Judges 4:18)
6. Moses (Exodus 32:26)
7. Hamor (Genesis 34:8)
8. Stephen (Acts 7:56)
9. Zechariah (Zechariah 13:7)
10. Pilate (Matthew 27:13)
11. Harbona (Esther 7:9)
12. Solomon (2 Chronicles 6:36)
13. Joseph (Genesis 44:23)
14. David (2 Samuel 16:10)
15. Agabus (Acts 21:11)
16. Jotham (Judges 9:8)
17. Hilkiah (2 Chronicles 34:15)
18. King Neco of Egypt (2 Chronicles 35:21)
19. Jehu (2 Kings 9:33)
20. Saul (1 Samuel 11:13)
21. Jehoshaphat (2 Chronicles 18:3)
22. Caiaphas (Matthew 26:63)
23. David (1 Chronicles 11:6)
24. Ahijah (1 Kings 14:6)
25. Ahab (1 Kings 20:11)
26. Shimei (2 Samuel 16:7-8)
27. Ehud (Judges 3:19)
28. The disciples (Matthew 17:19)
29. Jeremiah (Lamentations 3:22)
30. The daughters of Zelophehad (Numbers 27:3-4)

Bible Trivia

Provide answers for these Bible-trivia questions.

1. What tribe assisted the priests during religious duties?
2. Whom did David kill with a smooth stone?
3. Which of David's sons led a revolt against his father?
4. Who used a wool fleece to determine God's will?
5. What are the names of the two spies who wanted the people to conquer the Promised Land?
6. What country conquered and exiled the northern kingdom of Israel?
7. Who was king of Babylon when Babylon conquered Jerusalem?
8. What was the name of the miraculous food that God provided the Israelites?
9. How long did Abraham wait after God's promise until he had his promised son?
10. Who were Ishmael's parents?
11. What was the name of the prostitute who helped Israel's spies?
12. Where was Gideon when an angel appeared to him?
13. Who were the first recorded visitors of baby Jesus?

14. Who did Herod kill in order to keep a foolish promise?
15. What prophet had a donkey speak to him?

INTERMEDIATE

1. Why wasn't Moses allowed to enter the Promised Land?
2. Who was Uriah's wife?
3. Which judge was famous for being left-handed?
4. What woman leader in the book of Judges led Israel's army to victory?
5. Who led a group of exiles back to Jerusalem in order to rebuild the walls?
6. Who were the religious leaders of Jesus' day that did not believe in the resurrection?
7. Who was Hezekiah's wicked son?
8. Who became king of Judah at age seven?
9. What prophet restored a pot of stew that had been poisoned?
10. What Aramean soldier was healed of leprosy?
11. Who died for reaching out and touching the ark of God?
12. Abraham's first son was Ishmael. How much older was Ishmael than Isaac?
13. What was the name of Jeremiah's faithful scribe?
14. How did Jael murder Sisera?
15. Which of Noah's three sons (Shem, Ham, or Japheth) was an ancestor of Jesus?

ADVANCED

1. Whose staff grew almonds?
2. Who was Ruth's mother-in-law?
3. Who was David's great-grandmother?
4. Who was Saul's military commander?
5. Who wrote Proverbs 31?
6. Which of Solomon's sons became king?
7. Who was Solomon's mother?
8. How many plagues did God use against Egypt at the time of the Exodus?
9. What seer was hired to curse God's people?
10. Where did Saul hide when Samuel tried to introduce him to the people?

11. Who stopped David from killing her husband?
12. Who was king of Judah when Babylon conquered Jerusalem?
13. What prophet was protected by a heavenly army?
14. What man did the disciples choose to take Judas's place?
15. Which early church members died because they lied to Peter?

EXPERT

1. What Jewish chief priest prophesied that Jesus would die for his people?
2. How long did Joshua live?
3. What were the names of the two prophets that Jesus' family met in the temple?
4. How many years passed between the historical events of Genesis 50 and Exodus 1?
5. Who was Dagon?
6. Who are the two prophets who sat under a tree and wished to die?
7. What was Esther's Hebrew name?
8. Which psalm is considered to be the oldest?
9. Which two prophets were to deliver messages only to Nineveh?
10. How many songs did Solomon write?
11. Judah was once ruled by a queen. Who was she, and for how long did she reign?
12. Which of Joseph's brothers saved his life?
13. What men were overcome by the demons they were trying to exorcise?
14. If a Jewish man died and left behind a widow, who was she obligated to marry?
15. Who was the first person to create musical instruments?

Bible Trivia (Answers)

EASY

1. Levites (Numbers 8)
2. Goliath (1 Samuel 17)
3. Absalom (2 Samuel 14)
4. Gideon (Judges 6)
5. Caleb and Joshua (Numbers 13)
6. Assyria (2 Kings 17:6)
7. Nebuchadnezzar (2 Kings 25)
8. Manna (Exodus 16:31)
9. Twenty-five years (Genesis 12:1-4; 21:1-5)
10. Abram and Hagar (Genesis 16)
11. Rahab (Joshua 2:8-15)
12. Threshing grain in a wine press (Judges 6:11)
13. Shepherds (Luke 2)
14. John the Baptist (Mark 6:26)
15. Balaam (Numbers 22)

INTERMEDIATE

1. He had dishonored God when God told him to speak to a rock. (Numbers 20)
2. Bathsheba (2 Samuel 11)
3. Ehud (Judges 3)
4. Deborah (Judges 4)
5. Nehemiah (Nehemiah 2)
6. Sadducees (Matthew 22:23)
7. Manasseh (2 Chronicles 33)
8. Josiah (2 Kings 11:21)
9. Elisha (2 Kings 4)
10. Naaman (2 Kings 5)
11. Uzzah (2 Samuel 6:7)
12. Fourteen years (Genesis 21:4; 16:16)
13. Baruch (Jeremiah 32:12)

14. She drove a tent peg through his head. (Judges 4:21)
15. Shem (Luke 3:36)

ADVANCED

1. Aaron's (Numbers 17)
2. Naomi (Ruth 1)
3. Ruth (Ruth 4)
4. Abner (1 Samuel 14:50)
5. Lemuel (Proverbs 31:1)
6. Rehoboam (1 Kings 11:42-43)
7. Bathsheba (1 Kings 2:13)
8. Ten (Exodus 7–12)
9. Balaam (Numbers 22)
10. Among a pile of luggage (1 Samuel 10:22)
11. Abigail (1 Samuel 25:30-31)
12. Zedekiah (2 Kings 25)
13. Elisha (2 Kings 6:17)
14. Matthias (Acts 1:23-26)
15. Ananias and Sapphira (Acts 5)

EXPERT

1. Caiaphas (John 11:50-51)
2. 110 years (Joshua 24:29)
3. Anna and Simeon (Luke 2)
4. Four hundred years (Genesis 15:13)
5. One of the gods of the Philistines (Judges 16:23)
6. Jonah and Elijah (1 Kings 19:4; Jonah 4)
7. Hadassah (Esther 2:7)
8. Psalm 90, written by Moses (Psalm 90)

9. Jonah and Nahum (Jonah; Nahum)
10. 1,005 (1 Kings 4:32)
11. Queen Athaliah reigned for seven years (2 Chronicles 23)
12. Reuben (Genesis 37:21)
13. The seven sons of Sceva (Acts 19:13-16)
14. Her husband's brother (Deuteronomy 25:5)
15. Jubal (Genesis 4:21)

Celebrity Profiles

The clues below read much like the celebrity profiles found in popular magazines and newspapers. After reading the facts, guess the identity of each mystery person.

1. **Heritage:** My father is Abraham.
   Personal: I am my mother's only child.
   Favorite pastime: Playing with my twin boys (They couldn't be any more different.)
   Claim to fame: I was almost sacrificed by my father.
   Greatest life lesson: It never pays to favor one child over another.
   Biggest embarrassment: My son Jacob's treachery

2. **Heritage:** My dad was Isaac.
   Personal: I'm a twin.
   Favorite pastime: Real manly stuff, like hunting and fishing
   Biggest regret: I spent a lot of my life blaming my brother for my own mistakes.
   If I lived in the twentieth century: I might be stereotyped as a dumb jock.
   Biggest embarrassment: I traded my birthright for soup. (Pretty dumb, huh?)

3. **Heritage:** Abraham is my granddad.
   Personal: I am a twin.

Favorite pastime: Tricking my brother, Esau
Claim to fame: I got the birthright for the nation of Israel by trading a bowl of soup.
Personal philosophy: If you're smart enough to get it, it's yours.
Biggest embarrassment: Ten of my sons faked the death of my son Joseph.

4. **Heritage:** I was probably a Philistine.
   Personal: My name means "coquette."
   Favorite pastime: Playing with my boyfriend's hair
   Claim to fame: I was loved by a man who told me his deepest secrets.
   Personal philosophy: You gotta look out for number one.
   Biggest embarrassment: Samson lied to me and made me look bad.

5. **Heritage:** We are in-laws and both widows.
   Favorite song: "O Little Town of Bethlehem"
   Favorite pastime: Remembering the loved ones we have in common
   Personal philosophy: Follow God, and he will supply your needs.
   Biggest embarrassment: When we first came to town we had to eat others' leftovers.
   Claim to fame: One of us went out to get groceries and found a husband.

6. **Heritage:** I was a Philistine and proud of it!
   Personal: I loved a good fight.
   Favorite pastime: Having little Jewish boys for lunch
   Claim to fame: I was killed by a slingshot wound to the head.
   Personal philosophy: If they call you a giant, you better live up to it.
   If I lived in the twentieth century: I'd be the biggest playground bully you'd ever met.

7. **Heritage:** I was an Israelite.
   Personal: I was married to a brave man, but when he died I married the king.
   Favorite pastime: Beauty treatments in high places

Favorite song: "Splish Splash"

Claim to fame: My eldest son became the wisest king of Israel.

Biggest embarrassment: My lover had my husband killed.

8. **Heritage:** I was a Jewish maiden.

Favorite pastime: Competing in beauty contests

Claim to fame: I climbed from being an orphan to a queen.

Personal philosophy: Make the most of where you are. God can use you there.

Least known personal fact: My Hebrew name actually means "myrtle."

9. **Heritage:** My dad's name was Amoz.

Occupation: A prophet—a *major* prophet

Favorite pastime: Writing biographies of kings (I wrote two.)

Favorite outfit: A mourner's coat. It got me in the mood for work.

Memorable phrases I've coined: Wonderful Counselor, Prince of Peace

Personal philosophy: You don't always see the fruits of your labor, but you work anyway.

Biggest embarrassment: Naming my son Maher-shalal-hash-baz. What was I thinking?

10. **Personal:** I like to think of myself as a blueblood.

Confidant: A health-food nut named Daniel

Favorite pastime: I like to hear my dreams interpreted.

My favorite meal: Babylonian stew

Secret to success: I seek out wise people and listen to what they tell me.

Biggest embarrassment: I tried a Shake 'n Bake on three guys once, and ended up with *four* guys in the oven!

Special talents: I do an amazing cow imitation!

11. **Heritage:** We come from the same hometown.

Personal: Some people think we're pretty good looking.

Personal philosophy: We try to eat right.

If we lived in the twentieth century: We'd play beach volleyball.

Most awkward moment: Have you ever looked around and you're the only one standing?

Claim to fame: Playing with fire and not getting burned

12. **Heritage:** I was a son of Zebedee.

Personal: My brother and I were disciples.

Favorite pastime: There's nothing like a good fishing trip.

Little-known fact: I was the first of the twelve disciples to die for my faith.

Confidant: My brother, John, and Simon Peter.

Biggest embarrassment: Without thinking, I asked Jesus for a really selfish favor once. Boy, was I embarrassed!

13. **Heritage:** I was of the tribe of Judah.

Personal: I had to get married. A lot of people thought I was in trouble.

Favorite hotel: Believe me, they never have room. Stay with relatives.

Claim to fame: My son was a very important person.

Personal philosophy: Please God with your life.

Saddest moment: I saw my son die.

14. **Occupation:** Federal worker

Favorite pastime: Counting money

What I will be remembered for: Big tax refunds for those whom I cheated

Nickname: Shorty

Favorite woodland plant: Definitely the sycamore

Biggest embarrassment: When I met Jesus I was in a tree.

15. **Meaning of name:** Ruler of the people

Occupation: Scholar, Bible teacher, member of the Sanhedrin

A TV network I really would have liked: "Nick at Nite"

Favorite saying: "You must be born again."

Sermons that make me squirm: Any message about being a "secret disciple"

Friends with: Joseph of Arimathea

Little-known fact: I helped bury Jesus.

16. **Personal:** I'm good with numbers.

Confidant: I'm not really close with anyone, though I hang out with the disciples.

Favorite pastime: Watching my money work for me
Most memorable moment: A walk through a famous garden
Cause of death: Hanging
Biggest embarrassment: I betrayed the wrong man.

17. **Occupation:** A disciple
Confidant: Jesus
True confession: Sometimes I tend to see the glass half empty.
Personal philosophy: Seeing is believing.
Biggest embarrassment: When Jesus showed me my distrusting heart

18. **Heritage:** Greek
Occupation: I was one of the first deacons.
Real gift: Preaching (powerfully and pointedly)
Known for: Being full of faith and the Holy Spirit
Cause of death: Stoning
Claim to fame: Being the first person to die for my faith in Christ

19. **Heritage:** I was probably a native of Jerusalem.
Other name: John
Favorite pastime: Spending time with Jesus and the other disciples
Claim to fame: I penned one of the Gospels.
Personal philosophy: Always try again, even if you let someone down.
Biggest embarrassment: I got homesick and left Paul on a missionary journey. Also, some people claim I ran away naked when Jesus was arrested.

20. **Personal:** I am the mother of six boys and a daughter.
Confidante: My sister
Birth order: I'm the oldest child.
Personality trait: I always do what I'm told.
Physical appearance: Did I have weak eyes or beautiful eyes? No one seems to know.
One thing I'd change: I always lived in the shadow of my beautiful younger sister, Rachel.

Most interesting fact: I married my husband, but he didn't know it until the day after the wedding!

21. **Heritage:** I am the son of a Levite.
    Personal: I was a middle child.
    Biggest moment: Undoubtedly when I was named first high priest
    Claim to fame: My brother depended on me a whole lot.
    Favorite pastime: I enjoy public speaking.
    Biggest embarrassment: I helped build a relatively harmless golden calf.

22. **Family:** Tribe of Manasseh
    Personality trait: I'm a worrier, sort of a pessimist. I doubt myself sometimes.
    Greatest accomplishment: I beat a huge army with three hundred men who lapped water like a dog.
    Occupation: A soldier—not by choice, but by draft
    Personal philosophy: Stay away from ephods. They may look nice, but they'll get you in trouble.
    Nicknames: Jerub-baal
    Most memorable moment: I saw God do some incredible things with a sheepskin.

23. **Personal:** Professional soldier
    Confidant: Elisha
    Favorite pastime: Listening to my wife's stories about her servant girl
    Reputation: A mighty man of valor
    Personal philosophy: I'd rather have dignity with a disease, than embarrassment with health.
    Biggest embarrassment: Washing in a muddy river to get clean

24. **Heritage:** My father was king of Tyre and Sidon.
    Personal: I was married to King Ahab.
    Favorite pastime: Destroying prophets of Jehovah, stealing vineyards
    Claim to fame: I carried on a feud with Elijah, and I would have won, too, except for a few details.
    Personal philosophy: You've got to take what you want.

Biggest embarrassment: I was launched from a window only to become Dog Chow.

25. **Heritage:** My dad's name was Buzi. Can you believe that?
Personal: I was a priest. I lived with the other exiles from Jerusalem.
Biggest moment: God called me to prophesy through a vision.
Claim to fame: I was the inspiration for the song "Dem Bones, Dem Bones, Dem Dry Bones."
Personal philosophy: It's always worth it if you get to teach someone something.
Biggest embarrassment: I once ate a scroll . . . *and liked it!*

26. **Heritage:** I was married to a priest.
Personal: I had a child late in life.
Favorite pastime: Visiting with my sweet cousin who was pregnant at the same time I was.
Claim to fame: John the Baptist was my son.
Personal philosophy: Trust God and the impossible happens.
Biggest embarrassment: My husband wanted to name my son a name that was not in our family.

27. **Favorite pastime:** I liked to travel.
Biggest embarrassment: My parents' marriage was illegal; Mom was a Jew and Dad was a Greek.
Churches I've served: Churches at Philippi, Berea, Thessalonica, and many others.
Most significant early influence: My mom and my grandma
Confidant: Paul the apostle
Most interesting fact: Two books of the Bible were written as letters to me.

28. **Birthplace:** Palestine
Birth order: Youngest
Siblings: Eleven brothers and one sister
Saddest event: Mother died after giving birth.
Occupation: Family-owned business: herd administration

Biggest embarrassment: My big brother framed me for stealing.

29. **Little-known fact:** One of my grandfathers way back is Phinehas, who is Aaron's son, who is Moses' brother. Pretty cool, huh?

    Contemporary: Nehemiah is a contemporary of mine.

    Favorite pastime: I enjoy observing the reconstructed old temple.

    Claim to fame: I broke down emotionally in front of the temple.

    Personal philosophy: It doesn't matter if the outside looks good, if the inside is rotten.

    Biggest embarrassment: I thought the people were so great because they rebuilt the temple; then I come to find out, they weren't obeying God at all.

30. **Heritage:** I was a native of Chaldea.

    Personal: I was a direct descendant of Noah's son Shem.

    Favorite pastime: Spending time with my son Isaac.

    Claim to fame: I was called the father of the Jewish nation.

    Personal philosophy: If God says, "Move," I say, "How far?"

    Biggest embarrassment: My nephew's wife became the pillar of her community, so to speak.

INTERMEDIATE

1. **Marital status:** Married to my wonderful wife, Sapphira.

    Personal: I was part of the early Christian church.

    Cause of death: I lied myself to death.

    Claim to fame: I lied about the profits from a piece of real estate.

    Personal philosophy: Grab what you can and get out!

    Biggest embarrassment: Getting caught

2. **Place of service in the church:** Deacon (serving food to the elderly)

    Reputation: Full of the Spirit and wisdom

    Contemporary of: Stephen, the first martyr

Ministry highlight: Used by God to start a revival in Samaria
Site of most unusual ministry moment: The desert road to Gaza
Famous convert: The Ethiopian eunuch
Part of *Star Trek* I like the best: When they say, "Beam me up, Scotty."

3. **Occupation:** Wheat farmer
Confidantes: My wife and her mother-in-law
Famous family member: Great-grandson, King David
Economic status: Oh, I don't do too badly.
Personality trait: Generous to foreigners and strangers
Biggest coup: Meeting my wife-to-be in my own wheat field

4. **Personal:** I'm a softy when it comes to standing up for the underdog.
Confidant: Paul
Heritage: Native of Cyprus and from the tribe of Levi
Favorite pastime: Writing encouraging letters
Past business deal: I once sold quite a bit of real estate.
Reputation: I think people see me as a man of integrity.
Biggest embarrassment: I was once mistaken for the god Jupiter.

5. **Husband's occupation:** High-ranking Egyptian official (i.e. captain of the guard)
Weakness: Young, handsome men
My motto: "If you see something you want, get it!"
Warning: "Deny me what I want, and you will pay!"
Crime: Filing a false police report
Contemporary of: Jacob and Joseph
A TV show I would have loved: Any afternoon soap opera

6. **Father:** Jared
Famous offspring: Methuselah (the oldest man to ever live)
Number of candles on my cake at my last birthday party: 365
Claim to fame: Walking with God
Person I have something in common with: Elijah

Proud achievement: Making it into God's Hall of Fame/Faith in Hebrews 11
I saved money by: Never having to purchase a cemetery plot

7. **True confession:** I tend to bend the truth a little bit, every so often, when I feel like I need to.
Personal philosophy: Don't mingle with Canaanite women.
Memorable moment: I got a wedding proposal while I watered ten camels.
Personal: Mother of twin boys who had fought with each other since before birth
Biggest embarrassment: I favored one of my boys over the other.
Claim to fame: One of my sons is the father of the twelve tribes of Israel.

8. **Confidant:** I'm a confidant of many of the men here in my town.
Favorite pastime: Looking out my window over the countryside
Favorite color: Deep red
Most memorable moment: I hid two spies once.
Biggest embarrassment: Imagine my neighbors' faces when all their houses fell down, but mine was left standing!

9. **Occupation:** I was a judge among the Hebrews.
Personal: I went to battle, which in my day was man's work.
Favorite pastime: Sitting under my very own palm tree in the desert
Claim to fame: I did a duet with a guy named Barak.
If I lived in the twentieth century: I might have been a women's activist.
True confession: I was glad that Sisera got the reputation of being beaten by a girl.

10. **Confidant:** My youngest son (I have eight.)
Personal: My grandmother was a Moabite, but Grandfather loved her.
Favorite pastime: Watching a peaceful herd of sheep graze in the sun

Personal philosophy: When the prophet comes knocking, make sure *everyone* in your family is there.

Most memorable moment: Hard to say. Probably seeing my youngest knock some sense into this guy from Gath.

Biggest embarrassment: I had a son destined to be a king, and I only gave him harp lessons!

11. **Heritage:** I was in the royal line that ruled Judah.

   Personal: My name means "Jehovah is Strength."

   Favorite pastimes: Counting my kingdom as it grew; watching shadows go backward

   Most amazing memory: Seeing all those dead Assyrians outside of Jerusalem

   Claim to fame: My first act as king was to get rid of all the places of false worship and restore the temple.

   Personal philosophy: Not might is right, but might for right

   Biggest embarrassment: Acting like a big shot and showing those guys from Babylon the royal treasures

12. **Heritage:** I was a son of King Hezekiah.

   Personal: I became king at twelve years of age.

   Favorite pastimes: Ouija boards, seances, killing people for no reason

   Claim to fame: I had the longest reign of any king of Judah—fifty-five years of misery.

   Personal philosophy: Worship as many gods as you can. You might need them sometime.

   Biggest embarrassment: I am responsible for sawing Isaiah in half (though no one can prove it).

13. **My name means:** Begotten in Babylon

   Father: Shealtiel (but also an heir of my uncle Pedaiah)

   Claim to fame: An ancestor of the Lord Jesus Christ (Matthew 1:12-13)

   Nickname during the Exile: Sheshbazzar (Ezra 1:8, 11)

   Remembered for: Leading a group of exiles back to the Promised Land

   Career highlight: Becoming governor under Darius and overseeing the rebuilding of the temple

   Some people: Hear my name and think of "Barney Rubble"

14. **Location:** Many believed I worked first in Israel, then retired to Judah.
    Occupation: I was a prophet for about fifty-eight years.
    Favorite pastime: Spending time with my two boys and one daughter
    Claim to fame: I was the first of the minor prophets.
    Personal philosophy: If God tells you to marry a prostitute to teach people about love, you do it.
    Biggest embarrassment: My unfaithful wife and my unfaithful nation

15. **Heritage:** I was the grandson of Iddo.
    Personal: I was the eleventh of the twelve minor prophets.
    Occupation: I was a priest.
    Claim to fame: The book of the Bible named after me is a very messianic book.
    Personal philosophy: God desires obedience more than fasting.
    Biggest embarrassment: People are always getting me mixed up with the father of John the Baptist.

16. **Heritage:** My father is Abraham, but I'm not an Israelite.
    Personal: My name means "God will hear."
    Favorite pastime: Teasing my younger half brother
    Claim to fame: I was father to a nation who would be an enemy of the Israelites.
    Saddest event: Burying my father with my half brother, Isaac
    If I lived in the twentieth century: I would probably be in a gang.

17. **Profession:** Beggar
    Personal: I lived in Jericho a long time after the walls fell down.
    Favorite pastime: Guessing who was walking by, by the smell of their perfume
    Claim to fame: Jesus healed me by the roadside.
    Personal philosophy: It never hurts to ask. And keep asking if you have to.
    Favorite song: I love the first verse of "Amazing Grace," particularly the last line.

18. **Heritage:** I was a Jewish woman.
Personal: I was friends with Mary, Jesus' mom.
Favorite pastime: Watching my two boys—they are such good fishermen.
Claim to fame: My two sons, James and John (By the way, I had nothing to do with the beheading of John the Baptist!)
Biggest embarrassment: I once asked Jesus for a special favor. It was really inappropriate.

19. **Personal:** I am a member of the Jewish Supreme Court.
Favorite pastime: Estimating the Messiah's arrival
Contemporary: Nicodemus
Biggest embarrassment: I was only a secret disciple of Jesus.
Most interesting fact: I buried a friend in my own grave plot one time, but he only needed it for a couple of days.

20. **Occupation:** I was a Roman army officer.
Heritage: I was a Gentile by birth and a Jew by choice.
Contemporary: Simon Peter
Biggest moment: I was spoken to by an angel!
Claim to fame: It was through God working in my life that Peter came to see that salvation is for everyone, not just the Jews.
Reputation: I've always been known as a good man.

21. **Job:** Domestic servant
Employer: Mary, the mother of John Mark
Fond memory: Those late night prayer meetings Mary used to host
Traits: Excitable, joyful, faithful
People accused me of: Being "out of my mind"
Lesson learned: God often answers prayer immediately!
Miracle I witnessed: Peter's supernatural release from prison

22. **Heritage:** I was an Alexandrian Jew.
Contemporaries: Priscilla and Aquila.
Spiritual gift: Teaching is definitely one of them.
What would you be in the twentieth century: Either a televangelist or a motivational speaker

Personal philosophy: Be all that you can be.

Biggest embarrassment: I was preaching "The Messiah is coming!" after Jesus had risen from the dead.

23. **Heritage:** I was a Christian Jewess.
Favorite restaurant: My husband liked this Greek diner, of course.
Favorite place to shop: I know the marketplace in Lystra like the back of my hand.
Claim to fame: My son traveled with Paul the apostle!
Confidante: My mother Lois, a wonderful woman of faith
Greatest accomplishment: My boy, Timothy, became a great man of faith.

24. **Occupation:** I was superintendent of the churches on the island of Crete.
Associates: Paul, Barnabas, Timothy, and many others in the early church
Favorite pastime: Traveling with Paul on his missionary journeys
Claim to fame: There is a small book in the New Testament by my name.
Personal philosophy: Be faithful to your task and God will use you.
Biggest moment: Having my very own letter from Paul canonized into the New Testament

25. **Heritage:** I am Rebekah's brother.
Personal: My name means "white."
Favorite pastime: I love to show off my beautiful daughters.
Claim to fame: One of my daughters was going to get married, and on her wedding day I put her older sister in her place.
Personal philosophy: A younger sister should never get married before an older one.
Biggest embarrassment: I was bested by Jacob, my son-in-law.

26. **Heritage:** I married a Levite.
Personal: I had trouble getting pregnant.

Most difficult time: Putting up with my husband's other wife, Penninah

Favorite pastime: Visiting with Eli at the temple

Claim to fame: My wonderful son Samuel

Personal philosophy: Pour out your heart to God, and he will hear you.

Biggest embarrassment: I was accused of being drunk in the temple. Really!

27. **Heritage:** I was a native of Egypt.

    Favorite pastime: Sightseeing in the desert

    Claim to fame: My precious son, Ishmael. You might not hear it mentioned, but Abraham is his father.

    Personal philosophy: When you work in a family business, be careful what you do for your boss—it might backfire.

    Biggest embarrassment: My descendants and Sarah's have never played well together.

28. **Heritage:** I became part of a royal family.

    Personal: My husband died from shock, so I married again—this time, I got a real catch.

    Family business: We were into sheep herding.

    Claim to fame: I offered food and drink to King David during a war.

    Personal philosophy: It's best to make friends, not enemies, with powerful people.

    Biggest embarrassment: My numskull husband nearly got us all killed.

29. **Meaning of name:** God is Savior

    Little-known fact: I once (with God's help, of course!) parted the Jordan River and walked across.

    Favorite place for R & R: Shunem

    Awards I could have won: The Betty Crocker Prize (for salvaging a bad pot of stew); the AMA Medallion (for healing a leper); and the Forestry Association Commendation (for recovering a hopelessly lost ax head)

    Power even in death: A body was thrown on my grave, and it came back to life!

    Don't you dare call me: Chrome dome

    My hero: Elijah

30. **Heritage:** I was of the tribe of Naphtali.
    Confidante: Deborah, a judge of Israel
    Enemy: Sisera the Canaanite
    Claim to fame: I took a woman to war with me and not only did we win, but we lived to sing a duet about it.
    Personal philosophy: When you think God has his hand on someone, stick close to them.
    Personal: I appear in the Hall of Faith in Hebrews 11.

ADVANCED

1. **Occupation:** A priest and a prince rolled into one
   Personal: My daughter Zipporah married Moses.
   Favorite pastime: Hearing Moses tell the story about the burning bush
   Claim to fame: I once gave Moses advice that changed the way Israel was governed.
   Personal philosophy: If you delegate your workload, more gets done and less get tired.
   Little-known fact: I also went by the name Reuel.

2. **Heritage:** I was supposedly descended from Amalekite royalty.
   Personal: I was quite anti-Semitic.
   Favorite pastime: Persian politics
   Claim to fame: I was killed on the gallows I had built for someone else.
   Personal philosophy: You want to get ahead? You're going to have to step on a few people on the way up.
   Biggest embarrassment: Being ratted on by Queen Esther

3. **Occupation:** I was in the garment industry.
   Personal: I lived alone for part of my life.
   A movie about my life would be called: *The Color Purple*
   Claim to fame: I let Paul use my house when he needed to.
   Personal philosophy: Take responsibility for yourself and give back when you can.
   Little-known fact: I was a Jew by choice, not by birth.

4. **Heritage:** I was a Shuhite.
   Confidant: Job

Favorite pastime: Giving advice (I think I'm really good at it.)
Claim to fame: I gave three speeches to Job to try to make sense of his situation.
Personal philosophy: If something bad happens, I believe it's usually someone's fault.
Biggest embarrassment: My advice did Job no good whatsoever.

5. **Heritage:** I was a Levite, but I lived among the Ephraimites.
Personal: I was married to Hannah.
Biggest mistake: My wife was struggling with infertility, and I said, "Am I not enough for you?"
Claim to fame: I was Samuel's father.
Reputation: I was known as a godly man.
Contemporaries: Eli, Hophni, and Phinehas

6. **Heritage:** I was a son of Jacob and Leah.
Personal: It was from my descendants that Israel's priests were chosen.
Favorite pastime: Teaching my three sons the tricks of the trade
Claim to fame: I was one of Joseph's brothers who sold him into slavery.
Biggest moment: I avenged my sister Dinah's rape by a local prince.
Biggest embarrassment: My father spoke ill of me on his deathbed.

7. **Family business:** My dad and I were high priests.
Most famous relative: My uncle Moses
Most boring job: I helped take a census once.
Most meaningful moment: My dad and uncle passed on the sacred garments to me (it was a symbolic thing).
Biggest embarrassment: Not eating a sacrifice in the tabernacle's sanctuary, as Moses said I should.

8. **Heritage:** I was a tribesman of the tribe of Benjamin.
Personal: I was left-handed.
Most unusual job: I carried everyone's taxes from Israel to Moab.

Favorite souvenir: An eighteen-inch, double-edged dagger, but I don't have it anymore.
Favorite adage: Curiosity kills the cat.
Biggest embarrassment: I killed a king, but everyone thought he was, uh, indisposed.

9. **Heritage:** I was a wealthy Benjamite.
Personal: I was King Saul's dad.
Pet peeve: I have some donkeys that run away every chance they get.
Claim to fame: My son was taller than anyone else in our country.
Personal philosophy: When your son becomes king, you don't worry so much about runaway donkeys.
Biggest embarrassment: When it was time to anoint my son as king, he was hiding in the baggage.

10. **Hometown:** Joppa
Favorite pastime: Sewing for my friends
Favorite community service: Volunteering at the homeless shelter
Secret to success: Helping other people get ahead
Claim to fame: I died once, and Peter brought me back to life.

11. **Heritage:** My dad was the brother of King Saul's dad.
Confidant: I was the chief counselor for Ishbosheth, but I lost respect for him.
Favorite pastime: Picking the winning side
Claim to fame: I was a renowned warrior and commander in chief of Saul's army.
Personal philosophy: If someone's little brother is bugging you, kill him.
Cause of death: A deadly embrace from my chief rival, Joab.

12. **Heritage:** I was the sister of Absalom and daughter of King David.
Personal: I was raped while helping my supposedly sick half brother.
Favorite pastime: Playing with my nieces and nephews (with whom I lived)

Claim to fame: My brother Absalom avenged my rape and killed the man who raped me.

Little-known fact: I lived as a widow the rest of my life.

Biggest embarrassment: When I was raped, the perpetrator made it look like it was my fault.

13. **Heritage:** While I was not born to a royal family, I became king.

    Personal: I was of the tribe of Ephraim.

    Favorite pastime: I loved crunching numbers.

    Claim to fame: Succeeding King Solomon to the throne of Israel (forget Rehoboam—he doesn't count)

    Personal philosophy: A house divided against itself is a house I can control more easily.

    Saddest moment: Without doubt, the death of my son Abijah

14. **Heritage:** I was the son of Abijah, king of Judah.

    Personal: My name means "to heal."

    Favorite pastime: I enjoyed redecorating and fixing up the temple.

    Claim to fame: I greatly decreased idolatry in Israel during my reign.

    Personal philosophy: Clean everything up as much as possible, even if it means deposing your grandma (which I did).

    Biggest embarrassment: I died of a disease of the feet that I never thought of asking God to heal.

15. **Heritage:** I was a Danite of Zorah.

    Personal: I prayed to God about how to raise my son.

    Favorite pastime: To help my son increase his strength

    Claim to fame: My boy, Samson. He was a strapper.

    Personal philosophy: Kids! You raise them like you think you should, then you let them go.

    Biggest embarrassment: You should see the woman my son almost married!

16. **Occupation:** King of Judah

    Father: King Jehoshaphat

    Meaning of my name: Jehovah is exalted

How I'm remembered: As living just like all the wicked kings of Israel

Worst moment: Either contracting a painful, terminal bowel disease, or having Jezebel as my mother-in-law

My funeral: Poorly attended, because no one really cared that I died

17. **Heritage:** I was the son of King Asa.

    Little-known fact: My name is sometimes preceded by the words "great jumpin'."

    Contemporaries: Evil kings Ahab and Jehoram

    Greatest accomplishment: Defeating a collection of armies by using Levite musicians

    Reputation: I was known for seeking the Lord with all my heart.

    Occupation: I was the king of Judah.

    Biggest embarrassment: My son married a daughter of Jezebel.

18. **Heritage:** I prophesied in Palestine.

    Personal: I hoped to see the temple rebuilt.

    Contemporary: My young friend Zechariah. We did some work together.

    Claim to fame: I was tenth of the twelve minor prophets.

    Personal philosophy: Tell it like it is.

    Biggest moment: The completion of the temple

19. **Heritage:** For a time I was married to great King Ahaseurus of Medo-Persia.

    Personal: My husband divorced me and found another queen.

    Favorite pastime: Catching up on the palace gossip

    Claim to fame: Being replaced as queen by a young Jewish girl named Esther

    Personal philosophy: Stand up for yourself, but only if you're willing to pay the consequences.

    Biggest embarrassment: My husband wanted me to stand around so a bunch of men could gawk at me.

20. **Favorite pastime:** I did a lot of walking with a friend.

    Most famous friends: I knew Jesus' disciples.

Favorite place to shop: There's this place in Emmaus I just love.

Second biggest embarrassment: Jesus himself corrected my theology one time.

First biggest embarrassment: I didn't recognize Jesus walking down the road!

21. **Occupation:** I held an honorable office in Zedekiah's court.
    Confidant: My best friend, Jeremiah
    Favorite job: I was my best friend's secretary for a time (I even took dictation).
    Claim to fame: I wrote down all the prophesies of Jeremiah—*twice.*
    Personal philosophy: If you write a book and a king tears it up, just write another and add a curse on that king.
    Biggest embarrassment: I spent some time in prison. I was innocent, of course.

22. **Name:** My name fit me—it means "fool"
    Occupation: Wealthy owner of large herds of sheep
    Claim to fame: Marrying way out of my league
    A movie that could easily describe my life: *Beauty and the Beast*
    Qualities: Greed, stubbornness, and just plain old meanness
    Famous people I knew: King David
    Famous people I really ticked off: King David

23. **Heritage:** I don't have much heritage, or culture, either.
    Occupation: Some call it "the world's oldest profession"—and I don't mean farming.
    Claim to fame: I married a prophet named Hosea.
    Personal philosophy: If you can't be with the one you love, love the one you're with.
    Biggest embarrassment: They used my name for a sitcom about a naive marine.

24. **Occupation:** I was a priest, and probably part of my duties was to punish false prophets.
    Contemporaries: Nahum and Jeremiah were around. I was sent to talk to Jeremiah several times.

Death: I died in the capture of Jerusalem by the Babylonians.
Claim to fame: There is a book in the Old Testament that bears my name.
Personal: You would consider me a minor prophet.
Little-known fact: I was probably related to Hezekiah.

25. **Personal:** I was a ruler at the synagogue of Capernaum.
Confidant: Once I confided in Jesus.
Favorite pastime: Taking my little girl to the market with me
Biggest regret: Having only one child, a daughter
Secret to success: I went straight to the top and asked for what I needed, and I stuck with it until I got it.
Biggest embarrassment: Some guests in my home laughed right in the face of the Son of God.

26. **Occupation:** Priest
Favorite book: *Angels* by Billy Graham
Personal: My wife and I had a child very late in life.
Biggest fight with my wife: Over what to name our son
Claim to fame: My boy, Johnny. He was a good boy.
Biggest embarrassment: Seeing an angel, then not having a voice to make anyone believe me

27. **Occupation:** Governor
Confidante: My wife, Drusilla, who, by the way, was the daughter of King Herod Agrippa
Favorite pastime: Being recognized in the local Caesarean restaurants and watching a cartoon named after me
Claim to fame: The time my friend Claudius passed the buck to me and made me try Paul in my court
Personal philosophy: Even if you think a man is not guilty, you can still hope for bribes to free him.
Biggest embarrassment: I kept the apostle Paul in prison for two years.

28. **Reputation:** I was well thought of in Philippi and in Rome.
Confidant: Paul the apostle
Favorite pastime: Spending time with the people I loved
Claim to fame: I carried the contributions of the church at Philippi to Paul in prison.

Lowest moment: I got so sick while I was visiting Paul that I almost died.

Biggest moment: I carried the Philippian epistle back to the church at Philippi.

29. **Heritage:** I was of the family of the younger son of Aaron, who spoke for Moses.

    Personal: I was a mentor to Hannah's son.

    Favorite pastime: Teaching young Samuel was my most rewarding experience.

    Claim to fame: I was the first judge of Israel who was also a priest.

    My biggest mistake: I unjustly accused a woman of being drunk in church.

    Biggest embarrassment: My outrageous sons, Hophni and Phinehas

30. **Heritage:** Tribe of Judah

    Cause of death: Stoned and burned

    Personality traits: I had a weakness for fine jewelry and precious metals.

    Prized possession: I once happened onto a beautiful robe imported from Babylon.

    Most foolish mistake: Thinking I could bury something under my tent, and God wouldn't see

    Best known for: Getting my whole country in trouble for what I did

EXPERT

1. **Heritage:** I was the eighth son of Jacob.

   Personal: My descendants were a tribe of Israel that wandered through the desert between the tribes of Dan and Naphtali. My name means "happy."

   Claim to fame: The only one of my descendants that you would recognize is Anna, who recognized baby Jesus at the temple.

   Little-known fact: At one point my tribe was fifth of the twelve in size, but we declined until we were the only tribe west of Jordan that never produced a national hero.

Biggest embarrassment: My name is sometimes mistaken for one of the eight tiny reindeer.

2. **Heritage:** Gideon was my father.
   Personal: I had sixty-nine brothers.
   Favorite pastime: I loved to recite parables.
   Claim to fame: I was the only one of my brothers to escape the massacre by Abimilech.
   Personal philosophy: You need to do right by the memory of your ancestors.
   Biggest embarrassment: My half brother, Abimilech. He's not a good guy.

3. **Contemporary:** John, the beloved
   Personal: The apostle Paul had several acquaintances with my same name.
   Favorite pastime: I loved having get-togethers and hosting missionary families.
   Claim to fame: John's third epistle was written to me.
   My greatest influence: I was led to the Lord by John.
   Reputation: I was known as a man of integrity and obedience to God.

4. **Heritage:** I am King Saul's youngest son.
   Personal: My name means "son of shame."
   Family: My three brothers were killed in battle with my dad.
   Favorite pastime: Talking with my uncle Abner about how to rule Israel
   Claim to fame: I gave up the throne to King David.
   Biggest embarrassment: My uncle Abner betrayed me and let David become king.

5. **Occupation:** I was a servant.
   Favorite job: I worked for King Saul for a while.
   Personal: My name means "branch" or "twig."
   Claim to fame: King David used me to care for Jonathan's handicapped son's land.
   Biggest moment: The day I got half of my master's land
   Biggest embarrassment: I lied to King David, but he couldn't prove it.

6. **Reputation:** I was considered *very* wise.
   Greatest regret: I defected from King David.
   Favorite pastime: Playing board games and winning every time
   Claim to fame: I counseled first King David, then, foolishly, Absalom.
   Cause of death: I hanged myself.
   Biggest embarrassment: Because of David's prayers, my wisdom was turned to folly.

7. **Heritage:** I was born to a royal family.
   Cause of death: I was executed for treason.
   Birth order: I was the fourth son of King David.
   Claim to fame: If I had my way, King Solomon would have just been Solomon.
   Personal philosophy: If at first you don't succeed . . .
   Biggest embarrassment: My younger brother beat me out of the throne.

8. **Heritage:** My father was King Jehosaphat of Judah.
   Most memorable moment: I was anointed king by a young person who ran away right afterward.
   Favorite pastimes: Fast chariots and striking down idolatrous rulers
   Claim to fame: I destroyed the house of evil King Ahab.
   Personal philosophy: What is good for my country ultimately is good for me.
   Biggest embarrassment: God shortened my legacy because I left a few false idols around.

9. **Heritage:** My mom's name was Jedidah.
   Pet peeve: I just can't stand idol worship. It just drives me crazy.
   Favorite pastime: Knocking down those carved idol images
   Claim to fame: I became king when I was eight years old!
   Personal philosophy: Sometimes a pup is the best one to lead the pack.
   Biggest embarrassment: When we found the Word of God and realized we were breaking God's law all over the place

10. **Heritage:** I was the daughter of Ahab and Jezebel.
    Personal: I was married to Jehoram, king of Judah.

Favorite pastime: I loved to worship at the temple of Baal.
Claim to fame: After the death of Ahaziah I ruled Judah myself for six years—the only woman to do so.
Personal philosophy: What a man can do, a woman can do better.
Biggest embarrassment: I was assassinated and replaced by a six-year-old!

11. **Heritage:** My father was King Amaziah of Judah.
Personal: I became king of Judah at the age of sixteen.
One of my greatest influences: Zechariah, the prophet
Claim to fame: I was struck with leprosy because I wanted to worship God and do what only priests were supposed to do.
Personal philosophy: I'm a good king. I can do what I want to do.
Biggest embarrassment: Finishing out my reign in useless isolation

12. **Background:** A descendant of Shuah
Personality: Loud, insistent, very opinionated, impatient
My ideal job: A prosecuting attorney or a "fire and brimstone" preacher
A job not suited for me: Counseling
Friends: Eliphaz, Zophar, and Job

13. **Heritage:** My family was the first to become Christians in Greece.
Little-known fact: I was probably with Paul when he wrote 1 Corinthians.
Favorite pastime: Having missionaries stay at my house as they pass through
Claim to fame: Those in my household were the only people Paul baptized, besides Crispus and Gaius.
Personal philosophy: What goes around comes around. Spend your time doing good.
Biggest embarrassment: My church here in Corinth and the mess they're in

14. **Heritage:** My surname is Joseph.
Personal: I'm also known as Barsabbas.
Contemporaries: Jesus Christ and the disciples

Favorite pastime: Spending time with Jesus and the disciples

Claim to fame: I was one of the two men who were the choices to replace Judas Iscariot as a disciple.

Biggest embarrassment: I might have been a little embarrassed to not get picked as an apostle, but it was God's choice.

15. **Heritage:** I am of the tribe of Levi.

    Personal: I am very private. You won't find out a lot about my personal life.

    Favorite pastime: Singing in the temple choir

    Claim to fame: I'm quoted by Luke and Paul in the New Testament.

    Personal philosophy: I don't know why evil people get ahead, but I know ultimately God is in control.

    Biggest embarrassment: They called me a minor prophet, but I thought I was pretty major.

16. **Heritage:** My heritage doesn't matter because I am the wife of a ruler.

    Personal: I had a beautiful daughter who danced well.

    Favorite pastime: Going to royal parties with my husband

    Claim to fame: I was responsible for John the Baptist's death.

    Personal philosophy: If you can't get what you want through the front door, try the back door.

    Biggest embarrassment: My silver platter was ruined at one of my husband's parties.

17. **Confidantes:** Mary Magdalene, Joanna (Chuza's wife), among others

    Personal: Even though I was a woman, I had money of my own.

    Favorite pastime: I went along with Jesus and the disciples on their tour of Galilee, preaching God's kingdom.

    Claim to fame: The Bible mentions that I gave my own money to support Jesus and the disciples.

    Personal philosophy: Jesus made a difference in my life, even though the Bible doesn't give specifics.

Best-kept secret: That we women traveled with Jesus and the disciples.

18. **Occupation:** A New Testament prophet
   Confidant: The apostle Paul was a friend of mine.
   Favorite pastime: Telling the future—you know, famines and stuff
   Claim to fame: I foretold a Palestinian famine.
   Personal philosophy: If you've got a hunch, go with it.
   Little-known fact: I am believed to have been one of the seventy disciples of Christ.

19. **Heritage:** According to my name, I was a Roman.
   Confidants: Stephanas and Achaicus
   Favorite pastime: Helping and encouraging
   Claim to fame: I was friends with the first family to become Christians in Greece.
   Personal philosophy: Be good to the people who help you.
   Biggest embarrassment: The state of my home church, the church at Corinth

20. **Heritage:** I was the eldest daughter of Herod Agrippa I.
   Personal: My brother and I had a very dysfunctional relationship.
   Favorite pastime: Marrying different guys and then going back to live with my brother
   Claim to fame: The only time you would recognize me is when I heard Paul give his testimony before Festus (whom I never married).
   Personal philosophy: I've traded off my conscience too often to have a personal philosophy.
   Biggest embarrassment: While we could find nothing to accuse Paul of, we weren't convinced to become Christians.

21. **Heritage:** I was a Gentile.
   Personal: My names means "friend of God."
   Favorite pastime: Corresponding with friends
   Claim to fame: I am the person to whom Luke inscribed his Gospel and the book of Acts.
   Contemporaries: Paul, Luke, Jesus Christ
   Biggest moment: My conversion to Christianity

22. **Occupation:** Farmer
Personal: I have my own grape press. Not many can say that, can they?
Favorite moment: When I turned the tables on the Baal worshipers who were going to kill my son
Claim to fame: My son was Gideon, a man used of God
Personal philosophy: Stand up for your kids, even if you don't agree with what they've done.
Biggest embarrassment: That time my son used a sheepskin to test God. I mean, really . . .

23. **Heritage:** I was a Greek by birth and a Christian by faith.
Confidant: Paul, formerly Saul of Tarsus.
Favorite movie: *The Hiding Place*
Claim to fame: I was accused of treason because of my association with Christian missionaries.
Personal philosophy: Do the right thing and leave the consequences to God.
Biggest moment: Sneaking Paul and Silas out of town for their own safety

24. **Heritage:** I was from Athens.
Personal: I was led to the Lord by Paul.
Favorite pastime: Telling others about the Messiah
Claim to fame: I became a Christian at the same time as Dionysius.
Personal philosophy: Others can laugh, but when someone has been raised from the dead, I listen.
Biggest moment: I heard Paul speak at Mars Hill.

25. **Heritage:** I was a Jew.
Little-known fact: There are two men in the New Testament with my name. We might have been the same person, but then again, we might not have been.
Confidant: The apostle Paul
Favorite restaurant: There's a little breakfast place in Ephesus that Paul and I went to when we'd been up all night writing.
Claim to fame: Paul listed 1 Corinthians jointly in his name and mine.

Personal interests: I had an interest in the Corinthian Christians.

26. **Personal:** My name means "popular" or "ruler of the people."
    Hometown: Thessalonica
    Religious resume: A traveling companion of the apostle Paul
    Claim to fame: Mentioned in Paul's letters three times
    Weakness: Worldliness
    How I'm remembered: As the one who deserted Paul in his time of greatest need

27. **Personal:** I was a go-getter, a real achiever in early Bible times. I was the son of Cush.
    Hometown(s): Hard to say. I spent more time building cities that actually living in them.
    Claim to fame: I was called a mighty hunter in the Lord's sight.
    Biggest achievement: The first of the great empire-builders. I built Babel and Nineveh, later to become great cities. In my day, however, the capital was Resen.
    Biggest embarrassment: How did a proud name like mine become a slang name for a foolish or incompetent person?

28. **Personal:** I am a footnote in the sad history of Israel after Joshua died.
    Hometown: The hill country of Ephraim
    Favorite person: My mother. I stole a truckload of silver from her. After I admitted it, she made an idol in my honor!
    Most annoying person(s): Six hundred guys from the tribe of Dan.
    Personal motto: A person can never have too many lucky Levites.
    Biggest disappointment: Losing my priest to a band of ruffians. I gave him a good home and a fair salary, and this is how he rewarded me.

29. **Personal:** I have the dubious distinction of having the shortest reign in Israel's history.
    Favorite pastime: Conspiracy and regicide

Personal motto: If you're going to launch a coup, do it right! Make sure you kill *all* of the king's relatives.

Little-known fact: Jezebel called Jehu by my name just before her death.

Biggest disappointment: Apparently not everyone in the army agreed that I should take King Elah's place. A week just wasn't enough time, I guess.

When the going gets tough: Burn down your house around you.

30. **Personal:** I came from the area known as Shunem. My beauty brought me to the attention of kings.

    Little-known fact: A lot of people think I'm the young woman in Solomon's love song.

    Beginnings: I was summoned to lie next to old King David—just to keep him warm, mind you.

    Most difficult moment: Adonijah wanted to take me for his bride, but Solomon had him killed instead.

    Biggest embarrassment: My name sounds like an out-of-date carpet.

Celebrity Profiles (Answers)

EASY

1. Isaac (Genesis 22; 25; 27)
2. Esau (Genesis 25:29-34)
3. Jacob (Genesis 25; 27; 37)
4. Delilah (Judges 16:4-22)
5. Ruth & Naomi (The book of Ruth)
6. Goliath (1 Samuel 17)
7. Bathsheba (2 Samuel 11; 1 Kings 1:28-48)
8. Esther (The book of Esther)
9. Isaiah (The book of Isaiah)
10. Nebuchadnezzar (Daniel 1–3)
11. Shadrach, Meshach, and Abednego (Daniel 1; 3)
12. James (Mark 10:35-40; Acts 12:1-2)
13. Mary, Jesus' mother (Luke 1:26-56; John 19)
14. Zacchaeus (Luke 19:1-10)
15. Nicodemus (John 3; 19)
16. Judas Iscariot (John 12–13)
17. Thomas (John 20:26-29)
18. Stephen (Acts 6:1–8:1)
19. Mark (Mark 14:50-52; Acts 12:25)
20. Leah (Genesis 29)
21. Aaron (The book of Exodus)
22. Gideon (Judges 6–8)
23. Naaman (2 Kings 5:1-23)
24. Jezebel (2 Kings 9)
25. Ezekiel (Ezekiel 2:1–3:3; 37)
26. Elizabeth (Luke 1)
27. Timothy (2 Timothy 1–3)
28. Benjamin (Genesis 35; 42)
29. Ezra (Ezra 9:1-15)
30. Abraham (Genesis 11:27)

INTERMEDIATE

1. Ananias (Acts 5)
2. Philip (Acts 6:3; 8)
3. Boaz (The book of Ruth)
4. Barnabas (Acts 4; 9; 13–15)
5. Potiphar's wife (Genesis 39:1-5)
6. Enoch (Genesis 5:21-24)
7. Rebekah (Genesis 24–25)
8. Rahab (Joshua 2:1-21)
9. Deborah (Judges 4–5)
10. Jesse (1 Samuel 16–17)
11. Hezekiah (2 Kings 18–20)
12. Manasseh (2 Kings 21)
13. Zerubbabel (Ezra 1:8, 11)
14. Hosea (The book of Hosea)
15. Zechariah the prophet (The book of Zechariah)
16. Ishmael (Genesis 16; 25; 21:5)
17. Bartimaeus (Mark 10:46-52)
18. Salome (Matthew 20; Mark 15:40)
19. Joseph of Arimathea (Luke 23:50-56)
20. Cornelius (Acts 10)
21. Rhoda (Acts 12:6-17)
22. Apollos (Acts 18)
23. Eunice (2 Timothy 1:5)
24. Titus (The book of Titus)
25. Laban (Genesis 24–31)
26. Hannah (1 Samuel 1:1-25)
27. Hagar (Genesis 16)
28. Abigail (1 Samuel 25)
29. Elisha (2 Kings 2–8)
30. Barak (Judges 4–5; Hebrews 11:32)

ADVANCED

1. Jethro (Exodus 18)
2. Haman (Esther 5–6)
3. Lydia (Acts 16:14-15, 40)
4. Bildad (Job 8; 18; 25)
5. Elkanah (1 Samuel 1)
6. Levi (Genesis 34; 49:5-7)
7. Eleazer (Exodus 6:25; Leviticus 10)
8. Ehud (Judges 3)
9. Kish (1 Samuel 9–10)
10. Dorcas/Tabitha (Acts 9:36-41)
11. Abner (1 Samuel 14:50; 2 Samuel 2–3)
12. Tamar, David's daughter (2 Samuel 13:1-32)
13. Jeroboam (1 Kings 11:26–12:24; 14:1-20)
14. Asa (1 Kings 15:9-15)
15. Manoah (Judges 13:2-23)
16. Jehoram (2 Chronicles 21–22)
17. Jehoshaphat (2 Chronicles 20:1-30; 22:9)
18. Haggai (Ezra 5:1–6:14; the book of Haggai)
19. Vashti (Esther 1:1-22)
20. Cleopas (Luke 24)
21. Baruch (Jeremiah 36)
22. Nabal (1 Samuel 25)
23. Gomer (Hosea 1; 3)
24. Zephaniah (the book of Zephaniah)
25. Jairus (Mark 5:22-42)
26. Zechariah, John the Baptist's father (Luke 2)
27. Felix (Acts 24)
28. Epaphroditus (Philippians 2:25-30)
29. Eli (1 Samuel 1–4)
30. Achan (Joshua 7)

EXPERT

1. Asher (Genesis 48)
2. Jotham (Judges 9:1-21)
3. Gaius (3 John 1:1-6)
4. Ishbosheth (2 Samuel 3:6-12)
5. Ziba (2 Samuel 9:2-12; 16:1-4; 19:24-30)
6. Ahithophel (2 Samuel 15–17)
7. Adonijah (1 Kings 1:5-53; 2:13-25)
8. Jehu (2 Kings 9–10)
9. Josiah (2 Kings 22:1–23:30)
10. Athaliah (2 Chronicles 22:2–23:15)
11. Uzziah (2 Chronicles 26)
12. Bildad (Job 2:11)
13. Stephanas (1 Corinthians 1:16; 16:15)
14. Justus (Acts 1:21-26)
15. Habakkuk (Habakkuk 1)
16. Herodias (Matthew 14:3-12)
17. Susanna (Luke 8:1-3)
18. Agabus (Acts 11:28-30; 21:10-12)
19. Fortunatus (Acts 16:15-17)
20. Bernice (Acts 25:13–26:32)
21. Theophilus (Luke 1:1-4; Acts 1:1)
22. Joash (Judges 6)
23. Jason (Acts 17:1-9)
24. Damaris (Acts 17:32-33)
25. Sosthenes (Acts 18:17; 1 Corinthians 1:1)
26. Demas (2 Timothy 4:10; Philemon 1:24)
27. Nimrod (Genesis 10:8-12)
28. Micah (Judges 17:1–18:31)
29. Zimri (1 Kings 16:8-20; 2 Kings 9:31)
30. Abishag (1 Kings 1:1-4; 2:13-25)